EDI DEVELOPI

Infrastructure Delivery

Private Initiative and the Public Good

Edited by
Ashoka Mody

The World Bank
Washington, D. C.

The Economic Development Institute (EDI) was established by the World Bank in 1955 to train officials concerned with development planning, policymaking, investment analysis, and project implementation in member developing countries. At present the substance of the EDI's work emphasizes macroeconomic and sectoral economic policy analysis. Through a variety of courses, seminars, and workshops, most of which are given overseas in cooperation with local institutions, the EDI seeks to sharpen analytical skills used in policy analysis and to broaden understanding of the experience of individual countries with economic development. Although the EDI's publications are designed to support its training activities, many are of interest to a much broader audience. EDI materials, including any findings, interpretations, and conclusions, are entirely those of the authors and should not be attributed in any manner to the World Bank, to its affiliated organizations, or to members of its Board of Executive Directors or the countries they represent.

Because of the informality of this series and to make the publication available with the least possible delay, the manuscript has not been edited as fully as would be the case with a more formal document, and the World Bank accepts no responsibility for errors.

The complete backlist of publications from the World Bank is shown in the annual *Index of Publications*, which contains an alphabetical title list (with full ordering information) and indexes of subjects, authors, and countries and regions. The latest edition is available free of charge from the Distribution Unit, Office of the Publisher, The World Bank, 1818 H Street, N.W., Washington, D.C. 20433, U.S.A., or from Publications, Banque mondiale, 66, avenue d'Iéna, 75116 Paris, France.

At the time of writing, Ashoka Mody was principal financial economist in the World Bank's Cofinancing and Project Finance Department.

Library of Congress Cataloging–in–Publication Data

Infrastructure delivery : private initiative and the public good /
edited by Ashoka Mody.
    p. cm. — (EDI development studies, ISSN 1020–105X)
    Includes bibliographical references and index.
    ISBN 0–8213–3520–0
    1. Infrastructure (Economics) 2. Infrastructure (Economics) —
Finance. 3. Infrastructure (Economics) — Developing countries.
    I. Mody, Ashoka. II. Series.
HC79.C31516   1996
363—dc20   95–39451
                                                           CIP

Contents

Boxes

Tables

Figures

Foreword

As governments move toward increasing private provision of infrastructure, the benefits are evident in more and better services. However, the brief recent experience has also demonstrated that many challenges lie ahead. To effectively harness private initiative to meet the objectives of efficiency and fairness, governments themselves must gear up to deal with a new and sophisticated range of contracting, regulatory, and financial mechanisms. While much can be gained through a continued movement away from government to private provision, the benefits are unlikely to be either quickly or easily realized.

The essays in this book grew out of background papers for *World Development Report 1994*, which focused on infrastructure and development. Extensively revised and reworked, these essays present keen perspectives and policy guidance on the way ahead. They reflect on the historical experience of private infrastructure provision to identify factors leading to success. Lessons from the past have also led to modern analytical treatment of private incentives, regulatory design, and government risk management, which the book surveys in a widely accessible manner.

This book is part of the EDI Development Studies series and reflects EDI's commitment to present cutting-edge issues in a timely manner for policymakers and students.

Vinod Thomas,
Director
Economic Development Institute
The World Bank

Preface

The keen worldwide interest in increasing private participation in infrastructure has many facets—structuring new projects, introducing innovative regulatory practices, and designing and using new financial instruments. The World Bank's World Development Report 1994: Infrastructure and Development *described these exciting trends. Seven background papers written for that report (plus one paper written subsequently) form the basis of this book.*

The book explores several themes in greater depth than was possible in the *World Development Report*. The essays analyze from today's perspective the tension between harnessing private initiatives and protecting the public interest. This tension is conveyed in the Overview with a discussion of four mechanisms that discipline private providers of infrastructure: private incentives to operate efficiently, competitive forces that limit exploitation of consumers, regulation where competition is insufficient, and the control exercised by financial markets. Since no single mechanism is sufficient, combinations of measures are always needed to provide the required discipline.

The book does not intend to be comprehensive—given the many variations possible in the design and delivery of infrastructure and its supporting institutions. The variations in time and across spatial boundaries can be substantial and, due to differing histories and ideologies, can persist over long periods despite knowledge of "optimal" solutions. The book therefore explores certain themes and case studies in considerable depth to highlight the influence of history and ideas on the evolution of infrastructure delivery. In compiling these essays, we have made every attempt to bring the stories up to date, but many of the experiments described are evolving and bear watching.

The book does intend to satisfy a wide readership. While discussing complex concepts, every effort has been made to be clear and precise so that students of economics, politics, and public policy might benefit. Practitioners and students alike should find the analytical framework of the chapters and the case studies useful, including those that bring a historical perspective to current problems. Survey chapters probe in depth modern regulatory design and the management of contingent liabilities.

As editor, I would like to thank the authors for their continued efforts to refine the chapters. I would like especially to thank several reviewers who gave us the benefit of their thoughtful comments and advice: Michael Einhorn, David Haarmyer, Gregory Ingram, Christine Kessides, Dina Khatkhate, Subodh Mathur, and Lant Pritchett. Gregory Ingram's contribution goes beyond his comments: much of the work was initiated when he was staff director of the *World Development Report,* and his support has been critical to the completion of this book. Finally, the clarity of exposition and presentation owes much to the efforts of Andrea Brunholzl and Bruce Ross-Larson.

Contributors

Veronique Bishop is a financial analyst in the World Bank's Europe and Central Asia Department, where she manages telecommunications and other infrastructure projects. She has previously worked with Coopers & Lybrand's communications practice in London and with Citicorp Investment Bank in New York.

Barry Eichengreen is John L. Simpson Professor of Economics and Political Science at the University of California, Berkeley; a research associate of the National Bureau of Economic Research; and a research fellow of the Centre for Economic Policy Research. He has made major contributions to the study of international finance. Among his recent books are *A Retrospective on the Bretton Woods System: Lessons for International Monetary Reform* (with Michael D. Bordo, 1993), and *Reconstructing Europe's Trade and Payments: The European Payments Union* (1993).

Charles D. Jacobson is a policy historian with strong interests in environmental, telecommunications, and infrastructure issues. His recently completed manuscript, "Ties That Bind: Economic and Political Dilemmas of Networked Systems, 1800-1990" is still under review for publication by the University of Illinois Press. He is currently working as a researcher and consultant based in Washington, D.C.

Ashoka Mody is principal financial economist in the Resource Mobilization and Cofinancing Vice Presidency of the World Bank, where he advises widely on regulatory and financial policy and on project structuring. He writes extensively for scholarly and policy audiences and was on the core team of *World Development Report 1994*. He previously worked within the Bank on technology policy and international competitiveness. Earlier he worked at AT&T's Bell Laboratories.

Dilip Kumar Patro is a consultant with the World Bank's Resource Mobilization and Cofinancing Vice Presidency, where he works on international capital markets and assets pricing.

Thomas H. Pyle is managing director of Princeton Pacific Group, an investment banking consultancy specializing in project finance. He was formerly head of Merchant Banking of Bank Austria and associate director of Deutsche Bank's merchant banking activities in Hong Kong.

David E. M. Sappington holds the Lanzillotti-McKethan Eminent Scholar Chair in the Department of Economics at the University of Florida. Before joining the Florida faculty in 1990, Professor Sappington served as a district manager and member of the technical staff at Bell Communications Research. He has also served on the faculties of the University of Pennsylvania and the University of Michigan. Professor Sappington's research is focused on the design of incentive regulation. He has published widely on this subject and served as an adviser on the design of incentive regulation to a variety of firms and regulatory bodies. Professor Sappington currently serves on the editorial boards of five journals, including the *Journal of Regulatory Economics*, the *Journal of Industrial Economics*, and the *Journal of Economics and Management Strategy*.

Mark Schankerman is director of Policy Studies at the European Bank for Reconstruction and Development. He is presently on leave from the London School of Economics. Earlier he taught at New York University and he has consulted on telecommunications policy issues for more than a decade. His research contributions have been in the area of firm-level research and development and productivity growth.

Vinaya Swaroop is an economist in the World Bank's Policy Research Department. Before joining the Bank, he taught economics at the University of Wisconsin-Milwaukee. His main research interests are fiscal policy and growth, public sector pricing, and development economics.

Joel A. Tarr is the Richard S. Caliguiri Professor of Environmental and Urban History and Policy at Carnegie Mellon University. He has published widely on issues involving urban infrastructure and the urban environment, with a special focus on the use of history to inform contemporary policy problems. He has served on committees of the National Research Council and the Office of Technology Assessment.

Ning S. Zhu is an economist in the International Economics Department of the World Bank. He works on private debt restructuring in middle-income countries and official debt issues in low-income countries.

Overview

Infrastructure Delivery: New Ideas, Big Gains, No Panaceas

Ashoka Mody

Ideas efficacious at some times and in some human surroundings are not so at other times and elsewhere.

—William James
The Varieties of Religious Experience

World Development Report 1994 (WDR) spotlighted the incipient but strong move away from the overwhelming government domination of infrastructure delivery to private provision under increasingly competitive conditions. In chapters 3 and 5 of the WDR, technological change, advancements in regulatory design, and evolution of financial markets were identified as forces ushering in a new phase in the provision of infrastructure services. To elaborate on these forces of change—noting both their strengths and limitations—this book presents seven essays written as background to the two WDR chapters and one written subsequently. The first half of the book reviews the interplay of private initiative, competition, and regulation, while the second half traces the ongoing evolution of the financial tools used to fund the world's growing demand for infrastructure.

Government-run monopolies were once justified by the low production costs associated with large-scale operations and by the need to protect consumers from voracious private monopolies. But now there is growing recognition that private initiative—disciplined in part by competitive market forces—often has the upper hand in efficiently delivering infrastructure.

While the *government as a provider* is being outmoded (especially in sectors such as telecommunications and electric power) the *government as a regulator*—protecting the public interest—is acquiring a more prominent role.

Today there is a ferment of innovation in the tools governments use to safeguard the public interest. In the past, governments protected consumers from private monopolies by setting limits on their returns. This approach created no incentive to minimize the costs of delivering services, since compensation to the provider covered all operating costs and assured a "fair" return on investment. Now, by contrast, the restraints imposed by competition and so-called "incentive regulation" are being used to harness private initiative. Entrepreneurial governments are increasing the scope of competition by unbundling activities in which economies of scale have limited importance. Where scale economies continue to be severe, competition from substitutes or competition for the right to provide the (monopoly) services are being fostered. At the same time, regulatory instruments, such as price-caps, seek to limit service prices while maintaining private provider incentives for cost reduction.

Since the full range of changes—in ownership, sector structure, and regulatory regimes—takes time to implement, long-term contracts between governments and private providers are transitional devices that set the terms for financing urgently needed infrastructure projects. Projects under the build-operate-transfer (BOT) scheme and its many variants are the result. Such contractual arrangements have been most widely used to attract independent power generators, though they have also been applied extensively to toll roads and, increasingly, to water projects. The contracts are primarily regulatory instruments—spelling out the rights and obligations of private parties and the government—but they also serve to allocate risks and cash-flows and hence aid project financing. The financing innovation lies in using the cash-flows and assets of the project to attract the necessary funds—ideally, with limited or no recourse to the balance sheets of the private sponsors or to the government. In practice, governments continue to support projects with financial guarantees of key obligations and such subsidies as cash or land grants. The need, therefore, for accountability in government financing mechanisms has in no way diminished—it may even have increased due to the greater visibility of transactions undertaken.

Many of these new ideas are promising and valuable, but their novelty should not be overstated and their limits should be recognized. Today's changes are dismantling past structures, but they are also reviving earlier methods of financing and organizing infrastructure delivery (including those from the late 19th century). The expectation is that lessons have been learned and mistakes will be avoided. But however careful the design, no perfect solutions exist for all times and places. For example, incentive regulations—such as those seen in the United Kingdom in the 1980s and widely imitated elsewhere—overcome the ills of past regulatory schemes, but it is already evident that these methods must be continually tested and refined.

A framework proposed by Michael Jensen (1993) is adapted here to interpret and evaluate the current phase of infrastructure delivery. Jensen's framework identifies four mechanisms designed to induce business enterprises to keep their costs low while introducing new products and services and limiting the prices charged to consumers. These mechanisms include: private incentives for greater profits, competition, regulation, and discipline of financial markets. Importantly, Jensen notes that each mechanism has its limits and hence combinations of measures are required to address particular situations. Governments relying on private initiative in infrastructure—but seeking also to achieve public policy goals—need to consider the following possibilities and pitfalls:

- *Private incentives* replace diffuse systems of accountability under government ownership; however, private organizations also fail to operate efficiently where methods of corporate governance and internal controls are inadequate. Even where operations are technically efficient, monopoly prices lead to inefficient allocation of a society's resources.
- Thus, *competition in the marketplace* is a highly desirable complement to private incentives; but competition is not always feasible and may be slow to operate.
- *Regulatory oversight* limits egregious behavior where competition is unable to provide the required discipline; but regulation is cumbersome and brings ills of it own, such as special interest groups seeking to orient the system to their advantage.
- *Monitoring by financial markets* creates additional accountability and is a contrast especially to the lax standards for projects financed by government budgets; however, private financial markets can be excessively restrictive, rationing out desirable projects. Moreover, as noted, the need for government financing is rarely eliminated, and the combination of government and private financing in a project demands transparent mechanisms of limiting government exposure.

The sections that follow are organized to discuss, in turn, the operation of each of these disciplining mechanisms and how they interplay, providing a background to the essays in this book. While the essays fit this conceptual framework, not all aspects are necessarily covered, and some themes reappear from the different perspectives of the authors. Also, in various parts of this overview reference is made to portions of the *World Development Report* for the reader to follow up on specific examples and themes.

Public and Private: Not One—Always Both

Recent years have revealed a slow but definite shift from public to private delivery of infrastructure in most parts of the world. But these are yet experiments. Establishing a new—complementary—relationship between the private sector and public interests requires, like any relationship, a clear understanding of the strengths and weaknesses of each party, as well as their histories.

Purely economic arguments have rarely been influential in determining whether infrastructure should be under public or private ownership. Rather, at all times, infrastructure delivery has been conditioned by various —generally conflicting—ideals. In the opening chapter, Charles Jacobson and Joel Tarr trace over a century the prevailing influences on shifts along the public-private spectrum in the United States, Great Britain, and France. Besides economic development, infrastructure delivery has been shaped by other major forces, including the perception that "exclusion of nonpayers from some infrastructures such as roads and streets would amount to a denial of political and civil rights," a suspicion of concentrated economic power, concerns about the environment, and a view of the appropriate role of the state.

For much of the period between 1930 and 1980, in virtually all parts of the world, delivery of infrastructure was based on a particular constellation of ideas, leading to a particular social compact. In return for monopoly power, infrastructure providers were required to undertake several social obligations—most importantly, universal service at regulated prices. Monopoly providers were typically publicly owned. Even in the United States, where telecommunications and electric power were in private hands, urban transportation, water, and sewerage services were owned and operated by local governments. Often defended on narrow economic grounds— that large-scale operations housing complementary activities make delivery costs low—old ideas held their grip principally due to social and strategic objectives, which continue to be influential.

But their influence has not been enough to hide the cumulative economic failings of the old model. Operational inefficiency, lack of technological dynamism, and poor service to consumers widely characterize public infrastructure providers. Multiple goals and poor management accountability have resulted in substantial waste of resources, including overstaffing, as infrastructure provision became a source of political patronage in a system where the consumer had virtually no voice (World Bank 1994, chapter 2). Since the basic assumptions of economies of scale or lower costs from jointly delivering related services (economies of scope) were not valid in many parts of infrastructure, continuing monolithic government provision was based on shaky economic grounds in the first place. Even where gains from economies of scale and scope are available, these now need to be weighed against benefits from private profit incentives, competition between providers, arm's-length regulation, and the accountability demanded by shareholders. Most evidence has come from the privatization of the telecommunications sector where reforms are the most advanced. Shareholders and labor have benefited from increased value of the enterprise following privatization and consumers have benefited from more reliable and responsive service, even if they sometimes have had to pay sharply higher prices (Galal, Jones, Tandon, and Vogelsang 1994).

Perhaps the more striking indictment of the previous regime was its failure also to deliver on a key social objective. In an adaptation of the universal service goal, the model was justified in developing countries as an instrument for delivering public services to the poor—and to rural areas. However, a system was perpetuated that was neither efficient nor accessible to the poor (World Bank 1994, chapter 4). It is commonplace that the poor in developing countries have least access to infrastructure services—what use is subsidized piped water when poor households have no water connections? The result: poor families must purchase water from private vendors at "market" prices, several times the subsidized public utility prices. Similarly, small businesses that are unable to access power from the public utility install expensive and polluting power generators.

Today, as the system is questioned, its legacy is not easy to dismantle. Rates charged for services are often too low to meet costs and complex cross-subsidies exist among services and regions. Privileged consumers, including wealthy farmers in rural areas, and incumbent providers would like the arrangement to continue and often have the political backing to sustain the structure despite its failings. Certain long-held precepts must be discarded to eliminate the perverse incentives of the current system. A major casualty is likely to be universal service. It was never a realistic possibility in most developing countries, and it must be substantially abandoned for effective privatization (and even more so for the introduction of competition). While certain cross-subsidies to facilitate wider access to infrastructure networks will persist even under private provision—and explicit taxpayer funding of loss-generating activities is likely to emerge—the elusive target of universal access creates gross financial imbalances and is thus incompatible with financial accountability.

This is not to imply that economic efficiency will or must be the only objective. Both for tactical reasons—to facilitate the transition—and to achieve long-term social policy goals, objectives other than economic efficiency will rightfully exert significant influence. Both of these forces are observed in telecommunications sector privatizations as Veronique Bishop, Ashoka Mody, and Mark Schankerman document in chapter 2. Even in New Zealand, where the government has withdrawn from operations and scaled back its regulatory role, it has retained—through a "kiwi share" in the privatized telecommunications company—an option to guide sectoral development. Similarly, Malaysia—another pioneer of privatization—has extensively used a single, "golden" government share in telecommunications and in other sectors (World Bank 1994, box 3.8). Elsewhere, restrictions on foreign ownership have been maintained even as privatization has proceeded (in Mexico, for example). In all countries, the rights of the incumbent labor force have been protected through limits on labor redundancy, stakes in the privatized firm, and profit-sharing. The challenge is to keep these noncommercial objectives distinct and insulated so that private incentives are not diluted.

But will private incentives be sufficient? Drawing upon events over the past century, Jacobson and Tarr note that where market discipline has been high, performance by private firms has generally been better than where such discipline was absent or low. Using contemporary examples, Bishop, Mody, and Schankerman describe the opportunities for competition in all segments of the telecommunications sector. But competitive possibilities exist beyond telecommunications. Creative restructuring of sectors—eliminating regulatory barriers to entry—and rules for fair competition are needed.

Competition: One Size Does Not Fit All

Establishing competition in infrastructure requires three steps (figure 1). The starting point is to take a long, hard look at the structure of the sector, assessing how the services may be unpackaged. Unbundling feeds into the next stage, creating opportunities for competition in one or more segments of the sector. Where unfettered competition is possible, the process ends.

Figure 1. *Unbundling Activities Increases the Options for Competition and Private Sector Development*

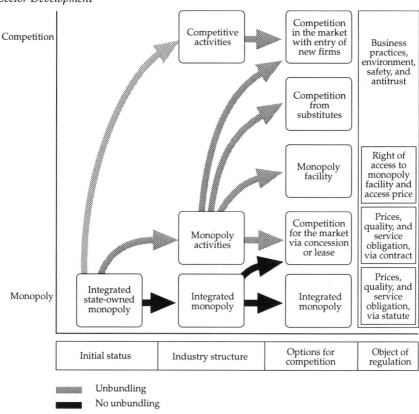

Source: World Bank (1994).

However, limited scope for competition implies that regulatory oversight is typically required to maintain fair competition and to protect consumers. The extent of unbundling, the exact nature of competition, and the objectives of regulation depend on the physical and institutional characteristics of the sector (table 1).

The sequential strategy set out here may seem at odds with a commonly held precept that "regulation must precede privatization." That may well be true when the only action contemplated is privatization of a state-owned monopoly. However, when a more fundamental restructuring of the sector is to be undertaken, a different perspective applies. The degree of competition and the relationships between final service providers and their intermediate input suppliers are primary in conditioning the behavior of market

Table 1. *Sectoral Strategies for Competition and Regulation*

	Water	Transport	Power	Telecom
Unbundling activities	Unbundling of bulk water from transmission and distribution.	Unbundling of track and services in rail transport; Unbundling of maintenance and service in roads— applies to all sectors.	Unbundling of generation, transmission and distribution.	Unbundling of local and long-distance services, or separation of network and delivery services.
Competition	For the market: through leases and concessions.	Concessions for natural monopoly activities such as track or toll road segments; Competition also from substitute modes of trnasport.	Direct competition in generation through "spot" markets or long-term contracts; Competition also in distribution through right of access to other distributors; Competition from substitute sources of energy.	Direct competition in virtually all activities.
Objects of regulation	Price, quality environmental protection, investment and service obligations.	Regulations of access and access pricing to railtrack; Safety and environment; Price regulation to be minimized where competition from substitutes exists.	Regulation of access and access pricing to transmission and distribution facilities; Safety and environment.	Regulation of access pricing; Consumer prices, where local telecom facilties are natural monopolies.

participants. Thus, to be effective, regulatory scope and form must reflect the sector structure and follow from the unbundling decisions. Consider Chile, where sophisticated regulation was established prior to privatization in electric power and telecommunications. But a lack of competition and the existence of potentially collusive relationships led to a reassessment of the regulatory strategy (Bitran and Saez 1994). Some aspects of regulation may well be implemented ahead of the full articulation of the sector strategy. But in Chile and elsewhere, regulation continues to evolve with changes in market structure.

Unbundling

A sector may be sliced *vertically*, delinking those who provide intermediate inputs from those who serve the customer. In telecommunications, ownership and operation of the physical network can be a different business from connecting customers to one another. In the electric power sector, generation, transmission, and distribution can each be under different ownership and management. Separation of track from rail services is another illustration of vertical unbundling. *Horizontal* unbundling occurs: (1) when entities are broken up to compete with each other and prevent economic dominance in the post-privatization phase and (2) when lines of business are separated by the customer served (such as passenger and freight) or by region. Horizontal unbundling creates the possibility of competition by comparison. In such competition, also referred to as "benchmark" or "yardstick" competition, the regulator uses information on all providers to determine price and performance levels.

By isolating the natural monopoly segments of a sector—where economies of scale prevail—unbundling promotes new entry and competition in other segments that are potentially competitive. Failure to unbundle can constrain an entire sector to monopoly provision even when numerous activities are ripe for competition. The trend is unmistakable: unbundling of infrastructure services is proceeding at a brisk pace.

Unbundling does involve trade-offs. Where economies of scope exist, it may be cheaper for a single provider to produce and deliver two or more services jointly than for separate entities to provide the services individually. A bundled sector—where all services are organized under one umbrella—allows exploitation of economies of scope and eases coordination among intermediate input suppliers and final service providers. An argument against unbundling also applies when a single provider benefiting from economies of scale (say, a power generator) is split up to induce competition (in power generation). However, even in such cases, gains from economies of scope and scale need to be weighed against benefits of cost-minimizing due to competitive pressures.

Moreover, gains from economies of scope need not always be lost through unbundling. Instead of a physical separation of activities, an accounting separation—such as between network provision and service provision in telecommunications—allows economies of scope to be preserved in the integrated firm, while new entrants can compete without fear of unfair pricing of intermediate inputs (Bishop, Mody, and Schankerman: chapter 2). Thus, interconnection pricing, or the pricing of networks—telephone networks, rail tracks, gas pipelines, and electricity grids—becomes a distinctive and critical element in an unbundled network.

Bundled systems have also been the mechanism for conveying subsidies to poor customers or those in remote areas. Unbundling is not sustainable where subsidies cannot be eliminated due to political pressures or to a lack of institutional capability in the previously subsidized segments. Still, unbundling is desirable ultimately because it makes cross-subsidies between different lines of business more transparent, identifies more precisely the subsidies needed to deliver services to the poor, and improves management accountability.

Options for Competition

Once sectors have been unbundled, competition can be used to achieve efficiency and new investment. In infrastructure services, the choice is not simply between unfettered supply in the marketplace and monopoly government supply. Intermediate arrangements for market-based provision are possible and often advisable.

Multiple providers may compete directly with each other, with regulatory control ensuring fair competition. A key requirement for fair competition is that all providers have equal access to the network (the phone or electricity grids or the roads). Access may be restricted by regulatory barriers held over from when monopolies were viewed as socially efficient. Regulatory barriers have come into question—even where economies of scale and scope favor a single provider—by the theory of contestable markets, which argues that the existence of potential rival suppliers limits the risks of monopoly abuse. Competing providers are common in various segments of telecommunications, in electric power generation, and in urban transport (World Bank 1994, chapter 3).

Barriers may also be commercially generated as when a large provider uses aggressive pricing or engages in other anticompetitive practices. Regulators must facilitate new entry by limiting restrictive practices. The ability of new entrants to interconnect to the existing network on equal terms with other providers is of increasing importance, especially in the context of unbundled networks. In telecommunications, electric power, and gas sectors, where transmission tends to be a natural monopoly, interconnection pricing is an evolving policy area where no firm principles have yet been established (Bishop, Mody, and Schankerman: chapter 2).

Although many developing countries have accepted multiple provision in electric power generation, that does not always mean that generators compete with each other. Most "independent power producers" sell to the transmission utility through long-term contracts, as in the Philippines. Among less developed countries, Chile and Argentina foster competition through sales by generators to a power pool, where a grid manager makes periodic determination of the cheapest supply sources to meet current demand. Competition is also maintained where generators are free to engage in long-term supply contracts directly with distributors, and the transmission company serves only as transportation. Bitran and Saez (1994), however, caution that significant opportunities for exercising market power may remain where ownership of assets remains concentrated. (A similar policy debate is evolving in the United Kingdom as major power generating companies seek to buy distribution companies.)

Further development of competition in the electric power sector is beginning to emerge in distribution segments in the United Kingdom and, more recently, in the United States. Direct competition in electricity distribution occurs when consumers are permitted to buy electricity from sellers of choice, and local distributors—whose wires link the customer's premises to the grid—are required to "wheel" electricity from competitors. Introduction of such competition, however, raises a transitional concern. Many distributors have signed high-priced long-term contracts with their suppliers so that when forced to wheel cheaper power supplied by other distributors, they are left "stranded" with past commitments incurred under a regulatory regime that allowed them to pass on the costs of power supply to consumers. Norms for resolving this concern have yet to be established.

COMPETITION FOR THE MARKET may be created through leases or concessions. Firms compete not for individual consumers in the market but for the *right* to supply the entire market. Where direct competition is impossible, competition managed through such contractual arrangements can increase efficiency. Contracts range from covering a specific service to long-term concessions that require operation, maintenance, and facility expansion.

Concessions have been especially important in water distribution and in toll roads, but they also could be effective in electricity distribution as a prelude to direct competition. A successful water concession was awarded recently in Buenos Aires, Argentina, where the possibilities of increased efficiency has allowed the successful bidder to lower prices below the level prevailing under public ownership and management.

The design and award of concessions requires substantial preparation. Bidders may engage in prolonged game-playing with each other and with the awarding agency when the relevant economic information (on costs and demand patterns) is not available or is withheld and when the bid evaluation process is complex and opaque. Careful prefeasibility studies, simple bidding and award criteria, and competitive access to all bidders facilitates efficient investment and operation.

Competition for the market occurs before the contract is signed and returns when the contract expires or is due for renewal. The winner of the contract thus faces no competition during the duration of the concession. The threat of being replaced at the end of the contract can, therefore, be an important disciplining force. However, as Jacobson and Tarr report (chapter 1), incumbents generally retain concession rights over long periods of time (Kwong 1994 reports the same for Hong Kong). The commitments in the concession contract substitute for a formal regulatory mechanism to protect the public interest.

Finally, *competition from substitutes* can be effective in certain sectors. A monopoly may appear to exist only because sectoral boundaries are drawn by physical rather than economic characteristics. The threat of losing customers to suppliers of substitute products provides motivation and discipline. Energy and surface transport are the two most important areas where competition from substitutes exerts pressure on the monopoly supplier. For example, a sole natural gas provider cannot keep power generation customers from using other fuels such as oil and coal. Instead of extending regulation to other related services, competition from substitutes can discipline the conduct of the perceived monopolist. The dangers of overregulation have been most noticeable in the transport sector. In the United States, for example, regulation of railways required controls on road transportation, which led to inefficiencies in both sectors. Hence the substantial abandonment of regulation in the late 1970s and early 1980s. For Hong Kong,

Kwong (1994) reports that in the effort to regulate urban transportation, competition between taxis, buses, and trains was thwarted while road congestion worsened.

Regulation: A Light Touch with Focused Goals

Market forces are potent, but not sufficient. With growing private delivery, the government's regulatory role is acquiring greater importance. However, regulation can be intrusive and is beset by imperfections of its own—such as vulnerability to capture by political and commercial interests. The trend is, therefore, towards regulation with a "light touch," in which the regulator steps away from detailed prescriptions and instead monitors outcomes.

The variety of regulatory practices that exist reflect the multiple goals and constraints for each sector, resulting in a wide range of public-private roles in infrastructure delivery. David Sappington (chapter 3) describes how regulators must balance different, often conflicting, objectives that evolve over time and vary by industry. The regulator must prevent abuse of a dominant market position, ensure new market entry, limit the prices charged to consumers, and establish norms for network interconnection rights and prices. Also included in the scope of regulation are quality of service, investment obligations, and information disclosure requirements. Not all of these objectives can be met simultaneously.

Regulatory Instruments

Where the main public objective is to protect consumers from monopoly prices, a traditional approach has been to set limits on the infrastructure provider's rate of return. Known as "cost plus" or "embedded cost" regulation, the method allows the provider to charge a price that covers costs and allows a "fair" return on the capital invested. The pitfalls of such a system are well-known: providers have an incentive to inflate costs, regulators are not well-positioned to determine costs, and wrangling over allowed costs and returns can protract regulatory decisionmaking.

The central problem in regulation has been the asymmetry of information—the regulator knows less than the firm being regulated. The question: How can a socially responsible regulatory regime exploit the private information available to the regulated firm? The answer: create incentives for the firm to use its information towards social ends.

To prevent regulation from becoming intrusive, "light," or incentive, regulation requires decentralization of regulatory activity—or the delegation of certain decisionmaking to the regulated firm—to exploit the firm's private information about consumer demand and production technology. Such delegation also economizes on the regulator's resources. However, to be truly effective, this approach must permit the regulated firm considerable discretion in conducting its business. As such, regulators must limit the goals they seek to achieve. For example, they may need to forgo restrictions on a firm's profits to allow incentives for low cost production.

One outcome of this line of thinking has led to price-cap regulation. Here, a cap is set on the rate at which prices can be increased. The allowable rate of increase is equal to the economy-wide rate of inflation, measured by a retail price index (RPI), less the X-factor, which measures the extent to which the sectoral productivity growth is higher than in the rest of the economy. Thus, prices are capped at the general level of inflation when the sector being regulated is experiencing productivity growth at the same rate as the rest of the economy. Where sectoral productivity growth is higher than average productivity growth, the gains are passed on to consumers through reduced price increases. With the consumer thus protected, regulatory resource use is minimized because regulation is not based on the firm's *costs*, which are difficult to observe, but rather on the prices charged, which are easily monitored. Since a limit is set on prices, an incentive is created to reduce costs beyond that implied by the predetermined X-factor, thus exploiting private information ultimately for public objectives.

That is the theory. Now the practice. In practice, such regulation has been effective in containing prices to the consumer. But its greatest success—rapid cost reduction, following from the incentives created—has also been a source of regulatory embarrassment. In the United Kingdom where such regulation was pioneered and is most extensively applied—in telecommunications, electric power, water, and soon the privatized rail system—practice is beginning to diverge from the conceptual ideal. A key principle of this regime is that the X-factor should be revised only infrequently—once in five to seven years. Otherwise, the regulator is implicitly back in the business of monitoring the regulated firm's costs. In the United Kingdom the telecommunications regulator has made "unscheduled" adjustments to the X-factor when profits have appeared to grow too rapidly (Bishop, Mody, and Schankerman: chapter 2). Also, the electricity regulator's actions have led to calls for a complete review of the present system. The regulator agreed to an apparently low X-factor—permitting high prices and profits—then within several months decided to review the decision after observing high profits.

Some have suggested that incentives for cost reduction can be maintained through the RPI-X method, and when profits exceed prespecified levels, a part of the excess can be passed on as benefits to consumers. At the other end, if profits fall too low, price increases would be allowed above the level set by the formula (Sappington: chapter 3). The caution against such an approach is that once measures of profit enter into the regulatory domain, the regulator is once again engaged in eliciting privately held information on revenues and costs.

Other practical matters arise. Adjustments to the RPI-X formula are sought to allow for social obligations. The major example here is in water regulation, where environmental standards require new capital investments for which the firm seeks a higher allowed price increase. In the United Kingdom, this has resulted in an additional "K-factor" that permits price increases over and above the basic RPI-X formula. Then, as Bishop, Mody, and Schankerman describe, there is the matter of defining the basket of services to go under a price-cap plan as well as determination of the X-factor.

While these practicalities are being ironed out in specific circumstances, new ideas continue to emerge (Sappington: chapter 3). In a further refinement of incentive regulation, a firm may be allowed to choose one compensation plan from a well-structured menu of alternative plans. Also, less scrutiny of the firm's proposed activities may be coupled with more severe penalties (such as lower prices or lower allowed rates of return) for marked differences between observed industry performance and the firm's predictions.

Light regulation is a step forward, but it does not eliminate trade-offs in the design of regulatory organization. Regulatory flexibility is valued, but so is commitment to fixed rules. Too much flexibility leaves room for strong interest groups to gain control of the regulatory process to their own benefit. Too rigid a regulatory framework limits needed adaptability to change and to correct mistakes. Rapid technological change favors flexibility, whereas insufficient government credibility requires strong commitment to rules. Alternatives to sectoral regulation—bearing their own limitations—include contractual agreements with individual firms and reliance on general anti-trust laws to maintain fair competition.

Establishing an Accountable Regulator

A regulator must be independent of the government and from those it regulates. Yet, it must be accountable. A new regulator is established, either as an autonomous agency or as a nonministerial government department, to administer the agreed on regulatory principles. The law creating the regulator confers security of tenure, spells out the regulator's duties, and defines operating procedures, including the regulator's authority to review the terms under which industry participants operate (for example, the license terms for interconnection and other matters affecting competition).

Regulatory independence helps avoid "capture" of the regulator, that is, undue influence by either the government or the regulated industry. The temptation for political interference is particularly strong in infrastructure because politicians are concerned that price increases (which contribute to inflation) will damage their electoral standing. The result in many countries has been extensive cross-subsidies and the suppression of price increases. Political involvement in sector policies also follows from a desire to influence personnel decisions or to spur investments and economic development within preferred jurisdictions. Autonomy from ministerial interference and accountability directly to the legislature are, therefore, highly desirable; in practice, however, ministerial authority in changing policy direction cannot be denied. Perhaps, the most effective—though still imperfect—insulation from political interference results when regulatory tenures do not coincide with those of the political cycle. Another concern is capture by those regulated. Consumer representation on regulatory boards and other avenues to voice concerns are required.

Once established, a regulatory body needs to develop rules and procedures of operation. The tradition in the United States has been to conduct lengthy public hearings and investigations to inform the regulator. While these are valuable, they can also be very costly. In particular, they can slow the introduction of new products and new pricing structures that better reflect production costs. Lagging firms can intentionally prolong hearings in order to suppress initiatives by an enterprising competitor. Consumers can be hurt by this process, and inefficient industry structures can result. Similarly, decisions are slower when made by a commission than by an individual regulator. But, in most developing countries, the slow speed may be preferable to the alternative of closed-door hearings by a single individual, which introduces the danger of opaque and arbitrary decisionmaking.

Alternatives to Sectoral Regulation

Where the resources and commitment do not exist to implement sector-wide regulation through an independent regulatory body, the obligations may be collected in a contract with the private infrastructure provider. This method has attracted many independent power producers where power generation shortfalls are large and new investments cannot wait for the development of sectoral regulatory authority—as in the Philippines. Often, the contracts have been backed by the financial guarantees from the government and from private sponsors (again, as in the Philippines). These guarantees specify compensation when contracts are not honored. Although effective in the short-run, the lack of a sectoral viewpoint means that investments may be inconsistent with the long-term strategy. (For example, high-cost power plants may be established or the flexibility to introduce competition later may be compromised by provisions of specific contracts.)

The decision may also be taken to abandon targeted sectoral regulation and instead rely on existing laws that govern general business practice, such as the telecommunications sector in New Zealand that relies on anti-trust laws for regulation. Soon after sectoral deregulation, the courts there were called to decide on the complex matter of interconnection prices (Bishop, Mody, and Schankerman: chapter 2). It is not easy to gauge the success of the model since the economic arguments for alternative approaches to interconnection pricing are still evolving (the court deliberations do, however, provide an engaging account of the ongoing debates). In most developing countries, complete reliance on the court system is not feasible, but the legal system will have an important role in the overall scheme of checks and balances, as will other indirectly related regulatory institutions, such as the securities and exchange commissions.

Government Finance—Off Again, On Again

Governments now provide or intermediate the bulk of infrastructure financing. Over 90 percent of financial flows for infrastructure are channeled through a government sponsor that bears almost all project risks (World Bank 1994, chapter 5). Infrastructure finance has generally drained government resources, since cost recovery has rarely been a serious goal as Vinaya Swaroop describes through several case studies in chapter 5. Private finance is needed to ease the burden on governmental budgets, but, equally, to foster greater accountability and closer monitoring of performance.

Tightly structured contractual agreements—laying out the financial obligations of all contracting parties—are critical to successful project financing. Where administrative capability is limited—rendering traditional financial intermediaries weak—such contractually based project financing best attracts private investors (figure 2). But infrastructure also stands to gain from parallel innovations delivering long-term finance through alternative institutions and instruments. The development of domestic capital

Figure 2. *Options for Financing Increase with Administrative Capacity and Maturity of Domestic Capital Markets*

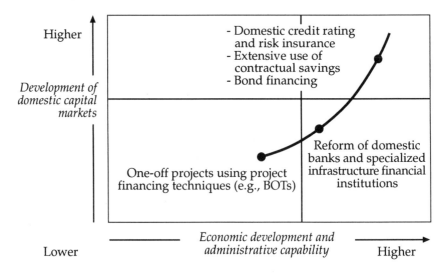

Source: World Bank (1994).

markets is the goal. Once credit rating and public regulation of financial markets are in place, options open up, including the use of long-term contractual savings.

Here—as in their regulatory function—governments are unlikely to wither away. Present trends indicate a new role for governments, one that marks a partial return to the ways of the late 19th century as described vividly by Barry Eichengreen in chapter 4. Then, as now, governments provided cash and land grants for infrastructure development and, most importantly, they mitigated private sector risks by providing financial guarantees. Risk mitigation is also a growing line of business for international financial intermediaries such as the export credit agencies and the multilateral development banks (see the account by Ning Zhu in chapter 6).

Eichengreen (chapter 4) shows that excessive guarantees in the late-19th century weakened private incentives to monitor financial performance and created a strain on budgetary resources. Today, a greater appreciation exists for the need to transfer substantial risks to the private sector and to better manage the contingent liabilities that arise from issuing guarantees (Ashoka Mody and Dilip Patro: chapter 8).

Project Finance

The financing of a project is said to be *nonrecourse* when lenders are repaid only from the cash flow generated by the project or, in the event of complete failure, from the value of the project's assets. Lenders may also have *limited recourse* to the assets of a parent company sponsoring a project or to the government through its guarantees. The use of such nonrecourse or limited recourse financing—also known as *project financing*—is a transitional response to activities recently brought into the orbit of the private sector. Thus, project financing, which permits sponsors to raise funds secured by the revenues and assets of a particular project, is often used in new ventures that have no track records.

To be successful, however, this financing technique requires a clearer delineation of risk than in traditional public projects. Hence, project financing can be complex and time-consuming because the interests of various parties have to be secured through contractual agreements. But new safeguards and conventions are evolving to deal with project risks and complexities. The expectation is that projects financed on a limited-recourse basis will, over time, develop a track record that will provide comfort for future investments. An important policy question is whether government tax revenues should be used to provide recourse, in the form of guarantees to lenders.

Parties to a private sector project financing include sponsors, arrangers, contractors, governments, end users, banks, lawyers, and consultants. The balance between financial players under project financing is outlined by Thomas H. Pyle (chapter 7). Equity typically forms less than 30 percent of the financing, of which foreign sponsors in developing countries take a 30 to 60 percent share. Technical majority control is generally maintained by local partners, though effective control remains with the foreign contractor. Stages of a project financing include market development and determination of need, assembling of sponsors, determining technical and financial feasibility, structuring, arranging and implementing the financing, and finally, monitoring performance.

Project finance is being used mainly in toll road and power plant projects under BOT and other, similar arrangements. The exact number of projects completed and in the pipeline is difficult to establish because no systematic recording method exists and because projects fall through even after being declared complete. However, an indicative assessment of the sectoral distribution is possible from table 2. Transportation projects, largely toll roads, dominate the numbers and the value of projects in high-income and developing countries (table 2). The more than two-thirds share of trans-

Table 2. Project Financing of Funded Infrastructure Projects, by Sector, October 1993

Country group	Number of projects funded	All projects	Power	Transport	Water and environmental infrastructure	Telecommunications	Other
World	148	100	13	60	16	2	10
High income	64	100	8	48	25	2	17
Middle income	77	100	16	69	10	3	3
Low income	7	100	29	57	0	0	14

Source: Public Works Financing (1993).

port projects in middle-income countries are in part due to the extensive toll-road programs in Argentina, Malaysia, and Mexico. As Pyle's case studies (chapter 7) show, however, power stations are better investments because economic returns are generally ensured through long-term contracts—and returns can be substantial.

Toll roads, by contrast, are often beset with problems. In Thailand, construction of highways in the Bangkok area has been troubled by lack of interagency coordination and lack of clarity in contractual arrangements (Pyle: chapter 7). The Mexican toll-road program illustrates the dangers of launching a major initiative with multiple objectives and insufficient preparation. The contract terms failed to pin the responsibility for construction time and costs on the private project sponsors. De facto flexibility in the concession period allowed sponsors to shift cost increases onto the consumer or the government. Creditors (mainly state-owned banks) failed to perform their normal appraisal and monitoring functions. The resulting high tolls have held down road use, although measures are now being introduced to improve the economics of these roads by lengthening concession periods, permitting a decline in tolls and hence an increase in usage.

Water and environmental infrastructure is another growth area—projects are being undertaken in middle-income countries (especially for waste water treatment), and their diffusion to low-income countries is imminent.

Today, project financing stands at a crossroads. While much has been achieved, the way forward depends as much on a new style of government functioning as on realistic expectations of private returns from infrastructure projects. While the need for sector-wide reforms is evident, greater attention to the terms on which private concessions are awarded and regulated is of critical importance. Project finance advisory services—including project and contract development—can provide high value, and the international official financial agencies can play an important role in disseminating best practice. But success will also require scaling back of private sector demands for monopoly rights—which prevents the advance of a sectoral reform agenda—and reducing claims on government guarantees, which are a finite resource.

Role of Governments

The conventional reasons for government involvement in infrastructure are economies of scale in delivery, public goods characteristics (as in roads), and external effects (especially in water and sewerage services). But government involvement does not imply recurring government subsidies. Principles of cost recovery, Swaroop (chapter 5) argues, should guide financing decisions. He even offers cautious support for earmarking of taxes, as when road and vehicle taxes are used for road investments and maintenance rather than being merged with general government revenues.

Eichengreen offers a more specific argument for government finance of infrastructure. Financial institutions and markets will often ration resources to risky infrastructure projects either because they are unable to monitor and control certain risks—including performance by their borrowers—or because they are unable to distinguish good projects from bad. In such a situation, if governments have better information (usually a big "if") or if they are better able to manage specific risks, then they can play a constructive role in stimulating infrastructure investment.

Today, the trend is towards governments providing guarantees that cover so-called "sovereign" risks. These include risks arising from government policy and regulatory actions that may go against the terms set in the original contract. In practice, risks being covered are substantial, due to a broad interpretation of sovereign risk. For example, when private independent power producers sell to a government utility under a "take-or-pay" contract (better described as a "take and pay or pay anyway" contract), the government's guarantee of that contract effectively provides coverage of market and credit risk. Private investors sometimes have legitimate concerns about the ability of utilities to pay their bills.

To transfer significant risks back to the private sector, governments need to introduce sectoral and enterprise reforms that place the utilities on a sound financial footing. Specific guarantee "fall away" provisions can be attached to indices of the utilities' financial performance. Guarantees must, therefore, be seen as transitional instruments that facilitate private investment while basic reforms are being undertaken. At the same time, prudent management of their contingent liabilities requires a more discriminating award of guarantees (including reduced coverage, where feasible), better monitoring of the performance of guaranteed projects, and an account of and reserve against the liabilities created (Mody and Patro: chapter 8).

Official Finance

As governments focus more on facilitating rather than financing infrastructure, international development banks—long the partners of governments in supporting traditional financing systems—also will need to experiment with new ways of doing business. The multilateral agencies are modifying their lending policies to encourage the expansion of both domestic and international private sector sources. Commercializing state-owned utilities, improving the legal and regulatory frameworks, and developing domestic financial markets are on the policy agendas of all international financial institutions.

Paralleling and complementing the efforts of host governments, a growing area of activity for bilateral and multilateral financial agencies is risk mitigation to facilitate private capital flows to infrastructure projects. Guarantees seek to assure lenders against defaults arising from inability to convert the local currency into a foreign currency and against political risk (the risk that policy and regulatory changes or expropriatory acts would render the project unviable). While such coverage is available from private companies, the rates are high and the amount of coverage is limited.

In this context, Zhu (chapter 6) explains the evolving roles of export credit agencies (ECAs)—national agencies that promote the export and investment interests of domestic firms. Leveraging on their traditional business as important underwriters and major financiers for the purchase of capital goods, ECAs are actively entering the project finance area. In their most limited form, export credit agency guarantees or insurance may be extended only against sovereign risk, making exporters or bankers responsible for commercial risks. In most cases, guarantees are extended to both types of risk, in part because it is difficult to distinguish between sovereign and commercial risks. The primary motives for setting up such insurance schemes are to support export industries (and thus employment) and to meet competition. So, export credit agency premiums have been highly subsidized (although premiums have been increased following losses in the 1980s).

Typically, ECA guarantees are backed by host government counterguarantees. However, reflecting government concerns to reduce their exposure in private projects, ECAs are beginning to provide guarantees that are not counterguaranteed. The Hopewell-Pagbilao deal for an independent power project in the Philippines marked the first time that a loan from an export-import bank was not backed by a government counterguarantee. Recently, the German agency Kreditanstalt fur Wiederaufbau (KfW) has financed projects with guarantees from local authorities but without guarantees from the federal governments in China and India (Zhu: chapter 6).

To attract international private capital to developing countries, several multilateral development banks, including the World Bank, the Asian Development Bank, and the Inter-American Development Bank, have also developed guarantee schemes to protect lenders. All these institutions operate on the principle that the guarantee must cover only those risks that the private sector is least able to bear. The World Bank's *partial risk* guarantees for project financing cover sovereign risks associated with infrastructure projects. Such a guarantee has been used for the Hub Power Project in Pakistan. (The World Bank also issues *partial credit* guarantees to facilitate long-maturity borrowing in international capital markets by guaranteeing payments in the later years. The proceeds from such loans can be used for infrastructure investments.) The World Bank requires counterguarantees from host governments, thus reinjecting the role of the government in determining project priorities and level of assistance to be provided. The other development banks do not require counterguarantees, but thus far have not done projects without them.

What the Future May Hold

The shift from public to private provision and from monopolies to competition is, for the present, a decisive one. Most evidence points to the benefits of the change—increased productivity, greater responsiveness to consumers, and reduced burden on governments. The good news is that private enterprise has been moving into a wide range of countries and projects. Legal and regulatory reform is underway. Flows of foreign direct investment by new infrastructure entrepreneurs are on the rise, as are international flows of portfolio capital. And the growth of domestic capital markets gives cause for optimism.

The transition is neither quick nor easy. Even in telecommunications, technological dynamism has not been sufficient to coax the institutional changes required. As Bishop, Mody, and Schankerman (chapter 2) note, Chile has spread its telecommunications reform efforts over two decades. Although lessons learned will speed institutional reform, the pace of change may still be soberingly long. In India, for example, the dominant network will be run by a government department for the foreseeable future. Competition through mobile telephony has been in the cards, but actual provision has been delayed for several years. A bold experiment in competition for local services is being attempted, but again, only time will resolve the intricacies of the tendering process. After that, the "rules of the game" and a credible regulatory body will have to be established to ensure effective competition.

Thus, technological dynamism—or the lack of it—is not the critical determinant of institutional innovations in infrastructure delivery. Progress will depend on the implementing capacity of the state and private sectors in different settings and their strategic visions. The constraints seem to lie mainly in overcoming the inertia to implement the individual changes and in coordinating the various components. These limits are largely explained by the continuing power of old ideas and established interests.

The present arrangements discussed in this volume are but experiments responding to a historical setting. Success in exploiting this transition and its new ideas lies in making sound technical decisions in market structure, regulation, and finance—and the more demanding task of building new, and often complex, relationships. The key players—policymakers with vision, private providers, and regulators—are in the process of developing new operating norms. The most significant lesson may be that sharp distinctions between public and private apply neither to practice nor analysis. Instead, public-private partnerships, more than a cliché, challenge us to think of new structures that blend private initiative with public accountability.

Bibliography

Bitran, Eduardo, and Raul E. Saez. 1994. "Privatization and Regulation in Chile" in Barry Bosworth, Rudiger Dornbusch, and Raul Laban, eds., *The Chilean Economy: Policy Lessons and Challenges.* Washington D.C.: The Brookings Institution.

Galal, Ahmed, Leroy Jones, Pankaj Tandon, and Ingo Vogelsang. 1994. *Welfare Consequences of Selling Public Enterprises.* New York: Oxford University Press.

Jensen, Michael C. 1993. "The Modern Industrial Revolution, Exit, and the Failure of Internal Control Systems." *Journal of Finance* XLVIIII (3): 831-79.

Kwong, Sunny Kai-Sun. 1994. "Infrastructural and Economic Development in Hong Kong." Background Paper to the *World Development Report 1994.* World Bank, Washington, D.C.

Public Works Financing. 1993. 67 (October).

World Bank. 1994. *World Development Report 1994: Infrastructure for Development.* New York: Oxford University Press.

1

No Single Path: Ownership and Financing of Infrastructure in the 19th and 20th Centuries

Charles D. Jacobson and Joel A. Tarr

The history of infrastructure provision in the United States, Great Britain, and France has been rich with institutional variation and experimentation. Yet certain consistent themes can be discerned. While direct competition between private firms has been uncommon in many infrastructure sectors, forms of market discipline have at times arisen from interproduct competition and other sources. Factors affecting private firm performance have included the presence or absence of such forms of market discipline, the degree to which measurement and monitoring difficulties are encountered in contracting for public goods, and contingencies of political and institutional development. Ownership and regulatory choices themselves have been influenced by pragmatic judgments concerning performance, economic development goals, and beliefs concerning the role of the state in society. In light of this history, attributes of markets served, the character of public purposes implicated, and the administrative capabilities of governments themselves all bear close examination in considering whether and how to increase roles played by private firms in furnishing different infrastructures.

Simple distinctions between "public" and "private" do not even begin to encompass the range of options used over the past 150 years regarding the ownership, financing, and operation of different infrastructures. User fees, levies on abutting property owners, and general tax revenues have been used to underwrite provision of both government and privately owned infrastructures. Government agencies have intervened in the operations of private firms in ways that have ranged from ongoing regulation over price and service terms to the break-up of monopolies and the mandated restructuring of supply and distribution arrangements. And private firms have played roles in government-owned infrastructures as builders, operators, and leasees of facilities.

This chapter surveys the complex and varied histories of a selection of infrastructures in the United States. The primary focus is on private, profit-seeking firms and on shifts back and forth between the private and public sectors. Relationships between forms of ownership, methods of underwriting provision, and responsiveness of service providers to changing public and private demands receive particularly close attention. To gain greater insight into roles played by political and institutional factors in shaping outcomes, brief discussions of experiences in Great Britain and France are included as well.

Although sometimes lumped together as desiderata in contemporary discussion, it is clear from the historical record that private ownership and operation of infrastructures, underwriting through user fees, and discipline on price and performance from market forces do not necessarily follow one from another. Private entrepreneurs, for instance, have undertaken construction of infrastructures (such as roads and streets) to reap profits not from user fees but from real estate development. At the same time, direct head-to-head competition between private firms has been uncommon, particularly for infrastructures such as water works in which consumers and producers are linked by facilities that are fixed, long lived, and expensive to duplicate. Owners of such facilities have typically not faced serious threats of being displaced by new entrants even when governments have opened markets to competing firms or put contracts or franchises recurrently out to bid.

But while limited direct competition and long tenures have been characteristic of many forms of private involvement in infrastructure provision, forms of market discipline could arise from other sources. During the late 19th century, for example, private electric utility firms aggressively vied with their manufactured gas counterparts for the business of lighting consumers. Similarly, the profits to be realized by increasing off-peak use of expensive capital facilities prompted both electric utilities and telephone companies during the middle years of the 20th century in the United States to cut prices in some markets and to aggressively promote and advertise new uses for their products.

In industries such as electric utilities and telephones, in which such market discipline has been comparatively strong, performance on the part of private firms has generally been better than in industries such as water works in which market discipline was weaker. Also important in shaping performance has been the role of government agencies in underwriting or contracting with private firms for the provision of avowedly public goods. Where output and quality of service was easy to specify and monitor, such contracting could function quite smoothly. Particularly under conditions of change, however, difficulties in specifying outputs and monitoring quality could cause severe problems.

In addition, the functioning of both private and public ownership arrangements has been affected by contingencies of political, institutional, and organizational development. Relationships between scale economies and the ability of organizations to exploit them have been particularly important. In early 20th century Great Britain, for example, jurisdictional limits on the size of service areas prevented both privately and municipally owned electric utilities from exploiting scale economies opened up by new technologies to the same extent as could privately owned utilities in the United States. This factor dwarfed ownership per se in accounting for differences in performance of British and American electric utilities.

The text that follows offers a more detailed historical discussion of changes and continuities in ownership, financing, and governmental oversight of different infrastructures. As shall be seen, many shifts have taken place both toward and away from forms of private involvement in provision of different infrastructures over the past 150 years. Much change has also occurred in which level of government furnishes infrastructures or oversees privately owned service providers. In the United States, shifts between city, state, and federal activity in the ownership and regulation of infrastructures have been common. In Great Britain and France, there have also been dramatic shifts over time in the activities of local, intermediate, and central governments. In all three countries, cycles or bursts of public and private spending on infrastructures have been followed by periods of retrenchment and stability.

Driving change in many instances have been the pragmatic judgments of political leaders and important constituencies that existing ownership and regulatory arrangements inadequately served economic development goals. Economic growth, however, has not been the only priority. Perceptions that there should be some domains of public and civic interactions free of market considerations have also shaped ownership and financing arrangements, as have concerns that exclusion of nonpayers from some infrastructures such as roads or streets could amount to a denial of political and civil rights. The rise of environmental concerns in recent years has made for additional complexities. Effects in the United States have included revision of pricing and regulatory arrangements, greatly increased government investments in infrastructures such as sewage treatment plants, and greatly reduced government investments in others such as large flood-control and hydro-electric dams.

Outcomes have also been shaped by ideas and ideals concerning the role of the state in society. Thus, in the United States, deeply ingrained suspicion of concentrated economic and political power contributed to the survival of private ownership of many infrastructures and to such interventions into private firm operations as the breakup of AT&T. In France and Great Britain, socialist ideals as well as specifically economic concerns were important in driving nationalization of electric utilities after World War II. During the 1980s, decisions on the part of the Thatcher government in Great Britain to reorganize and privatize the country's electric utilities were motivated by ideological and political, as well as economic, considerations.

Ownership and the Development of Infrastructures in the United States

Relationships between varieties of ownership and financing for different kinds of infrastructure, demand for public goods, and sources of market discipline can be seen in table 1.1. Ownership and financing of roads and streets and of sewerage and waste water treatment facilities will be considered first. Direct competition between owners of facilities has been minimal in these infrastructures. Any private ownership has mostly been in the hands of the property owners directly served. Choice of ownership and financing methods can be largely understood in terms of: (1) the links between service provision and property values, and (2) the degree to which infrastructure development has been intended to fulfill broader or more diffuse public roles.

In urban mass transit, water works, electric utilities, and telephones, decisionmaking has also been shaped at times by links between infrastructure, property values, and real estate development. But in contrast to roads and sewerage, user fees have consistently played a major role in underwriting provision. As shall be seen, private firms initially dominated ownership and operation of these infrastructures in the United States. In urban mass transit and water works, however, government agencies now serve the majority of the population, although some private provision does survive. In electric utilities and telephones, by contrast, the pattern is reversed and private provision continues to dominate. Examination and comparison of these contrasting experiences provides insight into the ways contracting factors, market forces, and public goods demands shaped outcomes.

Roads and Streets

Provision of roads and streets in the United States has been characterized by great diversity and much change over time in both financing and ownership arrangements. Amidst this diversity, however, broad patterns can be discerned. In shaping choice and driving change, close ties between property values and road and street access have been of critical importance. While user fees in the form of tolls have been employed for routes outside of cities in some cases, the bulk of financing for these facilities has come from other sources including contributions by land owners seeking to raise property values, governmental assessments on property, dedicated fuel taxes, and general tax revenues. Except for car parking charges, the levy of fees for traversing or use of either public or private streets within cities has been even less common.

Beliefs concerning the civic importance of roads and streets have also shaped outcomes. Views of mobility as an integral aspect of personal freedom and of roads and streets as public places to which all citizens deserve access as a matter of right have tended to militate against reliance on user fees in many situations. At the same time, however, turns to private ownership in some instances have been driven not by efficiency considerations, but by the desires of merchants or homeowners to exclude from their immediate locale people or forms of public expression that would have to be permitted on public streets.

With respect to routes outside of cities, the heyday of privately owned and operated roads supported by user fees came during the early decades of the 19th century. Many roads were built and maintained by state-chartered turnpike companies. Details of the charters and franchises varied, but in general both tolls and broadly defined standards of construction and maintenance were specified. Particularly in the less populated western areas of the country, such turnpikes served a developmental function with benefits accruing not only to facility users, but also to landholders in entire regions where improved access raised property values. In some instances, states issued private turnpike companies land grants so they could capture a portion of this gain and thus afford recompense for capital costs incurred during the early years when traffic volumes and revenues from tolls were often meager. But, unlike local and state governments, companies could not legally obtain

Table 1.1. *Ownership and Financing of U.S. Infrastructures*

Infrastructure	Type of ownership	Source of financing	Use of contracting and financing	Source of market discipline	Public good
Roads and streets	Real estate developers, property owners directly served (playing some role at all times).	Profits from real estate development. For longer term, assessments by property owners associations. Charges for parking.	n.a.	Contests for location advantage when development carried through by property owners or real estate developers.	Enhanced land values, public space, personal mobility. Particularly for major highways, negative externalities have become more important in recent years.
	Private turnpike companies (flourished in rural areas during early 19th century).	Tolls, profits from real estate development.	State charters and franchises for turnpike companies during the 19th century.		
	Different levels of government (predominated at all times).	Property tax assessments, dedicated gas tax and licensing fee revenue, general tax revenues. Charges for parking.	For public roads, contracts with private firms to build or maintain.		
	Governmental and quasi-governmental authorities owning toll roads (most established during mid-20th century).	Tolls.	Same as abaove.		
Sewerage	Real estate developers, property owners directly served (played some role at all times).	Profits from real estate development. For longer term assessments by property owners associations.	n.a.	Contests for location advantage when development carred through by property owners or real estate developers.	Enhanced land values when legally requiredCan reduce local nuisances
	Local governments and quasi-governmental authorities (predominated at all times).	Property tax assessments. Flat fees and user fees billed to property owners. General tax revenues with federal government playing increased role in recent years.	For government-owned systems, contracts with private firms to build or maintain. A few privately owned waste water treatment plants operating under contracts with local governments.		
Urban mass transit	Private firms serving paying customers and/or engaged in real estate development (initially predominated).	Profits from real estate development and user fees.	State charters and municipal franchises for private transit companies. Wide range of contract arrangements for subsidizing private provision.	Contests for location advantage when development carried through by property owners or real estate developers. Inter-product competition from automobiles and other forms of transport.	Enhanced land values, public space, personal mobility. Particularly for major highways, negative externalities have become important in recent years.
	Governments and quasi-governmental authorities (now predominates)	User fees, general tax revenues	For government-owned systems, contracts with private firms to build, maintain, and occasionally operate.		

Infrastructure	Type of ownership	Source of financing	Use of contracting and financing	Source of market discipline	Public good
Water works	Private firms serving paying customers and/or engaged in real estate development (initially predominated). Governments and quasi-governmental authorities (now predominates).	Profits from real estate development. Flat fees and user fees billed to property owners. Hydrant rental charges. Flat fees and user fees billed to property owners, property tax assessments. General tax revenues.	State charters and municipal franchises. Public lighting contracts. Contracts to build or maintain government-owned systems.	Contests for location advantage when development carried through by property owners or real estate developers.	Enhanced land values. Quenching of fire and prevention of conflagration. Purity and adequacy of supply important for public health. Cleanliness enhances dignity of citizens. Negative externalities have become important in recent years.
Contracts for fire protection	Private firms serving paying customers (predominated at all times). Governments and quasi-governmental authorities (played some role at all times).	User fees. Public lighting contracts. User fees. General tax revenues.	State charters and municipal franchises. Public lighting contracts. Contracts to build or maintain government-owned systems.	Demand elasticities and inter-product competition. Occasional head-to-head competition in distribution between government and privately owned utilities. Competition in generation for the business of distributors.	Cheap electricity sometimes seen as economic development tool. Negative externalities have become important in recent years.
Public lighting contracts	Private firms serving paying customers (predominated at all times). Cooperative or government-owned systems serving rural areas.	User fees. User fees. General tax revenues.	State charters and municipal franchises. Contracts with private firms to build or maintain.	Demand elasticities. Head-to-head competition in long distance service since 1980s. Increasing competition for local service from a number of sources.	Facilitating communication sometimes seen as politically and socially desirable. Good quality telecommunication can be important for economic development.

n.a. – not applicable

7

ongoing recompense from rising property values through the assessment of tax levies. Partly as a result of this handicap, and partly as a result of competition from canals and railroads, by the 1860s most private toll roads had been turned over to states and counties for operation from general tax revenues (Bruchey 1965).

Use of toll charges to underwrite the provision of major limited access roads outside of urban areas experienced a resurgence during the 1930s and 1940s. A major institutional arrangement employed was the public authority. Like the turnpike companies of the 19th century, such authorities were state chartered and deputed such governmental powers as the right to condemn land. But unlike them, ownership generally remained entirely in state hands, with private investors involved as holders of debt securities amortized from toll revenues rather than from equity. Examples of such roads built during this period include the Pennsylvania, Ohio, New Jersey, and Massachusetts turnpikes and the New York State Thruway. By 1973, there were 4,100 miles of toll road in the United States. Most limited access highways and virtually all other major roads in the nation, however, are not only government owned but free to users. Major sources of revenue include earmarked fuel tax revenues and road use fees for trucks and buses, usually assessed on a flat yearly basis. Private firms have been involved primarily as operators of food and fuel concessions at turnpike rest areas and as engineering and construction contractors rather than as owners of facilities (Keating 1989).

Inside cities, a wide variety of private, public, and mixed development strategies have been employed to draw upon increased property values to finance the construction and maintenance of streets and thoroughfares. Due to the substantial financial stakes involved and questions of access and privacy, choices have been highly contentious at times. In 19th century American cities, politicians were sensitive to the fact that decisions concerning streets could both attract support from influential businessmen, citizens, and neighborhood groups and provide them with opportunities for patronage and kickbacks. City councils usually responded quickly to requests for street openings or improvements that served commerce and could help downtown businesses prosper. General tax revenues were often used for this purpose, as were abutter assessments, and ownership was almost always secured in public hands.

Residential neighborhoods were a different story. Municipalities commonly undertook improvements only upon the petition of a certain proportion of abutting property holders; when the petitions were granted, the city would collect special assessments from all abutters. This approach had the advantages of reducing political involvement in infrastructure decisionmaking and insuring development. It had the disadvantage of leaving large areas of the city without services. Frequently, however, assessments were not fully paid and costs had to be covered from the general tax fund or the improvement was terminated (Einhorn 1991).

From the late 19th century onward, private real estate developers in many cities began laying out and constructing some streets and recouping costs through lot sales. In some cases, developers installed their own water supplies, sewers, and other infrastructures as well. Typically, these would then be deeded over to a municipal government to be maintained out of general revenues—most of which were themselves obtained through property tax assessments (Weiss 1987). In some instances, however, developers turned over streets and other infrastructure to private home-owner associations empowered to assess member fees for upkeep and maintenance rather than turning to municipal governments (Beito and Smith 1990). Although most residential streets in the United States continue to remain in the hands of local governments, provision by home-owner associations has increased rapidly in recent years. In both law and practice, however, the line between such home-owner associations (generally considered private) and municipal corporations (generally considered public but with quite similar powers to assess and to regulate), has been quite thin, with one form sometimes blending into the other (Monkkonen 1988).

Another development since World War II has been a proliferation of privately owned streets and common areas in commercial districts. Before World War II, privately owned streets in commercial districts were extremely uncommon. Over the past 40 years, however, private ownership and operation of entire commercial districts in the form of shopping malls has become ubiquitous. The entire property usually remains in the hands of one holder, with costs of maintaining common areas, streets, and parking lots recompensed as part of the rental fees paid by retail tenants. As parking is usually free to customers, infrastructure provision relies less on user fees than do public streets with parking meters.

At least in part, political and social factors may account for the continued growth of these forms of private provision. Private ownership of common areas in shopping malls as well as of residential streets makes it possible to control access and to exclude people or activities regarded as undesirable. Such control has been an important if difficult to quantify incentive for privatization. As a consequence, issues of the character of public and political life, of civil rights—as well as of efficient service provision—are raised by the increasing turn to private streets.

Sewerage Systems and Waste Water Treatment

As with roads and streets, ownership of sewerage systems and waste water treatment plants in the United States typically has rested with the property owners directly served or government agencies. Here too, outcomes have been shaped by links between infrastructure and property development and by broader public and political issues. The character of these issues, however, has differed. In roads and streets, debate and decisionmaking concerning public goods hinged largely on hopes for economic development, questions of access to avowedly public space, and beliefs in personal freedom and mobility. In sewerage and waste water treatment, by contrast, shifts in beliefs and concerns about local nuisances and broadly diffused public "bads" of water pollution have played dominant roles in shaping investment decisions and driving change.

Originally, in most American urban centers, people disposed of human wastes and used water in cesspools, privy vaults, or even in street gutters. Early in the 19th century, some public and private underground sewers existed in the larger cities (such as New York, Baltimore, and Boston), but these were intended for storm water street drainage rather than for human waste removal. By the 1820s and 1830s, most large cities had instituted periodic vault emptying either by private scavengers under city contract or by city employees. In many cases, cities "seesawed" between the use of municipal employees and the private contract system, with neither arrangement proving satisfactory (Tarr and others 1984).[1]

As cities grew in size and density, cesspool and privy vault capacities became inadequate. Municipal adoption of water works increased the stress on the cesspool/privy vault system, leading to increased nuisances. Different options were attempted to solve the problem but eventually most major cities adopted the so-called water carriage or sewerage system, a technical system that was supposedly sanitary and self-acting (Tarr and others 1984). Construction of municipal sewerage systems during the middle and later years of the 19th century was linked to a more general movement away from a piecemeal, decentralized approach to city building. Where private systems serving single streets or groups of houses existed, they were generally either integrated into the municipal system to prevent pollution or eliminated entirely (Peterson 1979).

During the 20th century, centralized sewerage systems have come to play an increased role in many suburban as well as urban areas, although

---

1.   This was also the pattern in regard to solid wastes.

septic tanks and cesspools are still employed in some suburban locales. By removing sanitary nuisances and health threats from urban areas, sewerage systems benefited localities; but rather than eliminate pollution, they merely sent it elsewhere (Tarr and others 1984). As early as the first and second decades of the 20th century, much technical knowledge about reducing pollution impacts existed, and municipalities constructed sewage treatment plants of various types, especially where sewage disposal methods created nuisances for the city itself. Investment was limited, however, and enormous volumes of raw or minimally treated wastes were dumped into the country's streams and rivers, posing a heavy public health burden for communities downstream.

In the last three decades in the United States, a national effort has emerged to tackle the problem. Federal and state water pollution standards have been tightened. Under the terms of the Water Pollution Control Act Amendments of 1972, the Federal Government began to provide municipalities with 75 percent of the money needed to plan and build waste treatment plants. From 1972 to 1984, the Federal Government spent more than $40 billion on the program, awarding about 17,000 grants (Helman and Johnson 1992). From 1976 to 1986, the proportion of the U.S. population served by waste water treatment facilities increased from about 67 to 75 percent (Helman and Johnson 1992). During the 1980s, however, concerns that some projects had been overbuilt and "gold plated," and beliefs that waste water treatment was primarily a local and state responsibility, led to cutbacks in federal spending. A federal role in financing projects then continued, but under the terms of the Water Quality Act of 1987. This role ended in 1994.

Many industrial plants in the United States treat their own effluent, but like the sewage systems to which they are appended, almost all waste water treatment plants serving municipalities in the United States are government owned. During the first half of the 1980s, a few cities chose to have private firms own and/or operate the treatment facilities because of tax advantages, lower costs, and the presumed greater efficiency of the private sector. Terms of arrangements have varied. In Auburn, Alabama, for example, the city formally evaluated proposals by four national firms. The winning firm proposed to provide construction, ownership, and operation under a 25-year contract, with the city paying an operations and maintenance fee. In Mount Vernon, Illinois, by contrast, the municipality retained ownership while a private firm upgraded and operated the existing facility in return for a fee adjusted for inflation and the volume of effluent processed (Helman and Johnson 1992).

The 1980 census showed that approximately 80 percent of the U.S. population was served by central sewer systems—a rise of 5 percent compared with the 1970 census—although the number of dwellings not served by central systems is actually increasing (EPA 1988). The absence of central sewerage systems is most common in rural and urban-fringe growth areas. These areas are largely served by private on-site systems, such as septic tanks, although new technologies such as holding tanks and mounds are slowly being adopted. Individual on-site septic systems, while usually inexpensive, often create pollution problems. The private home-owner is responsible for maintenance and emptying of the facility, as well as for transportation and disposal of the wastes. States and counties often neglect to rigorously enforce local sanitation and land-use codes in regard to these systems, creating potentially hazardous situations (OTA 1991).

Urban Mass Transportation

As with streets and sewerage systems, decisionmaking with respect to investment and ownership of urban mass transit systems in the United States has at times been shaped by specifically public goals and by close ties between property values and extension of service. Unlike the case in the infrastructures discussed previously, however, user fees have consistently been used to at least partially underwrite provision of urban mass transportation in the United States. The extent and the character of roles played by private firms have also differed. In both streets and sewerage, private provision largely consisted of individual property owners carrying through development to serve their own needs. In urban mass transit, too, entrepreneurs were far from oblivious to possibilities to reap profit from real estate development and land speculation. From the first, however, hopes of serving large numbers of paying customers played a major role in motivating private firms to build and operate transit systems.

The era of major private construction and operation of mass transit systems began in the 1850s. During the second half of the 19th century, urban mass transit underwent a series of technological transformations, shifting from horse car lines to cable, and then to electric traction. The new technologies made it possible for transit systems to be extended over far greater areas than before, but they were also more capital intensive than the old and required substantially more sophisticated management in order to function properly. Partially for these reasons, late 19th century electrification of transit systems was typically accompanied by consolidation of previously independent horse car lines and the emergence of transit monopolies.

Ownership, however, remained almost entirely in the hands of private firms. Even in cities such as New York and Boston, each of which built underground rapid transit lines with public funds during the late 19th and early 20th centuries, private firms actually furnished service under long-term lease arrangements (Cheape 1980). By the 1970s, however, the situation had changed radically. While private firms still owned just over half of the U.S. transit lines in 1978, government and quasi-governmental public authorities dominated in major centers and accounted for about 90 percent of the industry's patronage and operating revenues (CBO 1988).

Matters of financing have been more complex. From the first, both privately and publicly owned transit systems have obtained a portion of their revenues from fare-paying customers. But, particularly during the heyday of private transit development (late 19th and early 20th centuries), some of the greatest windfalls came not from fares, but from land speculation in areas served by the lines. This tie between transit development and land speculation explains much of the greater area expansion of American cities compared with European during this period. But land speculation generally provided only a one-time infusion of money, and this pattern of transit development came under increasing strain after the first years of the 20th century.

The rise of the automobile as a competing form of transportation was an important factor, as it siphoned off non-peak-hour ridership, but did little to reduce rush hour demands. Rigidity in franchising and contracting arrangements also made for difficulties. In many cities, franchises specified that fares be held at specific levels, such as five cents a trip. At the time such contracts were signed, price levels were stable or even declining. With the beginnings of inflation during World War I, however, the fare levels proved inadequate (Cheape 1980). By 1918, about one-third of the transit industry was in bankruptcy. In a few cases, struggling lines were able to gain release from fare caps in franchises and to access government subsidies (Wohl 1982). More customary, however, was streetcar company disinvestment in equipment and trackage. Beginning in the 1920s, as the cost of the automobile declined and ownership spread, public transit lines began to lose ridership and to suffer further financial damage. Between 1940 and 1979, the net operating revenues for the transit industry dropped from a profit of $96 million to a deficit of $2,380 million (Wohl 1982).

Increasingly, transit services became a responsibility of public authorities rather than the private market. In many instances, governments first subsidized privately owned transit lines and then acquired them. In 1964, Congress created the Urban Mass Transportation Administration and the Federal Government became a major actor in the game of transit provision. Reflecting concern over the loss of transit service in the urban core, the legislation authorized grants to modernize existing transit systems to attract riders and also to reestablish systems in the 105 cities that had lost transit service between the mid-1950s and the mid-1960s. Federal formula grants for mass transit became available in 1974, and in 1982 Congress authorized a mass transit account in the Highway Trust Fund. Despite this infusion of funds, the number of transit riders nationally continues to decline, as automobile usage increases for all types of trips (CBO 1988).

Although publicly owned and subsidized transit systems continue to dominate the field, a number of attempts have been made over the past few years to increase the role played by private firms. A few private, unsubsidized firms operate in market niches such as express bus services for commuters. The most common form of private involvement, however, is for governmental units to contract out particular operational or managerial tasks. Under President Ronald Reagan, attempts were made to spur privatization, and in 1984 the Federal Transit Administration issued a regulation requiring public transit authorities receiving federal aid to advance privatization in various ways. While contracting out for transportation services has increased, it still accounts for only a small proportion of total operations and is customarily limited to specialized and supplementary services (Gomez-Ibanez and Meyer 1992).

Water Works

Technologically, and in terms of functions served and public goods demanded, water works more closely resemble sewerage systems than any of the other infrastructures discussed so far. In terms of ownership and financing, however, the closest parallel is with urban mass transit. Initially, privately owned and operated systems dominated. But as the populations of major U.S. cities increased and their areas expanded, these cities consistently turned to direct government provision. By 1896, only 9 of the largest 50 cities in the United States still relied on privately owned water works. The only breaks in the trend toward government ownership came during periods like that following the Panic of 1873, when state-imposed restrictions on municipal authority coincided with a continued demand for water services (Anderson 1980).

Selection processes for private water works firms, details of the contractual or regulatory regimes under which they operated, and the scale and duration of private water works development differed substantially from case to case, as did the exact circumstances in which individual cities turned to municipal ownership. But certain consistent themes can be discerned. As would be expected given the natural monopoly attributes of water supply and distribution facilities, competition between operating water works firms seldom occurred, even in cases where there was no legal barrier to entry. In a few cities, a degree of competition for franchises to build and operate water works facilities occurred initially, but since substantial investments in fixed facilities such as water mains were required and the duration of contracts was typically long or even indefinite, recurrent bidding seldom took place.

In small communities in which population growth was modest, privately owned service providers and municipal governments sometimes managed to forge viable long-term relationships, even in the absence of ongoing competition for franchises and contracts. In larger and more rapidly growing urban centers, however, privately owned service providers and municipal governments frequently clashed over questions of new investments and issues of service quality (Blake 1956; Jacobson 1989). In many cases, these clashes played a major role in the turn to municipal ownership.

Arranging for provision of water for fire protection presented particularly intractable problems. Accurately predicting how a water works would actually perform in the event of a major conflagration was no easy task. Careful physical inspection and the exercise of considerable expertise and judgment by highly trained engineers was required (APWA 1925). Even when problems were identified, lack of an easily observed and objectively measured standard of performance made it difficult for a municipality to impose sanctions on an errant water works firm in an ongoing way. Urban growth compounded the difficulties. In order for private water works firms to be compensated for the investments required to serve growing needs, parties with directly opposing interests had to repeatedly come to terms over issues of facility design and quality of service, as well as price.[2]

In the case of government-owned water works, by contrast, public officials could arrange for construction of facilities serving specifically public

---

2.   Since the number of fire hydrants contracted for by a city bore little relationship to the amount of fire protection actually received, such commonly employed expedients as paying water works firms a set fee for each fire hydrant furnished did not solve the problem. A water company, for example, that replaced a system of four-inch water mains serving 400 hydrants fed by unreliable pumping stations with a system of twelve-inch mains serving the same number of hydrants fed by reliable gravity-form high altitude reservoirs, would have received *no* additional compensation for these investments under a per hydrant payment formula. Nor would it have any incentive for making such an investment.

and developmental needs without the sort of difficult bargaining between parties with directly opposing interests that occurred with private ownership. In addition, financing could be drawn from property tax revenues as well as from user fees. This recourse made economic sense because of the ways in which improvements in water supply and distribution facilities contributed to increased property values and other public benefits—even for those who consumed relatively little water. Despite these advantages, numerous cases can be enumerated in which government-owned and privately owned water works skimped on investments in facilities needed to reduce the risk of fire or to protect the public health. Ignorance and uncertainty took their toll, as did institutional and bureaucratic infighting and simple incompetence. Overall, however, government-owned water works in rapidly growing U.S. cities invested far more aggressively in water supply and distribution facilities than did their privately owned counterparts.

Over the past 30 years, economists have attacked this eagerness on the part of municipalities and other governmental entities to invest in large scale water supply facilities on efficiency grounds (Hirshleifer, De Haven, and Milliman 1960). Environmentalists have also taken up these themes, criticizing many large scale water projects as environmentally damaging and economically wasteful. The result has been an increasing use of markets in the pricing and allocation of water resources. Local and regional authorities are increasingly metering water, establishing markets for bulk supplies in water-short regions such as California, and reducing subsidies and raising prices to bring them more in line with marginal costs.

As in the past, however, government-owned systems continue to supply water to most of the urban and suburban areas where the bulk of America's population lives. As of 1989, about three-quarters of the people in the United States served by water works obtained their supplies from government-owned systems. While thousands of privately owned water works now operate in the United States, most of them are quite diminutive, serving small municipalities, unincorporated patches of metropolitan areas, or even single real estate developments (U.S. Congress, Office of Technology Assessment 1991). Some privately owned water works, however, are quite large and serve heavily populated areas. Examples include the Elizabethtown and Hackensack water companies in suburban New Jersey. These sorts of large, privately owned systems are most common in heavily populated suburban areas that are carved up into small political jurisdictions, thus making individual water works impracticable. In a sense, they represent a vehicle for regional service delivery.

Electric Utilities

Unlike the infrastructures previously described, electric utility service to private consumers in the United States has been funded almost entirely by user fees. Some interesting contractual issues have arisen in the provision of specifically public goods such as street lighting, but typically municipalities have paid for these and other public services on the basis of fee structures not dramatically different from those used by ordinary consumers. As with water works, private ownership predominated during the early years of electric utilities. Over time, a few large cities such as Seattle, Los Angeles, and Cleveland did turn to government ownership. But in sharp contrast to water works, private firms have mostly retained their hold in densely populated urban areas, and government ownership is found in a few small cities and in rural areas.

By almost any measure, privately owned electric utilities in most major U.S. cities have historically out-performed their water works counterparts in serving both public and private needs. One reason for this relatively good performance is that arranging for provision of specifically public goods such as street lighting did not present the sorts of contracting difficulties that bedeviled relationships between municipalities and privately owned water companies. Ease in measuring output and monitoring quality accounted for the difference.

As with water works, municipalities and privately owned suppliers of electric street lighting often found themselves enmeshed in long-term relationships, even when short-term contracts with provisions for competitive bidding were used. Unlike the case in water for fire protection, however, the output of public illumination furnished by a privately owned service provider could be specified with reasonable precision—the number of street lamps operating on a given night. Poor quality or unreliable service was not only immediately and indisputably apparent to municipal officials and members of the public, but could be easily sanctioned in an incremental and ongoing way simply through contract terms that provided a set penalty for each lamp outage (Boston Lamp Department 1892). Even more importantly, increases in demand for street lighting could be accommodated without having to renegotiate the terms of the simple per-lamp pricing structures typically employed (Jacobson 1989).

Market forces also played a major role in spurring electric utility firms to furnish high-quality service to consumers and to pursue aggressive marketing and investment policies. Particularly during the 1880s and 1890s when the industry got its start, electric utility entrepreneurs faced a highly unpredictable competitive environment (Platt 1991). Typically, municipalities issued nonexclusive franchises to electric utility firms which neither imposed significant constraints with respect to price or quality of service to private consumers nor protected companies against entry by competing firms. So long as such policies remained in place, the small size of generating facilities combined with the relatively low costs of stringing wire compared with laying pipe, meant that risks to incumbent firms from head-to-head competition were far greater in electric utilities than in water works.[3] Electric utility firms also faced far more intense interproduct competition than did their water works counterparts during this period. They had to contest for market share not only with well-entrenched gas lighting firms but with large consumers who could economically generate their own electricity (Passer 1953).

Over time, however, increases in economies of scale due to new technology hampered entry by new electric utility firms. Moreover, existing companies were encouraged to merge to avoid large-scale, expensive, and unprofitable duplication of expensive capital investments in generation and distribution facilities (Hughes 1983). By 1905 direct competition between electric utility firms no longer occurred in most major U.S. cities despite the absence of government-imposed restrictions on entry. Competition from gas for home and street lighting also declined during these years due to price reductions made possible by improved economies of scale, as well as technological improvements in lamp efficiencies (Passer 1953).

Nevertheless, powerful forms of market discipline on electric utility firms remained. Until the mid-1960s, capacity needs and growth in economies of scale provided incentives for electric utility firms to provide high-quality and reliable service and to aggressively extend their networks and develop new markets. Because electric utilities could not store significant amounts of power for future use, maintaining the ratio of average to peak consumption—load factor—at a high level was (and is) of critical importance for utilities to obtain a high level of remuneration from their increasingly expensive and large-scale capital facilities. At least in densely populated urban areas, these forms of market discipline meant that protection of consumer interests never depended on the efficacy of franchising and regulatory arrangements in electric utilities to nearly the same extent as with water works.

---

3.   Even during this period, episodes of direct competition rarely persisted for long. Nevertheless, price wars and the costs incurred in buying out competitors could result in significant financial strains on incumbent firms.

During the first decades of the 20th century, state regulation emerged as the most common form of government oversight over the electric utility industry. By 1935, 37 states and the District of Columbia had established regulatory commissions with jurisdiction over electric utilities. In general, the commissions possessed the authority to set rates and to protect electric utility firms against competition regarded as duplicative. In practice, however, state regulators generally did not constrain decisionmaking by privately owned service providers in significant ways. In nearly all states, commissions could not begin cases on their own initiative. In terms of the declining costs that characterized the industry, this worked to the advantage of utility firms because of the high costs of initiating and carrying through a complaint (Mosher 1929). Other constraints faced by regulatory commissions included inadequate staffing, lack of jurisdiction over wholesale interstate power sales, and the likelihood of disruptive, time-consuming, and inconsistent judicial intervention against any regulatory decision opposed by utility firms.

Steps taken by the Federal Government during the 1930s had a greater effect on the structure of the industry and the operations of private firms. Despite sharp opposition by private utility firms, Congress enacted legislation in 1935 that gave the Federal Power Commission authority to regulate wholesale prices for electricity marketed across state lines. At the same time, the Securities and Exchange Commission was given the authority to regulate the issue of securities by holding companies, to order them to simplify their corporate structures, and to require service organizations to serve operating companies at cost. Most importantly, the law mandated outright dismemberment for holding companies that did not serve geographically unified areas (Twentieth Century Fund 1948).

The New Deal years also saw the Federal Government take an increased role in producing and distributing electricity. Among the most important steps taken were the formation of the federally owned Tennessee Valley Authority—an experiment in combining electricity production with regional development—and the establishment of the Rural Electrification Administration. By sponsoring the formation of rural electric cooperatives and furnishing them with low interest loans, grants, and technical advice, the agency made possible the extension of electric utility service to the countryside on an unprecedented scale (Twentieth Century Fund 1948). Despite these initiatives, however, private ownership remained dominant.

In recent decades, both government and privately owned electric utilities have had to face new difficulties arising from technological, economic, and political change. During the late 1960s, the sorts of incremental advances in generating technology that had brought about steady increases in efficiency over the previous 50 years began to be played out. Efforts to lower costs through exploitation of scale economies also proved increasingly difficult, as new large plants proved more costly to build and less reliable than expected. The problems arising from scaling-up were particularly severe with nuclear power plants, but they also bedeviled conventional thermal facilities (Hirsch 1989). The rise of environmental concerns, soaring rates of inflation, and exploding fuel costs complicated the situation further.

Interestingly, reforms put in place as a result of these shocks broadened the roles played by both governments and markets in shaping electric utility development. Governments responded to environmental concerns by increasing the regulation of pollution discharges and by becoming involved in the siting of facilities (Hirsch 1989). In many states, shifts from declining to rising costs raised the political profile of electric utility issues and inspired unprecedented activism on the part of regulatory commissions in pursuing their traditional oversight of rates and service (Anderson 1981). Since the late 1970s, federal legislation has also played a role. Laws enacted in 1978 and 1992 have mandated that states take into account principles of marginal-cost pricing and least-cost planning in carrying through their own regulatory activities.

At the same time, the electric utility industry began to restructure itself along more competitive lines in response to the push of federal legislation. The Public Utilities Regulatory Policies Act of 1978 required utility firms to buy electricity from small, unregulated, independent cogenerating plants and facilities that relied on renewable resources to protect the environment and promote energy conservation. The Comprehensive National Energy Policy Act, enacted into law in 1992, extended the principles further. Largely motivated by a desire to increase competition in the electric utility industry, the Act reduced regulatory restrictions on independent power producers and enlarged the authority of federal regulators to order access to utility transmission facilities (Rosenzweig 1993). In principle, these changes could result in the emergence of true markets for electricity, with numerous generators, distributors, and purchasers buying and selling power over regional and even national grids. But while the role of the market has expanded in recent years, independent, vertically integrated private firms continue to dominate the provision of electricity in the United States.

Telephones

The history of telephone service in the United States both parallels and diverges from that of electric utilities. The two industries both began during the late 19th century. Consistently, in both industries, service to private consumers has been recompensed almost entirely by user fees. Growth trajectories have also been similar. Over the course of the 20th century, telephone as well as electric utility networks have spread across the entire country. And in both industries, technological improvements have dramatically driven down the costs of service provision. From the mid-1930s to the mid-1980s, for example, the number of simultaneous conversations that could be carried over a single coaxial cable increased from less than 500 to over 32,000. Development of microwave relay systems, beginning in the late 1940s, has contributed to further declines in costs of transmitting long-distance calls, as have recent developments in fiber-optic technology. Finally, deployment of increasingly sophisticated switching systems have greatly cut the costs of routing calls and have increased the range of communication services that can be furnished over the network.

But there are also differences. From the beginning, dominance by privately owned service providers has been even greater in telephones than in electric utilities. To a much greater extent than in electric utilities, development of telephone networks has involved the coordination of investment and operation on national and international scales, resulting in a different organization of the industry. In electric utilities, vertically integrated, privately owned service providers operating on a local and then, eventually, a regional scale have historically furnished the bulk of service. For telephones, a single firm has dominated virtually from the beginning.

Until 1984 that firm was American Telephone and Telegraph (AT&T). By the last decades of the 19th century, AT&T's management had succeeded in parlaying its access to large pools of capital and control of the Bell telephone patents into a position as the supplier of most of the local and long-distance telephone service in the United States. After expiration of the Bell patents in 1893, a large number of independent telephone companies were founded in both urban and rural areas. But by the end of the first decade of the 20th century, with the help of its control of long-distance lines and superior resources, Bell was able to buy out or eliminate most competitors in major centers (Garnet 1985). This dominant position would be maintained in subsequent years, as AT&T became the largest corporation in the United States.

During the first and second decades of the 20th century, the telephone company, like its electric utility counterparts, would come under the jurisdiction of state regulatory commissions. To a greater extent than in electric utilities, however, provision of service involved transactions that crossed state lines. As a consequence, federal involvement started earlier, beginning in 1910 with Congressional enactment of the Mann-Elkins Act, which gave the Interstate Commerce Commission (ICC) jurisdiction over prices charged for interstate and international telephone and telegraph and cable services. In practice, during the early years of its jurisdiction, the ICC made minimal efforts to set or control rates, but it did make valuation studies and set up a uniform system of accounts.

As in electric utilities, Depression era reforms would bring more extensive federal involvement. In particular, the framework of rate regulation would be elaborated more fully after passage of the Federal Communications Act in 1934. The Act placed regulation of interstate telephone service under the jurisdiction of a newly established Federal Communications Commission (FCC). The commission pursued a detailed investigation of the costs of telephone service and established a framework of continuing surveillance, under which rate levels would be set by informal negotiations in the future. But, unlike electric utilities, the Federal Government did not order a restructuring of the industry because of its belief that the telephone network was functionally integrated on a national scale in a way that the electric utility holding companies were not (Phillips 1988).

Nevertheless, from early in the 20th century, the dominance of AT&T was attacked as representing an undue and unaccountable concentration of political as well as economic power. Legal action centered mainly on efforts to prevent AT&T from buying out or destroying independent local service providers. In response to an anti-trust suit in 1913, for example, AT&T agreed to give small, independent telephone companies access to its long-distance network and promised not to acquire competing firms (Garnet 1985). The "Hall Memorandum," signed in 1922, reinforced these commitments, although by this date AT&T's dominance in major population centers was secure.

Since World War II, legal and governmental action has centered on increasing competition in those areas of the telephone industry in which economic considerations do not justify monopoly. In 1949, the Federal Government filed a civil anti-trust suit calling for the separation of AT&T and its equipment manufacturing subsidiary, Western Electric. At least in theory, such a split should have resulted in increased competition in the equipment manufacturing market and, ultimately, more choices and lower costs for consumers. The suit was settled in 1956 with an agreement by AT&T to pursue a more liberal licensing patent policy. The company was also restricted from entering non-common-carrier telephone businesses. Otherwise, the settlement left AT&T intact.

More radical change occurred in subsequent years. During the 1960s and 1970s, new technologies such as microwave transmission made it possible for firms to compete for long-distance business at relatively low cost. AT&T continued to furnish almost all long-distance service but, over time, a series of FCC decisions reduced legal barriers to entry, and competing firms such as MCI began to provide service in a few markets. Settlement of a civil anti-trust suit filed by the federal government in 1974 ended AT&T's monopoly in long-distance markets entirely and broke the links between AT&T's long distance and local operations. Since it was still regarded as a natural monopoly, local telephone service continued to be carried by regional companies. Long-distance markets, on the other hand, were opened to competition and, since divestiture in 1984, competition in long-distance markets has emerged as expected. These developments had taken place in a context of continued judicial and regulatory restraint on AT&T, restraint designed to prevent the firm from using its existing dominance to crush new competitors through aggressive pricing or other means (Phillips 1988).

Technological developments during recent years—such as the development of cellular and other wireless systems of telephony—promise to increase the potential for competition in local telephone service. Thus far, effects have been limited, and the vast majority of telephone calls are still carried through the lines and switches of the existing network. Future developments are uncertain, but based on existing experiences, changes in technology alone may be insufficient to sustain higher levels of competition in the future. In order to prevent new competitors from being "frozen out" by incumbent firms, restrictions on mergers and requirements for network access may remain necessary.

Comparative Analysis: Infrastructures in Great Britain and France

An examination of the histories of selected infrastructures in different countries can shed light on some of the ways in which ideas, institutions, and attributes of infrastructures have shaped choice and forms of ownership. As in the United States, the sheer range and variety of arrangements employed at different times and places has been enormous. In general, government ownership has been the dominant approach throughout the world for infrastructures such as roads and streets where user fees are seldom charged. The range of variation has been far greater, however, for infrastructures such as telecommunications networks, water works, and electric utilities where service providers are commonly recompensed all or in part by user fees. While provision of telegraph as well as telephone service in the United States, for example, has always been provided by privately owned firms, state ownership has predominated in France, Germany, Switzerland, and other European countries. In these nations, decisions on development as well as ownership of these systems have also been shaped by considerations of national unity and military need to a much greater extent than in the United States (Holcombe 1911; de Gournay 1988).

With respect to water works and electricity in Great Britain, the situation differed again. At the outset of the 20th century, as in the United States, oversight and direct provision of many infrastructures in Great Britain lay in the hands of a complex and deeply entrenched web of local municipalities and authorities. But, unlike the United States, Great Britain was and is a unitary state. In the British context, this has largely meant that a ruling party in the House of Commons could make decisions concerning the provision of infrastructures that were virtually unchallenged by independent courts, executives, or other legislative bodies. Until the 1980s, this power was generally applied by creating public bodies that could break through jurisdictional barriers and exploit scale economies in the provision of infrastructures.

For water works, the sequence played out as follows. As in the United States, a majority of Great Britain's urban population obtained its water from government-owned systems during the first decades of the 20th century, although a few private companies owned and operated systems under monopoly franchises. Since World War II, however, involvement by the national government in organizing the industry has been substantially greater than in the United States. Parliament approved a national water act in 1945 that provided inducement for municipal and local systems to amalgamate for efficiency purposes. Under the terms of the act, the number of separate water supply systems in England and Wales was reduced from 1,400 during World War II to 187 in 1974.

New legislation enacted in 1973 in England and Wales brought massive consolidation of both water and sewerage services. On the rationale that conservation and environmental protection require planning that takes into account the needs of entire regions and water sheds, management of the country's government-owned water works and sewage systems was placed in the hands of ten regional water authorities. In addition to providing water and sewerage services, the water boards were given responsibility for administering pollution control regulations. Under this regime during the 1980s, individual metering of households in Britain began for the first time.

Criticisms of the arrangement included claims that water works investment remained inadequate due to public sector borrowing limits and accusations that placing environmental regulation in the hands of service providers made for inadequate checks on the power of system managers (Maclean 1991).

As in water works, extensions of government ownership and the breaching of jurisdictional barriers that blocked exploitation of economies of scale went hand-in-hand in electric utilities in Great Britain. From the beginning, a far greater proportion of British than American municipalities established their own electric utility undertakings. From 1900 through 1948, municipal undertakings accounted for about two-thirds of electric utility sales in Great Britain. Municipalities dominated in densely populated urban centers, while private supply was more common in outlying areas—a pattern exactly the reverse of that in the United States (Hannah 1979).

In 1926, in response to problems and high costs arising from the small scale of both government and privately owned utilities, Parliament established a new quasi-public entity to build a national grid to link systems and to coordinate investment and operation of a generating plant. Under the plan, existing government and privately owned utilities retained ownership of generating and distribution systems, but a newly created Central Electricity Board was placed in charge of the construction and operation of a nationwide transmission network. The board determined the use of existing generating plants, bought the electricity produced by undertakings, and oversaw the planning of new capacity. In many respects, this organization resembled the public authority arrangements under development in the United States. The organization represented a form of public provision in that ownership was in the hands of the state. At the same time, the enterprise was self-financing and retained a degree of independence. While the Minister of Transport appointed board members, he could not dismiss them unless they completely absented themselves from their duties for more than six months. Managers and engineers were paid by the government but not considered part of the civil service (Hughes 1983).

In 1947, the newly elected Labor government nationalized the entire electric utility industry as part of a broader effort to reshape British society. With respect to government and private ownership per se, nationalization did not represent a change of revolutionary magnitude. By this time, the bulk of Britain's electric utility industry was already in government hands of one sort or another. However, the shift did make a difference in methods and scales of operation. At the time of nationalization, more than 600 franchised electric supply undertakings still operated in Great Britain despite the creation of the national electric grid during the

1920s and some consolidation during the following years. (Hannah 1979). Requirements for the Central Electricity Board to purchase electricity from these undertakings introduced both coordination difficulties and various rigidities. The act nationalizing the industry consolidated these undertakings into 12 new regional distribution corporations, with generating and transmission placed in the hands of a Central British Electricity Authority.

This legacy of consolidation in both water works and electric utilities in Great Britain has proven more enduring than that of the government ownership under which it took place. In the 1980s, as part of a broader conservative program to reduce the role of the government in the economy and to create an "enterprise society," Great Britain initiated a sweeping privatization program encompassing an array of infrastructures and industries, including both water works and electric utilities (Vickers and Wright 1989; Heald 1989; Grimstone 1989). For water and electricity, however, this has not meant a simple reversion to earlier patterns of industry structure and ownership.

In water works, on one hand, the 1973 division of the country into ten regional service areas survived. Privatization consisted of selling off equity in each region's monopoly water and sewerage provider to private investors. The policy did not envision direct competition in the provision or management of services. Parliament created a new national regulatory agency headed by a single individual (the Director General of Water Services), with responsibility for protecting consumer interests and ensuring that the service provider did not exploit its monopoly position. In addition, responsibility for environmental regulation was placed in the hands of a new National Rivers Authority (Maclean 1991).

In electric utilities, on the other hand, an effort was made both to preserve the economies of scale opened up by previous reform efforts and to simultaneously increase the role of competition in protecting consumer interests and inspiring entrepreneurial vigor. Two separate generating companies were formed in order to introduce at least a measure of competition. The twelve distribution companies created by the privatization were also given the authority to supply a small portion of their own electricity as a further source of competitive discipline in generation. Retaining a unified national transmission network was seen as indispensable if competition in bulk power markets was to develop. Ownership was placed in the hands of the twelve distribution companies to help ensure that a monopoly would not be abused by bulk electricity suppliers. As in water works, a new national regulatory agency (the Director General of Electricity Supply) was set up to oversee the entire arrangement.

Ownership of water works and electric utilities in France has evolved differently than in either the United States or Great Britain. In water works, the French scene is characterized by wide use of franchising and contracting arrangements. In most cases, private firms administer and operate the water works and collect charges from customers, while the physical facilities remain in the hands of local governments. As in the United States, 19th century French water works and other municipal infrastructures were either franchised out to privately owned service providers or were owned and operated by municipal governments. Over time, however, as Dominique Lorrain observes:

> . . . this dual pattern quickly underwent a number of modifications, all of which tended to attenuate the differences. Jurisprudence added guaranteed result clauses to the franchises. Other types of contracts were developed at the same time. Their common feature was that they combined private management with public financing and a transfer of ownership to the public sector for the most costly equipment such as water and waste treatment plants, and sewage stations (Lorrain 1992: 84).

The continued viability of private involvement in water provision in French urban centers is partially explained by factors similar to those that shaped the functioning of franchise and contract arrangements in U.S. water works and electric utilities. By allowing private firms to operate but not to own water works facilities, many French cities appeared to have sidestepped the difficulties in arranging for investment that plagued their American counterparts. While municipalities and privately owned service providers did develop long-term relationships, the French separation of ownership from operations enabled shorter contract lengths and may have increased the role of recurrent bidding as an inducement to good performance.

Furthermore, rapid urban growth and fire protection demands did not strain contractual relationships between local governments and private water works firms to nearly the same extent in France as in the United States. During the 19th century, French cities grew far more slowly than their American counterparts, remained geographically compact, and were built predominantly of stone and brick and other relatively fireproof materials. Hence, demands for water main extensions to serve outlying areas tended to be comparatively modest. Nor did protection against conflagration depend on water works to nearly the same extent as in U.S. cities with their densely packed urban cores and widespread use of wood in construction (Sutcliffe 1981; Rosen 1986).

Outcomes have also been affected by attributes of governmental arrangements and political culture. Like the United States, France has long had fragmented local government. From the French Revolution to the present, the country has been divided into more than 36,000 local communes that are responsible for many types of local service provision and other government functions. These units are often small in size and possessed of limited financial and administrative resources. In such a setting, private firms have found it possible to acquire greater technical and administrative capabilities and economies of scale in the construction and operation of water works and other infrastructures than have the communes (Lorrain 1992).

Initially, French electricity development also occurred under the jurisdiction of the communes with most systems both owned and operated by private firms. As in the United States and in Great Britain, during the 1920s opinion leaders began to call for the development of large-scale electric utility networks that were integrated on a regional or even a national scale. But with oversight in the hands of the communes, numerous jurisdictional and political obstacles obstructed such development (Frost 1991). World War II left France's electric utility industry with extensive physical damage to transmission facilities and generating plants. While reconstruction demanded large capital infusions, utility firms were nearly bankrupt. Indeed, the firms did not even have enough money to pay for the imported coal needed to fuel their existing generating plants. Faced with price controls and investor fears of expropriation, raising the capital needed to rebuild was out of the question.

But France, like Great Britain, possessed a unitary national government that could cut through such impasses, and in 1946 it enacted legislation nationalizing virtually the entire electric utility industry. Less radical steps, such as the lifting of price controls or the granting of subsidies to France's private utility firms, might have served to alleviate the immediate crisis, but many French elites across the political spectrum viewed the institutional bottlenecks that had obstructed industry development during the 1920s and 1930s as intolerable. French elites wanted abundant power for economic development and for building a new and better society in the post-war world. In addition, particularly on the left, nationalization was supported as a means to reduce class divisions, build a more egalitarian society, and eliminate the undue and corrupting influence of utility owners on politics (Frost 1991).

Conclusion

Private firms have played a wide range of roles in the provision of infrastructures as owners, operators, leasees, contractors, and facilities builders. Private firms and home-owner associations of various sorts have owned outright both toll roads and residential streets in the United States. Solid waste collection in American cities has been carried out by private firms paid for directly by consumers and under contract with municipal governments. Urban transit has been provided by private firms under a range of franchise, contracting, and regulatory arrangements in the United States and Great Britain. While water works facilities in France are predominantly government owned, private firms operate and manage the bulk of systems under an array of contracting and leasing arrangements. Throughout the world, portions of many of the infrastructures owned and operated by governments have been built by private firms.

Decisionmaking concerning infrastructure development, public goods demanded, and the roles played by private firms have been shaped by the values of politically important actors and the workings of governmental, political, and legal institutions. At times, goods defined as public have been provided free to users even though exclusion of nonpayers would impose few technical difficulties. U.S. examples include the interstate highway system, public parks, public libraries, and police and fire protection services. Rationales for defining such goods and services as public and worthy of free distribution have included perceived relationships to economic development goals and beliefs that there should be some domains of public and civic interaction free of market considerations. Also playing a role at times have been perceptions that exclusion of nonpayers from parks, streets, and other places defined as public could amount to a denial of political and individual rights. In recent years, growing environmental concerns have added a new element to the mix. Demands for environmental improvements have increased pressure for investments in certain types of infrastructures, such as waste water treatment plants. At the same time, new controversies have arisen due to the increasing attention paid to the public "bads" as well as the public "goods" of some infrastructures, including highways, large dams, urban water supply and irrigation, and conventional and nuclear thermal electric generating plants.

Choices as to private and governmental provision of infrastructures have also been shaped by ideas and ideals concerning the role of the state in the economy. For example, the far greater role of private firms in the provision of electric utilities in the United States, compared with Great Britain during the early years of these industries, can be attributed in substantial part to broad differences in beliefs concerning appropriate roles for government to play in furnishing and overseeing essential services. The much larger role of the state in furnishing telecommunications services in continental Europe compared with the United States can also probably be understood in these terms. Issues in other domains have also shaped debate and decisionmaking at various times. In both the United States and Great Britain, for example, public services contracting-out has been both supported and opposed because of its potential to break the power of public sector unions and to reduce workers' pay. In the United States, at least, issues of social and racial justice have also been involved because government employment has historically offered avenues of advancement to members of some minority groups. Privatization, it is feared by some, may choke off such opportunities (Suggs 1989).

Performance of ownership and regulatory arrangements has been shaped by contingencies of political and institutional development and idiosyncrasies of time, place, and circumstance. Constraints on geographical expansion faced by government and privately owned systems have been particularly important. In the case of electric utilities in the United States, for example, distribution by municipally owned systems has generally been confined to service within the boundaries of individual cities, while private firms could extend their lines with far less regard to jurisdictional boundaries. In such a setting, privately owned electric utilities exploited economies of scale opened up by new technologies in ways denied their municipally owned counterparts. In Great Britain, by contrast, both government and private systems faced constraints on expansion. Many private as well as government ownership advocates supported the creation of a quasi-public national grid in 1926 as simply the most practical route to break the log jam created by the industry's inefficient distribution.

Certain commonalties can also be seen in experiences with private provision of infrastructures. As would be expected by economic theory, lack of direct competition and provision of service through long-lived, capital intensive, and networked facilities have consistently gone together in a wide range of contexts. Where heavy facilities of this sort are in place, such as water mains and sewage lines, competition has been almost unknown. For telephone and electric utility networks in which costs of stringing wire are comparatively low, direct competition in distribution did at times take place. In most cases, however, such competition proved short lived, as rival firms quickly merged with the dominant service provider or went out of business altogether.

A second common theme has been longevity of tenure. In situations in which private firms actually own fixed and long-lived infrastructure facilities, displacement of existing service providers by new entrants has been quite uncommon, even in situations in which contracts or franchises have been recurrently put out to bid. Contract lengths can be shorter and recurrent bidding may be more powerful as a source of accountability under arrangements in which private firms operate but do not own facilities. Water works and other services in many cities in France are furnished under such arrangements. But even there, long tenures have been the norm. This theme is also consistent with theorizing by some economists (Williamson 1985).

Market incentives can arise from other sources, however, and in such cases the profit motive can be a powerful spur for efficiency, innovation, and responsiveness to consumer demands on the part of privately owned service providers. In the case of electric utilities in the United States during the first decades of the 20th century, for example, the increased profits to be realized by increasing off-peak demands and interproduct competition functioned as a market incentive for good performance.

Decisions as to pricing are also of crucial importance. In situations in which service providers are compensated entirely from user fees and a degree of market discipline is present, burdens of decisionmaking and enforcement faced by government agencies may be quite light. When a good or a service is subsidized or furnished free to consumers in order to achieve some public purpose, on the other hand, contracting arrangements of one sort or another may have to be relied upon. Such contracting can be a relatively straight-forward matter if output and quality of service is easy to specify and monitor. Even under static conditions, however, the problem of devising a workable long-term relationship between contractor and contractee may be far less tractable in cases where output and quality are difficult to specify. As could be seen in the case of water for fire protection in the United States, the difficulties ramify under conditions of change. Problems and conflicts in renegotiating contract terms with private vendors can result in rigidities that exceed those of all but the most rigid of public bureaucracies.

Clearly, attributes of markets and extents to which infrastructures serve public purposes both bear close examination in considering whether and how to increase the roles played by private firms. The findings also have some more subtle implications that relate to the administrative capabilities of governments. One of the major putative advantages of privatization is that it can reduce the role of government bureaucracies in performing entrepreneurial activities for which they may be poorly suited. But overseeing provision of specifically public services by privately owned service providers and ensuring that competition, if possible, does take place are also activities that require substantial expertise and well-developed administrative capabilities on the part of government agencies. Where market forces are weak and important public interests are at stake, therefore, the strengthening of governmental institutions may be a prerequisite of successful privatization.

Bibliography

American Public Works Association (APWA) 1958. *Refuse Collection Practice.* 2nd ed. Chicago: APWA.

American Water Works Association. 1925. *Water Works Practice.* Baltimore: Williams and Wilkins.

Anderson, Douglas. 1981. *Regulatory Politics and Electric Utilities.* Boston: Auburn House.

Anderson, Letty. 1980. "The Diffusion of Technology in the Nineteenth Century American City: Municipal Water Supply Investments." Unpublished dissertation. Northwestern University.

Armstrong, Ellis L., Michael C. Robinson, and Suellen M. Hoy, eds. 1976. *History of Public Works in the United States 1876–1976.* Chicago: American Public Works Association.

Beito, David T., and Bruce Smith. 1990. "The Formation of Urban Infrastructure Through Nongovernmental Planning: The Private Places of St. Louis, 1869–1920." *Journal of Urban History* 16 (May).

Blake, Nelson Manfred. 1956. *Water for the Cities: A History of the Urban Water Supply Problem in the United States.* Syracuse: Syracuse University Press.

Boston Lamp Department. 1892. *Annual Report of the Lamp Department for the Year 1891.* Boston.

Bruchey, Stuart. 1965. *The Roots of American Economic Growth 1607–1861.* New York: Harper & Row.

Cheape, Charles W. 1980. *Moving the Masses: Urban Public Transport in New York, Boston, and Philadelphia, 1880–1912.* Cambridge, Massachusetts: Harvard University Press.

Davidson, R. K. 1957. *Price Discrimination in the Selling of Electricity and Gas.* Baltimore: Johns Hopkins University Press.

De Bell, Garrett. 1970. "Energy" in Garrett De Bell, ed., *The Environmental Handbook.* New York: Ballantine.

de Gournay, Chantal. 1988. "Telephone Networks in France and Great Britain" in Joel A. Tarr and Gabriel Dupuy, eds., *Technology and the Rise of the Networked City in Europe and America.* Philadelphia: Temple University.

Einhorn, Robin. 1991. *Property Rules: Political Economy in Chicago, 1833–1872.* Chicago: University of Chicago Press.

Energy Policy Project of the Ford Foundation. 1974. *A Time to Choose: America's Energy Future.* Cambridge: Ballinger.

Frederick, Kenneth, and Dianna C. Gibbons. 1986. *Scarce Water and Institutional*

Change. Washington D.C.: Resources for the Future.

Frost, Robert L. 1991. *Alternating Currents: Nationalized Power in France, 1946–1970.* Ithaca: Cornell University Press.

Garnet, Robert W. 1985. *The Telephone Enterprise: The Evolution of the Bell System's Horizontal Structure, 1876–1909.* Baltimore: Johns Hopkins University Press.

Gomez-Ibanez, Jose A., and John Meyer. 1992. *The Political Economy of Transport-Privatization: Successes, Failures and Lessons from Developed and Developing Countries.* Cambridge: John F. Kennedy School of Government.

Gould, Jacob Martin. 1946. *Output and Productivity in the Electric and Gas Utilities: 1899–1949.* New York: National Bureau of Economic Research.

Grimstone, Gerry. 1989. "Privatization: Macroeconomics and Modalities" in V. V. Ramanadham, ed., *Privatization in Developing Countries.* London: Routledge.

Hannah, Leslie. 1979. *Electricity Before Nationalization: A Study of the Development of the Electricity Supply Industry in Britain to 1948.* Baltimore: Johns Hopkins University Press.

Heald, David. 1989. "The United Kingdom: Privatization in its Political Context" in John Vickers and Vincent Wright, eds., *The Politics of Privatization in Western Europe.* London: Frank Cass.

Hirsch, Richard. 1989. *Technology and Transformation in the American Electric Utility Industry.* Cambridge: Cambridge University Press.

Hirshleifer, Jack, James De Haven, and Jerome Milliman. 1960. *Water Supply: Economics, Technology, and Policy.* Chicago: University of Chicago.

Helman, John, and Gerald W. Johnson. 1992. *The Politics and Economics of Privatization: The Case of Wastewater Treatment.* Tuscaloosa: The University of Alabama Press.

Holcombe, A. N. 1911. *Public Ownership of Telephones on the Continent of Europe.* Cambridge: Harvard University Press.

Hughes, Thomas Parke. 1983. *Networks of Power: Electrification in Western Society, 1880–1930.* Baltimore: Johns Hopkins University Press.

Jacobson, Charles D. 1989. "Private Firms and Public Goods: Historical Perspectives on Contracting Out for Public Services" in Ann Durkin Keating, ed., *Public Private Partnerships: Privatization in Historical Perspective.* Chicago: Public Works Historical Society.

Jordan, Don. 1991."The Hidden Threat." *Public Utilities Fortnightly* March 15.

Keating, Ann Durkin. 1989. "Public-Private Partnerships in Public Works: A Bibliographic Chapter" in *Public Private Partnerships: Privatization in Historical Perspective.* Chicago: Public Works Historical Society.

Lorrain, Dominique. 1992. "The French Model of Urban Services." *West European Politics* 15(April).

Lovins, Amory B. 1977. *Soft Energy Paths: Toward a Durable Peace.* New York: Harper & Row.

Maclean, Mairi. 1991. *French Enterprise and the Challenge of the British Water Industry: Water Without Frontiers.* Aldershot: Avebury.

Melosi, Martin V. 1981. *Garbage in the Cities: Refuse, Reform, and the Environment, 1880–1980.* College Station: Texas A & M University Press.

Meyer, John R., and Jose A. Gomez-Ibanez. 1981. *Autos, Transit and Cities.* Cambridge: Harvard University Press.

Monkkonen, Eric H. 1988. *America Becomes Urban: The Development of U.S. Cities & Towns 1780–1980.* Berkeley: University of California Press.

Mosher, William. 1929. *Electrical Utilities: The Crisis in Public Control*. New York: Harper & Brothers.

National Council on Public Works Improvement. 1988. *Fragile Foundations: A Report on America's Public Works*. February. Washington, D.C.: U.S. Government Printing Office.

Passer, Harold C. 1953. *The Electrical Manufacturers*. Cambridge: Harvard University Press.

Persaud, Bishnodat. 1992. "Foreward" in Christopher Adam, William Cavendish, and Percy S. Mistry, eds., *Adjusting Privatization: Case Studies from Developing Countries*. London: James Currey.

Peterson, Jon A. 1979. "The Impact of Sanitary Reform Upon American Urban Planning." *Journal of Social History* 13(Fall).

Phillips, Charles F. 1988. *The Regulation of Public Utilities: Theory and Practice*. Arlington: Public Utilities Reports.

Platt, Harold. 1991. *The Electric City: Energy and the Growth of the Chicago Area*. Chicago: University of Chicago Press.

Rosen, Christine Meisner. 1986. *The Limits of Power: Great Fires and the Process of City Growth in America*. New York: Cambridge University Press.

Roth, Gabriel. 1987. *The Private Provision of Public Services in Developing Countries*. New York: Oxford University Press.

Rosenzweig, Richard. 1993. "The Energy Policy Act of 1992." *Public Utilities Fortnightly* 131(No. 1).

Scheiber, Harry. 1975. "Federalism and the American Economic Order, 1789–1910." *Law and Society Review* 10(Fall).

Suggs, Robert E. 1989. *Minorities and Privatization: Economic Mobility at Risk*. Washington, D.C.: Joint Center for Political Studies.

Sutcliffe, Anthony. 1981. *Towards the Planned City: Germany, the United States and France 1780–1914*. New York: St. Martin's Press.

Tarr, Joel A. 1984. "The Evolution of the Urban Infrastructure in the Nineteenth and Twentieth Centuries" in Royce Hanson, ed., *Perspectives on Urban Infrastructure*. Washington, D.C.: National Academy Press.

Tarr, Joel A., James McCurley III, Francis C. McMichael, and Terry Yosie. 1984. "Water and Wastes: A Retrospective Assessment of Wastewater Technology in the United States, 1800–1932." *Technology and Culture* 25(April).

Twentieth Century Fund. 1948. *Electric Power and Government Policy*. New York: Twentieth Century Fund.

U.S. Congress, Congressional Budget Office. 1988. *New Directions for the Nation's Public Works*. Washington, D.C.: U.S. Government Printing Office.

U.S. Congress, Office of Technology Assessment. 1991. *Delivering the Goods: Public Works Technologies, Management, and Financing*. April. Washington, D.C.: U.S. Government Printing Office.

U.S. Environmental Protection Agency. 1988. *Project Summary: A Statistical Abstract of the Unsewered U.S. Population*. April. Washington, D.C.: U.S. Environmental Protection Agency.

Vickers, John, and Vincent Wright. 1989. "The Politics of Privatization in Western Europe: An Overview" in John Vickers and Vincent Wright, eds., *The Politics of Privatization in Western Europe*. London: Frank Cass.

Weiss, Marc A. 1987. *The Rise of the Community Builders: The American Real Estate*

Industry and Urban Land Planning. New York: Columbia University Press.

Weiss, Marc A., and John W. Watts. 1989. "Community Builders and Community Associations: The Role of Large-Scale Developers in Private Residential Governance" in *Residential Community Associations in the Intergovernmental Systems.* Washington, D.C.: U.S. Advisory Commission on Intergovernmental Relations.

Williamson, Oliver. 1985. *The Economic Institutions of Capitalism.* New York: The Free Press.

Wilcox, Delos. 1915. *Report of Delos F. Wilcox, Deputy Commissioner, in Relation to the Queens County Water Company.* City of New York: Department of Water Supply, Gas, and Electricity.

Wittig, George. 1930. "Technological Developments" in *Census of Electrical Industries 1927: Central Electric Light and Power Stations.* Bureau of the Census. Washington, D.C.:U.S. Government Printing Office.

Wohl, Martin. 1982. *From Private to Public Transit: Lessons from Our 100-Year Experience in America.* Report SS-243-U.3-210. Cambridge: U.S. Department of Transportation.

2

Exploiting New Market Opportunities in Telecommunications

Veronique Bishop, Ashoka Mody, and Mark Schankerman

In most countries, telecommunications services have traditionally been delivered by a single, government-owned provider. Such state-owned monopolies have only rarely mobilized significant amounts of capital for the telecommunications network, and even in those instances they have a poor record of responding to the evolving needs of businesses and households. As a consequence, monopolies are giving way to a heterogeneous structure where competition exists in numerous market segments. Promoting competition requires liberal market entry rules. Also, to encourage entry by providers who may wish to supply only specific services, traditional cross-subsidization across services needs to be eliminated, which may require sectoral unbundling. The longer term regulatory task is to implement pricing rules that protect customers and that provide incentives to operators to reduce their costs. At the same time, a regulator in a pluralistic regime must establish rules and prices for the interconnection of the multiple networks—and this practice is still evolving. In countries undertaking reform, restructuring of the government-owned monopoly operator and regulatory reform are proving to be tandem efforts. Although the benefits of reform are often evident, the pace of change can be slowed by incumbent interests, and experience shows that sectoral reform has to be led by forces outside the traditional sectoral establishment. In that light, this chapter reviews policy reform in a complex sector where the physical elements of the network and institutional aspects are interdependent and where political economy considerations can be critical to success.

The telecommunications sectors of many developing countries are in transition from monopolies to multiple providers that compete with and complement each other. The transitions stem from the need to meet a huge suppressed demand for telecommunications, a dissatisfaction with traditional state-owned monopolies, and an unprecedented range of technological opportunities. The promise of a pluralistic market structure is great and may represent the only realistic hope of more than doubling telecommunications investments in the developing world to over $60 billion a year—a conservative estimate of the amount needed to meet the unfulfilled demand for conventional services and the growing demand for new services.

For the promise to be realized, however, coordinated measures will be needed to:

- Render incumbent providers more commercially oriented and subject to the same basic rules as other providers;
- Stimulate competition to increase efficiency and choice of services;
- Create a regulatory environment that protects consumers, ensures fair competition, and provides incentives for efficient investment; and
- Sensitively manage the interests of parties—such as traditional telecommunications workers—who are likely to lose from the reform process.

Each set of measures requires the creation of new incentive structures, embodied in new institutional forms. As a consequence, institutional innovation—rather than mere reliance on technological developments—is required to pave the way for successful transition to a competitive structure. Much of the experience to date comes from industrialized countries, but several developing countries have undertaken varying degrees of institutional reform, addressing their own special problems and, where possible, adapting lessons learned in advanced economies.

In most countries, telecommunications services have traditionally been delivered by a single, government-owned provider. Such state-owned monopolies have only rarely mobilized significant amounts of capital for the telecommunications network, and even in those instances have a poor record of responding to the evolving and varied needs of businesses and households. Large waiting lists are evident, especially in low-income countries. Moreover, a sizable latent demand lies concealed since prospective users do not even register on waiting lists until there is a realistic chance of receiving a phone connection.

Countries undertaking new initialives *restructure* the incumbent—typically the government-owned, monopoly operator—and, in tandem, institute *regulatory reform.* Restructuring and revitalizing the incumbent is undertaken to achieve both commercial and social goals, including the preservation of the government's financial assets and protection of the interests of workers in such enterprises. Moreover, restructuring is an essential aid to the process of sectoral reform: the incumbent operator's incentives need to be reoriented to compete on par with other operators, requiring corporatization, decentralization of activities into profit centers, and, ultimately, privatization.

Beyond enterprise restructuring lies competition. Under the pressures of accumulated inefficiencies and technological change that is reducing the economic benefits of large-sized operations, telecommunications monopolies are giving way to a heterogeneous sector structure where competition exists in many market segments (figure 2.1). While competition is most easily established in domestic long-distance services, the cartel in international services is being decisively broken, and the local loop linking the ultimate user to the network—and the last bastion of monopoly—is also witnessing growing competition.

Promoting such competition requires liberal market entry rules. It also requires the more complex and gradual task of redrawing the boundaries between different activities within the sector and realigning prices of different services to ensure efficient new entry. The sector needs to be unbundled to prevent cross-subsidization across services and to promote entry by new providers who may wish to supply only specific services. Such unbundling may be achieved by a physical separation of assets and operations, although an accounting separation—as between network and retail services—can also facilitate competition. Old tariff structures that embed large cross-subsidies have to be phased out and replaced with ones more conducive to competition. During the transition, the incumbent operator maintains a dominant position and thus can prevent fair competition; however, the incumbent is also saddled with service obligations that new entrants often do not have, and for which it must be compensated.

Competition is considered its own best regulator, but everywhere regulatory bodies are being established to ensure fair competition and to protect the public interest. The regulatory task is to implement pricing rules that protect customers while providing incentives to operators to reduce their costs. More importantly, a regulator in a regime with multiple operators must establish rules and prices for the interconnection of the various networks—and this practice is still evolving.

Although the benefits of reform are often evident, the pace of change can be slowed by those benefiting from prevailing shortages. Telecommu-

Figure 2.1. *Direction of Liberalization of the Telecommunications Sector*

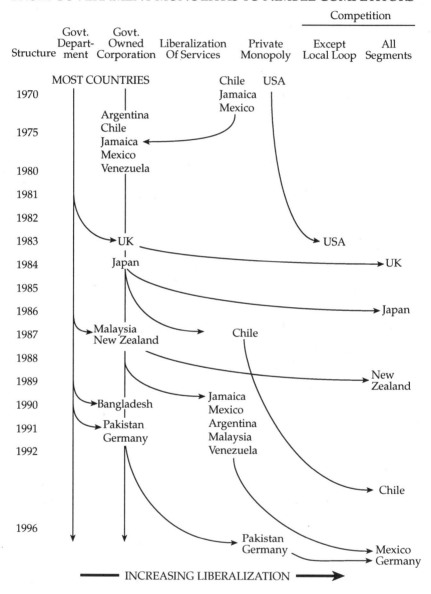

Source: Compiled by the authors from various sources.

nications reform thus has to be led by forces outside the sectoral establishment. For example, established interests often invoke, in a self-serving manner, the potential displacement of workers as a reason for holding back. In practice, this tactic has been undermined by a variety of measures that have successfully mitigated the potentially negative effects on workers. No doubt, the diffusion of reform has been accelerated by user demand for technological advances. But it has taken the commitment of senior government leadership to realign interests in favor of consumers and away from the old telecommunications establishment.

In what follows, we deal successively with the large gap between supply and demand, restructuring the incumbent to face the market test, new opportunities for competition, the new regulatory regime, and the political economy of institutional change.

The Supply-Demand Gap

The large unfulfilled demand for telecommunications in developing countries—seen in long waiting lists and poor service quality—imposes a severe cost on the operations of firms and households. In addition to "plain old telephone service," applications tailored to customer needs are being pioneered in developed countries, but their relevance is as great for developing country enterprises, especially those with international transactions. Addressing this supply-demand gap will require substantial new investments, possibly as much as $60 billion a year.

Evidence of Suppressed Demand

Figure 2.2 shows a familiar relationship: phones per capita increases with income per capita. More important, a comparison of the regression lines for 1981 and 1991 reveals that this gap in telephone use between the high-income and low-income countries has increased over the last decade. Such a gap could suggest that the telephone is a luxury indulged in by the rich (President Charles de Gaulle of France scorned it as a gadget) or that telecommunications are more productive in the more information-intensive, rich countries. We find persuasive evidence, however, that the gap arises in large part from severe underinvestment in telecommunications services in developing countries.

Today, no one can seriously assert that telecommunications is a luxury. For firms competing in international markets, the demand is particularly acute.

Figure 2.2. GNP vs. Main Lines The Gap between the Telecom Haves and
Have-Nots is Growing in Low- to Middle- Income Countries, 1983 and 1992

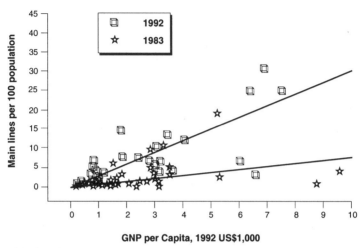

Source: ITU (1994).

Empirical studies have shown that both the quantity (lines per population) and the quality of telecommunications are extremely important for
generating exports and for attracting foreign investment (Boatman 1991;
Mody and Yilmaz 1994; Wheeler and Mody 1992). In some respects, developing countries depend even more on telecommunications infrastructure
than developed countries. Exports of products that are characterized by
rapidly evolving demand (such as apparel) are particularly sensitive to the
availability of a telecommunications network. In addition, the export of intermediate products (such as auto parts) requires close contact with customers who need to minimize their inventory levels. In the newly industri-
alizing economies of East Asia, advanced applications of telecommunications for the movement of documents and goods are being developed to
bolster their competitive advantage in traditional exports such as garments,
footwear, auto parts, and electronics goods (Mody and Reinfeld 1994). This
implies an accelerating increase in demand for telecommunications services.

Telecommunications investments in developing countries have shown
high economic rates of return. For World Bank projects, they were estimated at 27 percent on average, which is substantially higher than the average on the Bank's portfolio (World Bank 1991). These estimates make
conservative assessments of the consumer surplus from telecommunications investments and do not account for spillover benefits.

Failure to keep pace with growing demand has been especially evident in low-income developing countries, where suppressed demand is highest. According to International Telecommunication Union, registered waiting lists for new telephone service represent 27 percent of the installed base in developing countries (ITU 1994). The situation is most acute in Sub-Saharan Africa, where the average waiting list is 60 percent of the number of installed lines. In many cases, the waiting times exceed ten years. In contrast, the upper half of middle-income countries have waiting lists of 19 percent (figure 2.3).

NEW LINES. Pent-up demand in developing countries can be conservatively estimated at 45 million lines, the total of registered waiting lists (ITU 1994). This is conservative in that: (1) not all countries report waiting lists and (2) discouraged "waiters" are not reported. The existence of discouraged waiters is illustrated by the increase in waiting lists that typically occurs as more phones are provided and the prospect of receiving a phone improves (ITU 1994). This phenomenon is strikingly illustrated in India where the number of new lines installed in any year of the past decade has served at least one-quarter of the waiters (a naive interpretation being that the wait list would be eliminated in four years), yet the waitlist has continued to grow (figure 2.4). In Chile, the number of lines increased by more than the size of the waiting list between 1989 and 1990, yet the waitlist remained (figure 2.4). Similarly, according to one report, for every new telephone installed in China, two new applicants join the queue for telephones (*Communications International*, July 1994).

Figure 2.3. *Waiting Lists as a Percentage of Main Lines, 1992*

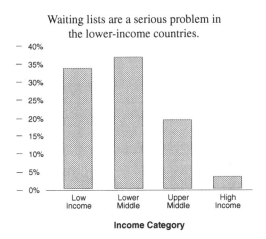

Source: ITU (1994).

Figure 2.4. India and Chile: Wait Lists and Main Lines

As phone availability increases, so do waiting lists

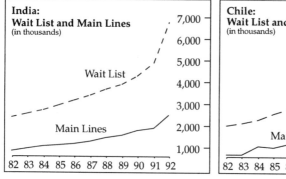
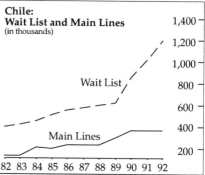

Source: ITU (1994).

SERVICE QUALITY AND ENHANCED SERVICES. Underinvestment and poor maintenance has also resulted in poor service quality. Fault rates of 20 per month for every 100 lines are not uncommon in developing countries, compared with fault rates of 2 per 100 lines per month in developed countries. Low call-completion rates for domestic and international services increase costs for users and depress revenues for the provider. According to an estimate for Ghana in 1992, call completion rates were less than 50 percent; the average number of lines not working at any time was 20 percent, and the average duration of faults was 30 days—though for rural connections repair could take over a year (Anderson Management International 1993).

The Magnitude of Suppressed Demand

An estimated $60 billion in annual investment is required to meet the demand for telecommunications services in developing countries, representing 1.36 percent of the annual GDP of these countries (table 2.1). In the early 1990s, developing country telecommunications investment was just under $30 billion a year. The required investment of $60 billion a year encompasses three components: (1) historical growth; (2) satisfying the current wait lists; and (3) providing new and improved services.

Projected developing country investment in basic telecommunications networks is $32.1 billion per year (ITU 1994). This estimate, however, is based on past supply trends—an inaccurate guide for the future. Impor-

Table 2.1. Annual Telecommunications Investment Requirements for Developing Countries (billions of dollars)

| | Developing-country income group | | | |
	Low	Lower-middle	Upper-middle	All
New Lines— ITU estimate	11	10	11	32
New Lines— to supply current wait list by 2000	2	5	4	11
Quality improvements and enhanced services	2	6	9	17
Total	15	21	24	60
Percentage of GDP	1.52	1.82	1.10	1.36

Source: ITU (1994) and author's calculations (see text).

tantly, it excludes investments required to meet the demands of those waiting for telephones.[1]

Supplying just the 45 million officially waitlisted for a telephone (thus not counting the discouraged demand) would cost an additional $67.5 billion (assuming the ITU cost of $1,500 per line), implying an investment of $11 billion per year if the existing waiting lists are to be eliminated by the year 2000.

In addition to the high demand for "plain old telephone service," there is a growing demand for many specialized and "intelligent" services.[2] Although

1.   ITU's calculations are based on the assumption that investment to the year 2000 will continue at the rate experienced in previous years (at a cost of $1,500 per line): "Projection [is] based on average annual growth rate in main lines and population over the last 8 years" (ITU 1994: 3).

2.   Many businesses urgently need packet-switching facilities, X.400 messaging services, electronic data interchange, and paging and mobile services. To overcome these shortages, dedicated bypass networks have been or are being created to enable companies with local and international needs to transfer data. In India, these include networks belonging to the Indian Railways, the Steel Authority, the State Bank, Reliance Corporation, and others. In Ghana, Barclays Bank has dedicated lines for its data transfer between branches.

no accurate measures of investment requirements for quality improvements and enhanced services exist, we have estimated that high-income countries invested some $81 billion in these areas in 1992, or $200 per installed line.[3] Given the lower sophistication of developing country networks, we could assume that their required investments in quality improvements and enhanced services were only half the high-income country levels, or $100 per installed line—creating an increased appetite of $17 billion a year.

The Transition from Old Ways to New

Today, the challenge is to provide the large network investment required without imposing a burden on government resources.[4] At the same time, opportunities unfold as domestic and international capital markets play a more important role in financing infrastructure. Joint-ventures add another set of opportunities, with leading international companies allowing transfer of expertise. For such capital and expertise to be efficiently deployed, services must be oriented towards the needs of consumers, with an emphasis on greater pluralism in the network.

Given the growth of needed investment in the sector over the past decade, state-monopoly telecommunications provision has diminished to make way for more open, competitive structures. As figure 2.1 demonstrates, there is a marked trend towards liberalization. In a dozen countries, the sector has evolved from the government monopoly model prevalent in the 1970s to one in which a broadening array of services is being "unbundled" from the dominant operator. During the mid-1980s, many of these entities were reorganized so that telecoms were separated from postal services, operators were corporatized, and in some cases, these government-owned corporations were privatized. Meanwhile, certain services were opened to competition, but generally only those outside of basic network services. This limited unbundling

---

3.   ITU estimated total investment in high-income countries at $100 billion in 1992, during which year 12.6 million new lines were installed. Using the ITU benchmark of $1,500 per line, the new lines would have cost $19 billion to install. The balance, $81 billion, spread over 406 million installed lines, implies an average investment in quality and service enhancement of $200 per line.

4.   A handful of government-owned monopolies have successfully enlarged their networks. France transformed one of the smallest and most backward networks in Europe into one of the most modern in the world, trebling the number of main lines in a decade from 7 million in 1975 to 25 million in 1985 (Ergas 1992: 2). Turkey's PTT similarly trebled its network, but in an even faster six years. And Korea's network has grown by 1 million lines per year since the early 1980s (Kim, Kim, and Yoon 1992).

typically occurred in the following order: equipment, value-added services, data transmission, and cellular and private circuits. In the late 1980s and 1990s, competition was finally opened in network services—primarily domestic long-distance, but in a few local services as well.

Enterprise Restructuring

The restructuring of the incumbent operator is critical for both economic and political reasons. Increased autonomy—with incentives for commercial orientation—can greatly improve overall performance. Typically, such autonomy is achieved through corporatization, but often the further step of privatization is needed to minimize governmental interference in operations. Privatization also is used, in practice, to achieve goals beyond enterprise performance, including the development of capital markets. Successful privatization requires sensitivity to maintaining national ownership and continued adherence to social goals. Where constraints to privatization exist, contractual arrangements—through build-operate-transfer (BOT) schemes and their variants—can draw new investment and improve efficiency.

An important premise of enterprise restructuring is that the regulatory functions must be separated from network operations from the start to create a level playing field for all operators. It is often argued that a regulatory framework must precede privatization, or even corporatization; however, in practice, the two tasks proceed side-by-side.

Corporatization and Decentralization

Corporatization is often a prelude to privatization. The major objective of corporatization is to convert the telecommunication department into an autonomous organization that is owned by the government, but runs on a commercial basis. By placing the telecommunications operator at arm's length from the government, corporatization permits telecommunications operators to respond directly to the market. Checks on the operator may be instituted at this stage through licensing conditions that stipulate the conditions of operation. The goal, often not realized, is that all requirements placed on the corporation by government be explicit, thus eliminating the need to respond ad hoc to government intervention.

Following corporatization, one strategy for improving efficiency is to decentralize operations. This practice allows greater responsiveness to customers and increases managerial accountability. Regionally based profit centers or separation into lines of business have been mechanisms for decentralization in New Zealand, Indonesia, and Mexico.

NEW ZEALAND. To create Telecom Corporation of New Zealand Ltd. (TCNZ), the government passed the State Owned Enterprise Act in December 1986, and the Telecommunications Act in July 1987. Under these laws, TCNZ became a corporation fully owned by the government. Following corporatization, TCNZ decentralized decisionmaking responsibility into subsidiaries so that managers closest to the customer would be accountable for their needs and for unit profitability. Four new regional operating companies were created to provide local telephone service, and one subsidiary was created to provide domestic and international long distance service. There were also nine small, entrepreneurial "New Venture" companies, each focusing on a specialized market segment. New managers with commercial business experience were recruited and appointed to the boards of the newly created subsidiaries.

INDONESIA. In 1991, the legal status of P.T. TELKOM was changed from a government enterprise to a limited liability company. The new company's shares are still held wholly by the government, but this structure allows future transfer of shares, perhaps in tranches, to private entities. TELKOM is in the process of decentralizing its organization with the ultimate goal of creating several regional subsidiaries, plus a long-distance and a cellular operator under a holding company. The subsidiary companies will, in turn, form joint ventures with experienced telephone operators. Another company is likely to be established to manage the PALAPA satellite system.

The restructuring dovetails with the goals of investment mobilization and stimulation of competition. The new structure encourages competition in two ways. First, decentralization creates "benchmark competition" among the regional subsidiaries. The managers of each subsidiary will be responsible for the relative profitability of their subsidiaries. Second, a new wireless company will provide long-distance and local cellular service in competition with TELKOM.

MEXICO. In 1987, to prepare for privatization, Telmex's corporate structure was decentralized and separated from ministerial control. Functions were also restructured into geographic or service-related profit centers. Managers at the regional level could make decisions without relying on central approval and were more accountable for regional profitability. "This change accelerates decisionmaking, clarifies responsibility, helps to allocate capital...serving the needs of Telmex's different customer groups" (Casasus 1994: 10).

Meanwhile, administrative control of Telmex was transferred from the Communications Ministry to the Finance Ministry, which was managing the privatization program. The Finance Ministry allowed greater autonomy in operations and Telmex gained more financial autonomy through the large price increases of 1988 and 1990. Telmex could then self-finance a larger proportion of its investment. Through innovative new securitization transactions, Telmex gained access to international capital markets and' raised over $900 million in three years.

Privatization of the Government-Monopoly Operator

The objectives of efficient operation can, in principle, be met through corporatization and restructuring the organization into profit centers. But the further step of privatization has increasingly been taken. Transfer of ownership to the private sector is justified for a variety of reasons, including additional insulation of operations from political whims, greater efficiency of operations, and creation of a level playing field for other private operators.

Evidence shows that post-privatization efficiency improvements benefit shareholders and labor and that consumers gain from rapid network expansion—but they often pay more for services that were heavily subsidized. A study of total welfare gains (sum of monetary gains to shareholders, employees, and consumers) found that the gains as a proportion of pre-privatization sales were 12 percent in the United Kingdom, but were much higher in Mexico (50 percent) and in Chile (155 percent) (Galal, Jones, Tandon, and Vogelsang 1994: 532).

To provide quick consumer access to new lines, privatizations are often accompanied by a requirement to undertake certain minimum investments. These so-called "roll-out" obligations are exemplified by the service conditions imposed on Telmex, the privatized Mexican telecommunications provider. Network development targets built into the concession required Telmex to achieve a line growth rate of at least 12 percent a year—twice the growth rate achieved during the late 1980s. In addition to line growth requirements, the concession also required improvements in service quality. Telmex exceeded the targets. Similar roll-out conditions were used in Argentina and Venezuela where the privatized utilities also outperformed obligations. For example, CANTV in Venezuela (privatized in December 1991) expanded its network by

50 percent in the following two years and virtually all targets for service improvements were met. Since the levels of service provision are now so low in developing countries and the incentives to expand so enormous, roll-out requirements may be unnecessary. Moreover, when roll-outs are used to secure the provision of services on uneconomic terms to particular areas or consumers, they can distort pricing.

The privatizations thus far have shown great sensitivity to political and social concerns. The message: while efficiency gains are likely to be achieved through privatization, the central concerns of policymakers are local ownership, redistribution of ownership and rents to employees and other socioeconomic-economic groups, and availability of service to weak consumers. Also, externalities—such as the development of capital markets—are an important objective in privatizing utilities. These lessons are illustrated by the privatization experiences in Mexico and New Zealand.

TELMEX CAPITAL RESTRUCTURING FOR PRIVATIZATION. The capital restructuring process for Telmex in Mexico had several objectives: (1) to transfer part of the ownership to Telmex employees, (2) to attract equity interest from experienced foreign operators, but retain Mexican control of Telmex, and (3) to develop the ability to raise capital using new international financial instruments.

First, the government sold 4.4 percent of its A shares (or voting shares) to the company's employees, of which 1.6 percent were sold to its managers (Dougan and Bruno 1991). These were paid for through an eight-year credit provided by the government's development bank, on favorable terms.

Second, a controlling block of shares was sold to a private Mexican-led consortium on December 20, 1990, for $1.76 billion. Foreign operating companies were allowed to participate as minority partners (in keeping with the foreign investment law). The winning group included Grupo Carso, a diversified Mexican group in association with the minority investors Southwestern Bell and France Telecom. Although the group acquired only a 20.5 percent ownership of Telmex, its voting rights were 51 percent.

Third, to further attract foreign capital but retain Mexican control, new shares with limited voting rights were issued in an international public stock offering to investors in the United States, Europe, and Asia for $2.2 billion in May 1991. This was a landmark deal, representing the largest global stock offering by any Latin American company. It was also the first time a privatization was carried out through a public offering of shares in Latin America, and the first time that more than 85 percent of the shares being offered were placed outside the home country. Mexico's government, now a minority Telmex holder, sold a 14 percent stake in the company. The offering placed the single largest injection of foreign money to date into Mexico's government coffers (Dougan and Bruno 1991).

Finally, in May 1992, the Mexican government sold an additional 4.7 percent of the company in an international and domestic offering, and now retains about a 4.8 percent holding. Overall, the government received some $6 billion from the Telmex privatization. (Casasus 1994, Galal, Jones, Tandon, and Vogelsang 1994).

THE "KIWI" SHARE IN NEW ZEALAND. In privatizing TCNZ, the Government of New Zealand sought to limit foreign ownership to 49.9 percent to ensure coverage of local service areas. Through a "kiwi" share, it maintained leadership in policymaking.

In September 1990, the government took a dramatic step: 100 percent of TCNZ shares were sold through open bidding to a consortium led by two New Zealand managers (with 0.5 percent ownership) and owned by two American regional operating companies (Ameritech Corporation and Bell Atlantic). To ensure that the government's objectives would be met, it attached several conditions to this sale. The agreement stipulated that the owners would: (1) sell back 10 percent of the stock to a New Zealand corporation, and (2) reduce ownership below 49.9 percent by spring 1994 through public subscription.

A special share—the "kiwi share"—issued to the Crown gave the finance minister specific rights to control overseas ownership and other key articles of incorporation. The articles require that half of the directors be New Zealand nationals. Moreover, the government instituted service obligations in the "Telecom Pledge," including continued free local residential calling, residential line rental price increases limited to the consumer price index, equal pricing for rural and urban areas, continued universal access, and the requirement to publish quality-of-service records (New Zealand Ministry of Commerce 1992).

Contracting-Out: The Thai Example

Where political or other constraints exist to full privatization, yet another method for increasing network size and improving efficiency is contracting-out, which brings in private initiative under the existing government operator's umbrella. Such contracting-out has been used to provide local telecommunications services in Thailand (Augenblick, Stern, and Sullivan 1994; *Financial Times*, April 6, 1994).

To help meet the growing demand for telecommunications services, the Telephone Organization of Thailand (TOT) has granted two build-transfer-operate (BTO) concessions to private operators to provide a total of three million new telephone lines by 1996 at an estimated cost of $5 billion. The first concession, granted in 1991, provided for the installation of two million lines in the Bangkok area. The winner of the concession was a Thai-owned multinational (Charoen Pokphand group, an agro-industrial corporation), which subsequently formed TelecomAsia, in partnership with Nynex, an American regional operator (which took a 15 percent equity position). Nynex appoints the chief operating officer and other key executives.

Under the BTO scheme, TelecomAsia is installing the new lines, will transfer ownership to the government, and then operate the system for 25 years under a revenue-sharing agreement. This agreement specifies that TelecomAsia will pass 16 percent of total service revenues to TOT. The system will consist of an overlay network that interconnects with both the 1.2 million-line TOT network and Communications Authority of Thailand's international gateway. Construction is underway and is expected to be completed in five years. TOT has agreed not to compete with TelecomAsia before 1997.

A second BTO was awarded in 1992 to Thai Telephone and Telecommunication Co. (TT&T), an affiliate of the Loxley group—with Japan's Nippon Telegraph and Telephone holding a 20 percent interest—to install and operate one million new lines in the rural northern provinces or "up country," centered on Chiang Mai. In the 25-year concession agreement, TT&T will take 56.9 percent of revenues collected, and TOT will take the rest. The larger revenue-share for TOT, compared with the 16 percent for TelecomAsia, is justified on the grounds that provincial lines generate more revenue through long-distance calls.

The Thai BTO schemes prove the potential for attracting private financing to telecommunications projects, even for local networks. The projects have been financed with a combination of supplier credits, loans, and project cash generation. The two BTO companies have since raised funds through public offerings on the Thai capital market and form—along with other telecommunications listings—16 percent of the Stock Exchange of Thailand. Similar schemes are now being attempted in other developing countries, notably Indonesia.

Bringing in Competition

Until only a decade ago, in most countries the telecommunications sector was dominated by a single organization that provided a variety of goods and services with very different economic characteristics. Scale economies (the cost advantages of large size) and scope economies (the savings realized from the joint production of services) were used to justify the single provider. But economies of scale and scope have generally declined with technological progress and, even where they exist, such economies may no longer justify government-mandated monopolies. There is compelling evidence that competition is possible in virtually all segments of telecommunications.

Do Natural Monopolies Exist?

When one provider can serve the market at a lower cost than two or more providers could, a natural monopoly is said to exist. It is also common for these providers to supply a number of services, only some of which benefit from economies of scale. A natural monopoly in one service, however, may allow the provider to gain an advantage in another service that could be competitively provided.

The telecommunications sector was long considered to exhibit both scale and scope economies because of the "lumpiness" of the required investment and the adaptability of the physical infrastructure to multiple uses. But evidence now shows declining economies of scale in the provision of telecommunications services. In switching, or the routing of calls, increased modularity means that being small has less disadvantage in cost. After being switched, calls are traditionally transmitted over underground copper cables, but wireless technologies reduce the minimum efficient size of investment for long-distance communications. Very small aperture terminals (VSAT), for example, are a low-cost, satellite-based alternative for long-distance communication. Radio-based, cellular technologies that provide service to a small customer base in a local area are available at increasingly competitive prices. Optical fibers do not conform to this trend—once laid in the ground their very large capacities render parallel investments uneconomic from a social view point. However, even with fiber optics, software makes it possible for competitors to "share" the fiber in transparent and fair ways.

The evidence on economies of scope in the telecommunications sector is weak at best. Economists attempting to measure scope economies for the former Bell system in the United States came to very different conclusions on this question, although subsequent evidence has tended to favor the view that while scope economies do exist, they are relatively limited (Evans and Heckman 1984; Charnes, Cooper, and Sueyoshi 1988; Banker, Chang, and Majumdar 1992). The physical evidence also undermines economies of scope. For example, common standards embodied in switching software (such as Open Network Architecture) seamlessly interconnect networks and services offered by numerous suppliers and permit the charges from these suppliers to be itemized on a single bill. Such software allows use of common facilities by multiple providers.

With economies of scale and scope declining, the question is: how much competition can the telecommunications sector sustain? Although telecommunications markets with numerous suppliers are still rare, competition among a few rival providers can lower costs and prices. The theory of contestable markets says that even where economies of scale and scope favor a single provider, potential rival suppliers that contest the market limit the risks of monopoly abuse. Thus, all new entrants should be allowed to provide services, letting the market decide how many providers can operate profitably. Potential competition is most effective where new entrants have limited sunk costs of market entry—that is, when entrants can recover their investments by selling their assets if they decide to pull out of the business. By permitting easier redeployment of assets—through developments in switching, VSAT, cellular, and software systems—technological change is undermining monopoly provision of telecom services.

Ways to Unbundle

Competition is facilitated by unbundling the sector, either physically or in its accounting. Separation along business lines allows prospective entrants to compete in those segments open to multiple providers. Moreover, unbundling allows for the market to test economies of scale and scope, rather than allowing regulators to predetermine which segments should remain bundled.

Vertical unbundling occurs when two activities—one of which is an input for the provision of the other—are institutionally separated. For example, since long-distance operators need local networks to reach their customers, the separation of local and long-distance services is vertical unbundling. Separation can also occur between provision of network services (an intermediate input) and retail services (a final output).

Horizontal unbundling separates activities by markets—either geographically or by service category. Telecommunications lends itself to this form of unbundling as well. The operation of rapidly growing radio-based cellular services is typically separated from the provision of traditional telephone services. In some cases, horizontal unbundling, or divestiture, into a number of producers allows direct competition. In other cases, when divestiture leads to regional monopolies, horizontal unbundling allows for better performance comparisons and, consequently, more efficient regulatory monitoring.

But the distinction between vertical and horizontal unbundling is not always sharp. When specialized providers sell information services using communication links owned by traditional network operators, vertical unbundling between the provision of networks and the supply of information services is needed to allow fair competition between horizontally separated service operators.

Constraints to unbundling are technical and economic. Attempting to force activities that are closely interdependent into distinct boxes can impose high transaction costs because once coordination runs smoothly within a single firm, it becomes more difficult and less effective when handled between firms. And having separate, vertically linked monopolies—each charging a markup over costs—may result in higher charges than those of a single, vertically integrated firm.

But even where the technology accommodates unbundling, legal and administrative institutions often limit the possibilities. In Hungary, a telecommunications law enacted in 1992 separated long-distance (including international) services and local telephone services, which are under the jurisdiction of municipal authorities (Bruce, Harrell, and Kovacs 1993). Under the law, private concessions for local services were to be granted on a competitive basis. But practical problems intervened. As in other countries, local rates are very low, attracting few investors to that part of the network. And investors in the long-distance service faced the prospect of bargaining with group after group of local government officials on terms of interconnection to local networks. A compromise awarded long-distance services and 60 percent of the local network to a single franchise. Competition for the rest of the local network was opened to companies having demonstrable financial strength and sound business plans.

Possibilities and Implications of Competition

A telecommunications market appropriately unbundled opens up competition in virtually every segment. Competition in any one segment lowers tariffs in that segment, which changes the prospects for *other* segments. For example, competition in domestic long-distance telephony and international telephony has often substantially lowered the traditionally large margins in these services so that they can no longer subsidize local services. The consequent rise in local rates, together with developments in wireless technology and the entry of cable network operators, is gradually, but definitely, making local services amenable to competition.

Box 2.1. *China Introduces Competition*

China has announced an historically unprecedented expansion of its network from about 30 million lines to 120 million lines by the year 2000. Investment by the monopoly operator, the Ministry of Posts and Telecommunications (MPT), is expected to be about $8 billion in 1994—aggregate telecommunications investment in China could rise to $15 billion a year to meet the ambitious targets.

To mobilize such large investments, the State Council has abolished MPT's monopoly by licensing a new provider, China United Telecommunications (Unicom), to operate a nationwide network, including both long-distance and local connections. Unicom is a partnership of three Chinese ministries—railways, electric power, and electronics. The expectation is that the networks already operated by the railways and power ministries would form the nucleus of the new enterprise. The Ministry of Electronics brings its expertise in modern communications technologies to the venture.

Other steps towards opening the telecommunications market include: permission to the Ministry of Electronics in January 1994 to compete with MPT in data services, allowing the People's Liberation Army to use its radio network for commercial ends, and the separation of regulatory and operation functions within MPT to ensure that the incumbent and dominant operator does not enjoy undue advantage over new entrants.

Though joint-venture partnerships with foreign companies for the provision of services are, at present, not permitted, the indications are that such partnerships will soon be allowed. Nynex, a regional operator in the United States, has established an advisory relationship with Unicom. Cable and Wireless of the United Kingdom, through its subsidiary Hongkong Telecom, has been nominated a "preferred partner" by MPT. The expectation is that these partnerships will be formalized and used to construct and operate regional or functional networks, possibly on a BOT basis.

Source: Financial Times, July 21, June 23, May 27, May 20, and April 20, 1994.

LONG-DISTANCE COMPETITION. Unbundling—either induced by the market or mandated by the regulator—begins with long-distance service because this segment has high profit margins, which are typically used to subsidize local services. The recent history of competition in telecommunications begins with MCI's challenge to the venerable AT&T with the aid of microwave technology for transmitting long-distance communications signals.

Long-distance services are also an important arena of competition in developing countries.[5] Two significant developments are occurring in China, which has recently licensed a second operator (box 2.1), and in Mexico, where competition for long-distance services will commence on January 1, 1997 (box 2.2).

---

5.   India is an exception. While maintaining a monopoly of long-distance, Indian decisionmakers have divided the country into 18 regions, and, in each, a second operator will be eventually allowed to compete with the incumbent. For such competition to be realistic, local rates would need to be substantially revised upwards.

Chile, also having begun with long-distance competition, now has introduced full-fledged competition. In Chile, two companies have dominated the market. Compania de Telefonos de Chile (CTC) provides local telecommunications service to over 90 percent of the population, and as such is the main interface with the customer. Additionally, CTC provides a limited amount of long-distance service, operates cellular networks in the two major urban areas (Santiago and Valparaiso), and offers a variety of other services. Empresa Nacional de Telecomunicaciones (Entel) is the primary long-distance phone company in Chile, though its share of the market has fallen to 70 percent as new entrants have been allowed to provide long-distance service in the past few years. A third company, Telex-Chile, controls about 25 percent of the long-distance traffic through its subsidiary Chilesat.

From this unbundled, yet monopolistic position, Chile is moving towards a multi-carrier structure that is highly competitive. In mid-1994, new legislation permitted CTC to extend into long-distance services, and hence compete (through its subsidiary Chile-MUNDO), while allowing Entel to provide local telephone connections. Other existing and potential providers will similarly have rights to provide integrated services. For the Chilean customer, this implies choice of telephone companies, both on a call-by-call basis by dialing an access code and through pre-subscription to a specific company. Initially, primary competition is likely to occur between CTC and Entel; however, Chilesat was successful in

---

Box 2.2. *Long-Distance Competition in Mexico*

In Mexico, Telefonos de Mexico (Telmex) enjoys exclusive rights to provide long-distance communications until January 1, 1997, and local service through 2026. In anticipation of the opening of the long-distance market, the government is preparing to sell concessions to new operators. At the start, 60 of Mexico's most important cities will benefit from competitive provision of long-distance services, growing to over 200 cities by 2000.

Some prominent international operators—Bell Atlantic, Sprint, and MCI Communications—are said to be negotiating joint-ventures with Mexican partners to bid for these concessions. Telmex, in the meantime, is gearing up provide interconnection to the new operators. While details of the interconnection pricing are not known, they are expected to reflect the costs of providing interconnection linkages and to follow "international norms" of transparency and nondiscrimination between operators.

By licensing cellular operators in 1989, Mexico had already created the basis for competition. Cellular providers that are not subsidiaries of Telmex have formed an association, which has sought to establish precedents on interconnection standards and prices.

Source: Reuters, July 1, 1994.

signing customers for integrated service even in anticipation of the changed policy, serving notice of significant competitive possibilities. Another major company likely to join the fray is Bell South, one of the major U.S. regional operating companies.[6]

Prospects for long-distance competition continue to improve with developments in satellite technology. In Indonesia, the use of satellite transmission for private, dedicated networks (using VSAT technology) is increasing. Recently, Malaysia announced the acquisition of a satellite explicitly in the context of entry by a second telecommunications company (*Journal of Commerce*, May 18, 1994). In the Philippines, Philippine Global Communications Inc. is expected to set up a domestic satellite network in the near future (*Journal of Commerce*, June 30, 1994).

INTERNATIONAL COMMUNICATIONS. The growing competition in international services does not stem, as yet, from any major technological breakthroughs and would not be worth remarking upon if it were not for the devastating impact international competition will have on the traditional rate structures. Until recently, international services were a carefully managed cartel of national telecommunications authorities. By restricting other channels of international communications flows, national authorities had devised a system of high international service rates, which they then shared ("settled") according to arcane accounting rules. The huge profits from international services subsidized domestic, especially local, phone services.

The pressures on the international cartel have been many. First, the settlement arrangements between national telecommunications authorities led to large anomalies in pricing. And creative uses of technology are being used to exploit the anomalies. For example, in the deregulated U.S. market, which offers among the lowest international rates, over 100 "call-back" bureaus have mushroomed. The overseas caller disconnects after the first ring. The intelligent switch in the bureau automatically calls back with a dial tone, permitting the user to place a call as if from the United States (*Financial Times*, August 15, 1994).

---

6.   Competition will be maintained through continued regulatory and judicial oversight. The Chilean Supreme Court confirmed a recent antitrust ruling requiring Telefonica Internacional (a subsidiary of Telefonica de Espana) to sell one or the other of its holdings in the two leading Chilean phone companies, CTC or Entel. Telefonica has since sold a 15 percent stake of the 20 percent it held in Entel, while maintaining its 44 percent interest in CTC. Also, in the transition to full competition, rates charged by the different companies, especially CTC, will be capped by the regulator.

Second, powerful pressures from firms operating in a global market-place have forced most major telecommunications companies to form formal and informal alliances that supersede national barriers. With growing competition among the different alliances for the business of multinational companies, old rate structures are receiving a further blow (*Financial Times*, June 16, 1994).

Third, increased international transmission capacity has further frayed the cartel. Availability of alternative transmission services—such as satellite and undersea fiber optic cables—has facilitated bypassing the channels controlled by national authorities. International services have traditionally been carried by publicly owned satellites, principally Intelsat, but other satellite-based services are growing at a rapid pace (O'Brien 1994). In addition to a number of regional initiatives in Europe and Asia, Panamsat, Intelsat's chief global competitor, launched the first of three satellites in July 1994. The three new satellites will give Panamsat between six and seven times its current capacity. Competition in satellite-services would be greatly reinforced if the exotic low-earth satellite ventures, such as Iridium, were to materialize.

Growing competition in international services has triggered new public policy concerns. For organizations like Intelsat and Inmarsat to perform effectively in the new competitive environment, they may need to be privatized (*Wall Street Journal*, July 29, 1994). More importantly, in place of maintaining a cartel for provision of international services, greater resources are being devoted—in service negotiations under the General Agreement on Tariffs and Trade—to seek enhanced access in foreign markets (Broadman and Balassa 1993).

LOCAL COMPETITION. The advent of radio-based cellular telephone networks has introduced a major competitive element, especially in developing countries. These networks have relatively low capital costs, which makes them readily contestable. Radio-based telephones compete with existing local networks—and in many countries with one another. Sri Lanka had licensed four cellular operators, which has decreased its tariffs to among the lowest in the world—connection costs of $100 and operating costs of 16 cents a minute. Compare those costs with the more typical costs charged by a monopoly provider in El Salvador—$1,000 and 35 cents a minute.

Cellular telephony, which uses radio waves for communications, is largely used for mobile communications, but it can also be used for "fixed" telephones. According to one commentator, the imminent development of fixed radio networks for local communications is a "revolution waiting to happen" (Adonis 1994). In the coming years, it is expected that the cost of fixed radio connections for the local loop will plummet, making them competitive with traditional, wireline networks. In the United Kingdom, Ionica, an aspiring competitor to British Telecommunications and Mercury, plans to build local loops throughout the country using such radio technology (*Financial Times*, August 19, 1994). In Indonesia, Ratelindo, a joint-venture between the state-owned operator and a private company, has been licensed to provide 280,000 fixed radio connections, principally in Jakarta.

Although radio-based mobile telephony already provides a measure of competition in local telephony, the traditional wire networks for providing the final connection to the customer appear immune to significant competition. However, the beginnings of increased competition is evident even in this segment. Two types of competition to consider are benchmark (or yardstick) competition and direct competition. In benchmark competition a country is split into regions, each of which has a monopoly local operator. For example, Argentina has two regional operators (Telecom Argentina in the north and Telefonica de Argentina in the south) and the United States has seven (called the Regional Bell Operating Companies). This type of competition allows regulators to check that one operator's prices are not significantly out of line, without having to address the complex issues surrounding interconnection and natural monopoly. But since there is no competition within the local market, benchmark competition does not create direct incentives for businesses to cut costs and improve efficiency.

Direct competition in local service is rapidly approaching. The British government decided to permit new entrants to the local market in 1991, prompting cable TV operators and regional electricity to plan expansion of network services, using their existing infrastructure, which already supplies individual customers. Over 100 companies have been licensed to provide local services, but British Telecom still dominates with a 90 percent market share. In the United States, several states have passed legislation to permit local competition (Baumol and Sidak 1994) and recent federal legislation is accelerating the process. In Chile, although local competition has been opened as noted, CTC still controls over 90 percent of the local telephone lines.

Weighing the Benefits of Competition

Where economies of scale exist, it can be socially wasteful for competing providers to lay duplicate networks—a traditional argument in favor of restricting provision to a single operator. However, even where a natural monopoly exists, competition may increase operating efficiency and consumer choice. There is increasing consensus on the benefits of competition outweighing losses incurred from the persistent natural monopoly characteristics of the telecommunications network (Cave 1991).

Contemporary experience with direct competition is only a decade old, but both the early experiments with competition and recent results validate its benefits. Data for the United States during the early decades of this century show that "competition stimulated growth, extended service to unserved or underserved areas, and created pressures which improved both the development and the application of telephone technology" (Mueller 1991, p. 8). Following the divestiture of AT&T in 1984, several new entrants invested in network capacity in the United States (Crandall 1989). After the introduction of a number of major deregulatory initiatives over the past two decades, greater competition has led to lower prices or better services for consumers—while efficiency gains and new technologies or business practices led to sustained profitability (Winston 1993). Outside the United States, evidence of falling prices, better quality, and greater responsiveness to customers comes from Japan, New Zealand, and the United Kingdom (Takano 1992; Oniki, Oum, and Stevenson 1990; Williamson 1993; Bell and Cave 1991). In each of these countries, however, gains from competition cannot be easily separated from efficiency improvements following the privatization of the state-owned monopoly.

In the developing world, the experience of competition is still limited. Competition exists primarily in cellular telephony. There, the evidence from Sri Lanka already cited is most striking. And not only are the service costs low, but the cost of a cellular phone declined from $2,500 to $250 in one year (due in part to a decline in import duty), and the number of subscribers is reportedly growing at 8 to 10 percent a month (*Reuters*, September 11, 1994). In Chile, even in the short period since the introduction of multiple providers, rates have fall sharply, making them among the lowest in the world (*Reuters*, April 7, 1995).

Regulatory Reform

In parallel with enterprise restructuring and more liberal entry rules, three regulatory tasks are undertaken to induce efficient investment, to protect consumers, and to maintain fair competition. First, traditional cross-subsidies are gradually eliminated through *rate rebalancing* to ensure that new entrants do not "cherry pick" and leave the incumbent saddled with least profitable services. Local rates are raised to promote investment in the most underserved section of the network. Second, where competition is not feasible, consumer interests are protected through a regime that places a *cap on price increases*—such a regime also induces the operator to improve operating efficiency. Finally, the successful operation of an unbundled network requires rules for *fair pricing of interconnection* between network segments. Ideally, rate rebalancing should be completed early, otherwise the effectiveness of other tasks is constrained.

Rate Rebalancing

The structure of telephone tariffs influences the segments of the telecommunications market to which investors are attracted. In the past, long-distance telephone calls were priced high enough to allow monopoly suppliers of telecommunications services to earn reasonable profits while keeping down the price of access to the network and of local calls. When telecommunications markets have been opened up, new investment has typically flooded to long-distance service—where tariffs are significantly above costs—rather than to network services where investment needs are more urgent but tariffs are below costs. In Japan, for example, several new investors entered the profitable long-distance market, while none wanted to compete with NTT's loss-making local service.

Alternative approaches exist to deal with the related issues of rate rebalancing and fostering new entry. Rebalancing can be achieved directly by raising local rates and all countries seeking to introduce competition have to go through this process. It is typically infeasible to raise rates in one shot, although Latin America has seen substantial increases over the short-run. For example, when Mexico's Telmex was awarded a six-year monopoly under a concession agreement in 1990, rates for local services were raised three or four times over original levels. In light of impending long-distance competition, Telmex further rebalanced rates during the period of the concession. The result: long-distance rates have fallen (though they still remain high) while rates for local services have risen steadily. The Philippines, by contrast, has chosen to encourage new entry immediately, though rate structures will change only gradually. New operators are prevented from serving only the lucrative international services market and are required to provide 300 less profitable local exchange lines for each connection to the international gateway.

Another transitional approach is to embed the cross-subsidy in the access price. For example, when a new entrant is providing the more lucrative long-distance service, the incumbent who has access to the final consumer can charge an access price that reflects some of the costs of maintaining the local network (see discussion on access pricing). This approach does not solve the problem of encouraging new entry in the local network, but it does facilitate competition in long-distance services without putting the incumbent at a disadvantage due to its local service obligations.

Consumer Pricing Rules

Competition provides incentives for suppliers to charge the lowest profitable price. So if barriers to entry were eliminated, in theory, there would be no need to control prices. In reality, however, competition in the telecommunications sector is imperfect, so price regulation is generally required in some segments. As noted above, Chile has maintained a price-cap regime for the dominant providers despite substantially liberalizing entry.

Utilities have traditionally operated under rate-of-return regulation—as was the case for the U.S. telephone company AT&T until 1989 (Braeutigam and Panzar 1993). Such regulation, also referred to as "embedded cost regulation" or "cost-plus" pricing, was used to cover operational costs and to permit an agreed return on investment. The agreement sought to protect consumers from excessive prices while ensuring adequate investor returns. This regulatory device not only creates no incentives to limit costs, it perversely encourages higher investments and cost inflation to increase total returns.

A move has thus occurred toward so-called "incentive regulations" that focus on fostering efficiency and technical progress in the network (Sappington: chapter 3). An important application of incentive regulation has been "price-cap" regulation, which sets the maximum allowable rate of price increase. The allowed rate of increase is the general rate of inflation in the economy, measured by the retail price index (RPI), minus an X-factor—the productivity offset. The X-factor is the difference between the rate of growth in total factor productivity (TFP) in the selected service (or group of services) and in the aggregate economy. The purpose of the X-factor is to reflect the whole range of diverse factors that cause changes in the unit costs of service delivery, apart from the input prices—including the technological advances and shifts in demand that influence costs through economies of scale, scope, and density.[7]

---

7.   To prevent strategic behavior aimed at influencing the productivity offset, the value of the offset must be based on industry wide indicators and not be tied to the operational and investment decisions of individual firms. Moreover, the productivity offset should be based on long run movements in productivity growth. Measurement of "best practice" producivity growth must be based on recent historical data, rather than forecasts (since, in competitive markets, price changes follow unit cost reduction rather than anticipating them and also because forecasting is impractical).

First applied in the United Kingdom, the price-cap system has been adopted around the world because of its expected benefits in encouraging efficiency improvements while allowing the operator to better predict its revenues. Empirical investigations of these benefits have been few because price-caps are recent and adequate benchmarks for comparison are not available. One study based on interstate differences in regulatory regimes in the United States showed that the presence of a price-cap regime significantly lowered service prices (Mathios and Rogers 1989). Many U.S. states instituting price-caps have also simultaneously required operators to increase deployment of digital infrastructure (Greenstein, McMaster, and Spiller 1994). As may be expected, price-caps do not have any influence on price in a competitive situation such as that in cellular telephony (Shew 1994).

Improvisation has been an obligatory feature of price-cap implementation across and within countries to allow for varying conditions. Introduced in 1984 for governing prices charged by British Telecom in the United Kingdom, the X-factor was set at 3 percent and applied to one basket of services comprising line rentals and tariffs for local and national calls (OFTEL 1992). The first review in 1989 raised the X-factor to 4.5 percent. An interim review in 1991 brought the highly profitable international services within the basket and raised the X-factor to 6.25 percent. Finally, in 1993, the X-factor was placed at 7.5 percent and should remain at that level until 1997. In parallel, a specific cap (or sub-cap) was placed on line rentals (the X-factor was negative, implying an increase in real prices). Also, private circuits, which had no price control because they were believed to be competitive, were covered under a new basket in 1989 with an X-factor of zero.

Telmex in Mexico became subject to price-cap regulation in January 1992, a year after privatization. A single price-cap is applied to the overall weighted average price of Telmex's services. The X-factor is zero, implying that prices on average can keep pace with inflation. The X-factor is much lower than in the United Kingdom because the X-factor reflects not just productivity differentials, as it should in theory, but also seeks to compensate for historically low prices for certain services. As noted above, Telmex can decide how to rebalance its rates, keeping in mind that it will be subject to competition in long distance services in 1996.

In the United States, the price-cap plan for AT&T has three baskets to discourage cross-subsidy between the baskets while allowing flexibility within a basket. The real price of services in each basket has to be lowered by 3 percent. Over time, as particular services become more competitive, they are freed from regulation. For example, services have been steadily removed from basket three, which contains such business services as private line networks and data transmission.

No clear practice has emerged on pricing new and innovative services. It may generally be expected that such services are subject to competition, but this is not always the case (for example, call waiting and forwarding for residential customers remains largely the domain of the dominant local provider). However, placing price-caps on new services runs the danger of reducing incentives to innovate. The appropriate treatment of new services is related to the more general question of partitioning services into baskets. One approach may be to cover all services—new and old—under one basket, as in Mexico. Provided average price commitments are met, application of the price-cap to a single basket of services allows the alleged monopolist pricing flexibility across services. However, this raises the danger of inefficient cross-subsidies, leading to an argument for a larger number of baskets. Fewer baskets are preferred since they reduce the administrative burden of negotiating and monitoring a proliferating set of productivity offsets, as happened in certain U.S. states (Schankerman 1994).

To summarize, as with any regulatory regime, price-capping, while a step in the right direction, is not perfect. The operator retains monopoly profits when cost reduction is greater than the agreed productivity offset. There are also practical problems in implementation. Inevitably, renegotiations of the productivity offset occur, leading to reexamination of the fairness of rates and hence effectively a reversion to the rate-of-return type calculations that the system sought to avoid. Thus, though the productivity offset legitimately needs to be updated, the offset preferably should be left in place for several years— at least five to seven—to maintain the incentive benefits of the price-cap mechanism. Regulators also face a trade-off between administrative simplicity (one basket) and protection of consumers (many baskets). Ultimately, the goal must be to phase out price regulation, as competition develops. For that, mandatory interconnection with nondiscriminatory and fair pricing is needed.

Interconnection Pricing

Interconnection pricing is in its infancy, particularly in developing countries (box 2.3). In practice, rough and ready norms for revenue sharing between different components of the network are adopted. However, as the number of providers increases and as networks become more complex, the basis for interconnection pricing will be tied more to the costs of interconnection.

A primary economic objective of the interconnection pricing regime is to facilitate efficient new entry. The incumbent operator has an incentive to

---

Box 2.3. *Interconnection in Poland*

The interconnection issue is acquiring increasing importance in developing countries, and especially in Eastern Europe where multiple operators have been licensed. In Poland, for example, a 1990 telecommunications law allowed independent operators the right to develop networks in regions not served by the government-owned telecommunications provider Telekomunikacja (TP SA). Three large independent operators have been licensed to provide local services, in addition to almost 60 other small providers.

Interconnection between TP SA and the independent operators involves establishing a means of providing access to each company's network and sharing revenues from this access. To date there is no one standard interconnection agreement between TP SA and the independents. The telecommunication law states that each independent company must negotiate its own separate agreement with TP SA. This lack of standard agreement has prevented the majority of the independents from further pursuing the development of their local network. Without interconnection, outside investors are hesitant to commit any resources until a strong and fair contract is established.

Revenue-sharing between operators is likely to be the most practical solution since reliable measures of cost do not exist. Under such a system, the revenue is shared between the local operator originating the call, the long-distance operator, and the local operator completing the call. The share received by each of the three parties is a matter of negotiation. However, the expectation is that the long-distance operator will receive somewhat less than one-third of the revenues, with the remaining revenues shared equally between the local operators. Such sharing is presumed to reflect costs incurred by the different parties.

Source: Personal communication from Dan Craun-Selka and Norman Nicholls.

---

limit competition by restricting physical interconnection or charging a price so high that new entrants cannot operate profitably merely by connecting a set of new customers to the existing network. Although lower interconnection costs make new entry profitable and induce greater competition, it is a mixed blessing. When interconnection costs are low, the new entrant has less incentive to build its own network—to lay its own cables, establish new wireless links, or install new switches—since it has cheap access to an existing network. This may be appropriate where the existing network is already well-developed since duplication is considered undesirable. In that case, new entry is primarily a means for fostering greater efficiency.

The lessons learned from interconnection regulation in developed countries are only just beginning to emerge. Low interconnection prices in Japan, set at the level of highly subsidized local call rates, have resulted in only limited network expansion. Where networks are sparse, as in many developing countries, the objective of new entry is not only to create a more competitive environment but also to expand the basic network. Thus, an interconnection price should at least cover the incremental costs (fixed and traffic-sensitive costs).

A distinction is made between *directly attributable costs* (or the incremental costs of conveying a call) and the *opportunity costs* along the interconnection link (or the profits foregone from renting the interconnection link to a competitor). Directly attributable costs are not precisely measurable since the facilities are typically used in conjunction with other parts of the network when providing multiple services. Thus, cost allocations between services—an arbitrary exercise in practice—and conventions of more or less accuracy are used to overcome this problem.[8]

The greater controversy lies in the appropriate definition and measurement of opportunity costs. There are two distinct problems here. The first is a transitional issue, related to the historical structure of tariffs. As discussed above, prices for services have been unbalanced: local services have typically been unprofitable, requiring recovery of costs from long-distance (and especially international) services. This legacy has a direct impact on interconnection charges. A new entrant has the greatest incentive to provide long-distance service where prices are above costs, where they can "skim the cream." If the incumbent charges only for the conveyance costs, then profits in the long-distance business will erode, while losses in local telephony remain. To overcome this, interconnection charges must include some of the foregone profits in long-distance. In the United Kingdom such charges are referred to as access deficit charges. Similarly, in Australia new entrants are required to contribute to a fund for providing universal services. To stimulate new entry, however, the U.K. regulator, OFTEL, has often chosen to discount or even waive these access deficit charges (Armstrong and Doyle 1994).

Opportunity costs remain even after rates are rebalanced to reflect their hidden cost and significant deficits in the provision of particular services no longer exist. The *efficient components pricing rule* is an economically efficient way of pricing interconnection, under certain conditions. The rule specifies that the price of interconnection equal the opportunity cost to the provider on the particular route, where opportunity cost is measured as the revenue the provider would obtain from final consumers of telecommunications services minus any cost savings achieved if the new entrant incurred some of the operational expenses in establishing that link.

---

8. The directly attributable costs of interconnection have two components: fixed and variable. Fixed costs are the costs of providing the physical access and refer to the hardware installed for creating access for other carriers as well as software (including the relevant databases on subscribers). Variable costs, or the costs of actually conveying the call, depend upon the volume of traffic and, in practice, are determined by the level of traffic during the busy hours when congestion in the network is likely to be the greatest. See Mitchell 1994. Ultimately, the fixed costs should be transferred to subscribers, as part of their rental charges, as has gradually occurred in the United States.

This pricing scheme compensates the incumbent not only for direct costs incurred but also for profits that are lost when the entrant takes away the incumbent's customers. The rule also provides some competitive discipline, since only those competitors able to undertake operations at a lower cost than the incumbent will enter (Baumol and Sidak 1994). Moreover, if followed strictly, the rule is simple and the information required for implementation (the price charged by the incumbent and incremental costs along that route incurred by the entrant) relatively easy to acquire, and the specific problems associated with determining costs to the incumbent and the allocation of such costs are eliminated.

In practice, the rule has not been easy to implement. In New Zealand, the rule has been challenged on the grounds that opportunity costs include monopoly profits of the incumbent provider and, as such, is relevant only when competitive conditions already prevail or when the final price charged to the consumer is regulated (box 2.4). The application of the rule is further complicated by practical considerations. For example, customers gained by the new entrant are not necessarily customers lost by the incumbent.

Box 2.4. *Legal Test of Efficient Components Pricing*

In New Zealand, the "efficient components pricing rule" is under dispute. Telecom Corporation of New Zealand (TCNZ), the incumbent, has proposed this rule which requires the new entrant, Clear Telecommunications (Clear), to pay the direct incremental costs to TCNZ of providing the interconnection as well as the opportunity cost of that interconnection (which is the profits forgone by TCNZ when it allows Clear to use its communication lines). Applied to the local loop (the link from the customer to the nearest phone exchange), this requires in effect that Clear's customers pay TCNZ the same line rental charge as do TCNZ's own customers (TCNZ would also receive payment for incremental costs of linking to Clear's network less costs saved due to Clear's investments in the local loop).

Although considered a fair pricing rule by the High Court of New Zealand, it was found later by the Court of Appeal to violate section 36 of the Commerce Act since the price included *monopoly* profits. The Court of Appeal agreed with the principle that the incumbent should be compensated for lost profits, provided these were profits earned in a competitive set up and not in a monopoly situation. Alternatively, if the final price to the consumer were regulated at approximately the level prevailing in a competitive market, then it would once again be appropriate to charge for profits forgone.

The Privy Council determined that the judgment of the High Court had been the appropriate one. It reasoned that charging an interconnection price that included monopoly profits did not violate the Commerce Act since a "level playing field" existed and TCNZ effectively charged itself the same price for interconnection as it charged competitors. The matter of controlling monopoly profits was a separate one and needed to be addressed independently. In arriving at this judgment the Privy Council noted that it had not resolved the interconnection dispute but had only concluded that TCNZ's position was consistent with the objectives of the Commerce Act.

Source: Baumol and Sidak (1994); *Telecom Corporation of New Zealand, Ltd., and Others v. Clear Communications, Ltd.,* The Court of Appeal of New Zealand (1994).

By identifying new customers and catering to their special require-ments, the entrant can expand the size of the customer base, enhancing the value of the incumbent's network. In such a case, the estimate of profits foregone by the incumbent needs to be scaled down to reflect the contribu-tion made by the entrant in attracting new business.

Alternative approaches have been suggested to overcome the difficul-ties associated with a dominant operator. One is to mandate the break-up of the dominant operator into several companies, such as New Zealand's TCNZ (Mueller 1993). In this proposal, each company would have a re-gional base but would compete for all services with other companies. The limitations of such an approach are: (1) the break-up will be arbitrary to a degree, (2) the cost efficiencies from the broader scope of activities enjoyed by large companies will be dissipated, and (3) no barriers will exist to pre-vent the reemergence of one or more dominating operators.

A different approach to this problem with greater relevance to a mod-ern interconnection regime is emerging. In this model, no attempt is made to break up the operator regionally or to isolate local and long-distance pro-vision (as in the United States). Rather, separation occurs between *network* and *retail* services. In Rochester, New York, for example, the local phone company has voluntarily agreed to separate its business into a service com-pany and one that provides the network infrastructure. The new service company will use the infrastructure on the same terms as other entrants. The United Kingdom is moving in the same direction. OFTEL has proposed an accounting separation between the network and service operations of British Telecom.

Ultimately, as with price-capping, the expectation would be that man-datory interconnection with regulated prices would no longer be required. This would happen when alternative carriers are available to provide the interconnection to the customer (within narrowly specified geographic ar-eas), thus breaking the monopoly on interconnection services. Dispensa-tion with interconnection regulation could occur even when there are only two providers of interconnection services (Schankerman 1994).

Making the Regulatory Transition

Empowering independent bodies with policymaking and regulatory ca-pabilities—and ensuring their separation from the dominant operator—checks the power of the operator. Policymaking sets the broad agenda based on the needs of users, whereas regulation enforces the goals set by policy-makers. Thus, the first task is to unbundle the various roles of the government. Box 2.5 describes the range of actions required and the process followed in Mexico and Malaysia for this unbundling.

The regulatory objective, in turn, can be undertaken in alternative ways, including: (1) establishing an independent regulatory body and (2) embodying regulatory provisions in contracts. An independent regulator implements policies with respect to new entry, handles various aspects of pricing, acts as a source of information to both sides in a transaction, and arbitrates contracts and disputes between parties. However, in practice, regulatory provisions are also incorporated into the charters of operating companies and other company-specific contracts, laying out the rights and responsibilities of operators. Examples of such provisions include the "kiwi share" in New Zealand or a similar "golden share" in Malaysia through which the government ensures social obligations of the dominant provider. Also, as in Mexico and Argentina, the roll-out obligations of the provider are embodied in the concession agreement between the provider and the government. Where limited regulatory capacity exists or relevant legislation limits the scope of action, such contracts take on additional importance.

Box 2.5. Unbundling the Government's Role in Mexico and Malaysia

Before reform, Mexico's Ministry of Communications was responsible for policymaking, regulation, and some aspects of operation of telecommunications services. This permitted the Ministry to influence Telmex's operating and financial decisions. When the government privatized Telmex and introduced competition, the policy-making, regulatory, and operating functions needed to be separated.

The government's efforts to streamline and reform the regulatory framework had three major thrusts. First, the regulator relinquished direct participation in the construction of networks, and it privatized telecommunications services that it had previously provided directly, such as the federal microwave network. Second, the rules under which Telmex operated were reformed. Price cap regulation and targets for network expansion and quality were applied, with a commitment to gradually opening up competition among all telecommunications services. Telmex was also granted a concession to operate a cellular communications on a duopoly basis. Third, a new set of telecommunications regulations was passed to complement the General Communications Law. These laid out the limits of intervention by the government and the conditions for competition in the sector.

In Malaysia, the legal frameworks for the regulation and corporatization of telecommunications were established simultaneously through three legal acts. The 1985 amendment to the Telecommunications Act of 1950 reformulated the Telecommunications Department of Malaysia as the sole regulatory authority and defined its functions and powers within the sector. The Ministry of Energy, Posts, and Telecommunications retained the right to license operators. The 1985 amendment to the Pensions Act of 1980 made a special provision to preserve the retirement benefits of staff members. The Telecommunications Service (Successor Company) Act of 1985 transferred the telecommunications operating business and associated assets and liabilities from the former Telecommunications Department to a new operating company. In addition to these legal acts, the government used administrative means to enable the new operating company to function as a viable concern.

Source: Casasus 1994 (Mexico) and bin Isahak 1989 (Malaysia).

Developing regulatory capacity requires an ongoing commitment to provide resources for regulatory skill development as well as ensuring the independence and authority of the regulator, as the Argentinean example shows. Charged with regulatory responsibilities in November 1990, the Comisión Nacional de Telecomunicaciones (CNT) in Argentina did little until the end of 1991 (Hill and Abdala 1993). CNT's failure to formulate standards and processes for issuing licenses retarded the development of new telecommunications services. Meanwhile, a number of radio operators and telephone cooperatives, faced with a delay in receiving licenses and little or no policing of their operations, started operations without licenses. Consumers also suffered from CNT's inability to effectively address service complaints. Efforts to reform CNT have, however, improved its performance. A team of outside consultants working with CNT from early 1992 to May 1993 made progress in developing strategies and procedures. CNT's top staff, previously political appointees, have been chosen through a competitive selection process since October 1993. The Philippines has also undertaken measures to make the regulatory process more autonomous and accountable. A draft bill in the lower house of Congress defines the role of the National Telecommunications Commission, increases the number of commissioners, assigns a fixed tenure, and increases access to operational funds.

Experience in industrial countries shows that as regulators become stronger, "regulating the regulators" may be required. In the United Kingdom, for example, the National Audit Office audits regulators under a larger mandate to determine "value for money" in public service, and the Monopolies and Mergers Commission hears appeals of decisions by sectoral regulators.

Political Economy of Reform

As most policy reformers know, not all efficient solutions are adopted, and achieving change depends on dealing with relevant interest groups. The greatest threat is posed by those who merely derive rents from the existing, artificially induced shortages. Successful implementation of reform requires that these powerful, but nonproductive parties—those who dispense phones in short supply—be rendered less influential through creating a stronger consumer constituency. Then there are those whose skills could be rendered obsolete by the changes initiated. Mechanisms for increased labor ownership are needed to ensure that all productive players share in the long-term gains, even though some may endure short-term losses.

Creating New Constituencies

It is to be expected that the threat of dismantling a large telecommunications monopoly will generate considerable resistance to change, often at the highest administrative levels. The loss of unofficial perquisites and diminished power can motivate considerable opposition. Usually, there are few people outside of the government operator with adequate knowledge of the workings of the sector and thus the operator can use its knowledge and experience to advantage to raise issues and concerns designed to block or delay the reform momentum.

In those countries where reforms have been successful, telecommunications has been approached from the user perspective. This approach forces reform initiatives to shift out of the traditional telecommunications ministries or departments. Where major changes have been implemented, ministries representing user interests have been in the forefront of change. Finance ministries, for example, were prominent both in New Zealand's and Mexico's reforms.

Australia created an independent regulatory body (Austel) and then wedged a reformist bureaucracy between Austel and the government. Austel was an arm's length authority that created an appeal mechanism for mediation of conflicts between the government and market players. The reformist bureaucracy took a proactive approach by creating communications between various interested parties. Australia also developed two other interesting consensus-building mechanisms: (1) a parliamentary caucus committee and subcommittees including those members of parliament who had worked in the sector, and (2) a ministerial advisory committee, acting as an extra-parliamentary mechanism to bring all interest groups—operators, potential operators, and labor—inside the tent to sound out ideas and generate consensus.

Users have also directly pressed for reform. The Australian Telephone User Group (ATUG) lobbied government continuously to erode the power of the telecommunications monopoly and to seek improved conditions for business. ATUG then took an active role in providing a user perspective during the reform implementation phase. In Argentina in 1987, 17 banks had joined together to push for new network facilities in Buenos Aires, preferably by a new operator (Cowhey 1990). Potential foreign investors and multinational development agencies have alerted the government to the international community's interest in becoming involved in improving India's telecommunications services.

Labor Acceptance of Reform

Organized labor can block reform or privatization of a state-owned telecommunications operator. Telecommunications workers everywhere fear that restructuring might mean layoffs or harsher working conditions. This concern is justified, especially since many monopoly operators are highly inefficient. Staff levels of 70 staff per 1,000 lines are not uncommon in developing countries, compared with 5 or 6 staff per 1,000 lines for efficient, developed country operators. For example, India's telecommunications operator employs nearly half a million workers (or about 56 staff per 1,000 lines). The staffing ratio of Tanzania's state telecommunications operator is over 70 per 1,000 lines, and the ratio has been increasing over the past several years (World Bank 1993: 16).

Obtaining labor buy-in for the reform process first requires involving labor representatives in the analysis of policy options and preserving some of their major benefits (especially pensions). But reforms also provide an opportunity for radical rethinking of labor-management relationships, especially by giving labor a greater stake in the restructured operation (ownership stake or potential participation in increased profitability). To be effective, the more radical approach requires programs to increase the skills and flexibility of the workforce by offering: (1) training and re-training, so that all workers can keep up with the demands of new technologies, (2) job placement programs to allow flexible redeployment of staff, and (3) incentives to increase skills using methods like "productivity clauses" that offer merit-based pay raises (World Bank 1993:16).

In many cases, labor has been persuaded to accept liberalization. In Mexico, a number of measures were taken to protect labor, and as a result, "the telephone workers' union (STRM) supported the idea [of privatization] almost unanimously" (Galal, Jones, Tandon, and Vogelsang 1994: 443). These protective measures were as follows:

- A government commitment not to reduce staffing, made clear from the start;
- Worker participation in the capital of Telmex, where 4.4 percent of the company's shares were sold to the union;
- Simplifying the bargaining process and reducing the number of contracts to be negotiated in a year;
- Reducing the number of job categories from 500 to 41 by streamlining job titles to increase worker mobility from one function to another;
- Increased spending on worker retraining and skills development;
- Productivity clauses to reward workers for high performance.

In the end, the total number of workers declined only marginally, and Telmex's real labor productivity, after stagnating from 1981 to 1988, rose sharply from 1989 through 1991. This balance was reached by growing the network at least 12 percent a year, introducing new labor-saving technology, retraining workers to operate the new equipment, and implementing a union agreement that permitted re-assignment of workers. Labor gained significantly from the privatization process as well. One study found that the aggregate welfare change as a result of the privatization was worth 50.7 percent of sales; of this, Telmex workers received 15.9 percent—just less than one-third of the total gain—through salary increases, profit sharing, and stock appreciation (Galal, Jones, Tandon, and Vogelsang 1994).

In Malaysia, one goal of the overall privatization process was to prune the civil service, and telecommunications workers saw this as a threat. But Telkom Malaysia was restructured without layoffs—99.9 percent of Telkom's government employees accepted the package offered by the new corporation. The package was attractive because of Telkom's commitment to no retrenchment for five years and to terms no worse than pre-privatization in pay, benefits, and pensions. In fact, both skilled and unskilled workers are better paid in the privatized Telkom than they were prior to privatization.

In the United Kingdom, labor relations prior to privatization were difficult not only within British Telecom but all around the country. British Telecom has been reducing its labor force since 1981, when management unilaterally announced a plan to reduce the work force by 15,000 over a five-year period. Bargaining between the company and the unions continues to be hard, with at least one industrial action in 1987. Labor still gained marginally from the privatization (Galal, Jones, Tandon, and Vogelsang 1994). Employees saw share bonuses and large wage increases in return for changes in working practices that allowed the company greater flexibility in labor allocation decisions.

Looking Ahead

The challenge of coordinating the various aspects of reform explain why the move to new structures—even in a technologically dynamic sector—can be so slow. Chile, which has moved the farthest, stretched its telecommunications sector reform over almost two decades. Mexico, which initiated reforms in the mid-1980s, expects to have full competition perhaps a decade from now. At each new stage of the process, new institutions (or rules) are required, which in turn require the consent of various parties.

Certain patterns emerge regarding the sequencing of reforms: restructuring of the incumbent monopolist has been a central concern since its dominant political influence against liberalization is often the major obstacle to reform. But there has been no one way of restructuring. Corporatization generally precedes privatization; however, contracting-out bypasses the need to address the power of the incumbent while it allows a growing private presence. Ideally, transparent regulatory rules should precede privatization and new entry; in practice, regulation evolves with the market structure.

The lesson, therefore, is not that reform should be sequenced in a particular (and rigid) manner, but rather that market forces should be introduced early to drive the pace of reform. The stream of technical advances will be best exploited when regulatory restrictions on new entry and operations are minimized. In the past, governments have often prepared the ground by first restructuring and privatizing the existing operator before allowing competition. But especially where telephone penetration rates are low, the early appearance of new players (operating on level terms with the incumbent) can provide much needed phones, spur better performance from the incumbent, and reduce, though not eliminate, the burden of regulation.

The irony is that reform often proves most difficult just where phones are most scarce and where the creation of a new telecommunications regime might seem easiest because of the small installed base.

The message of this survey is that change requires institutional savvy, which balances many conflicting goals and interests. Although certain practical measures to negotiate these conflicts were described, a heavy burden is placed on policymakers and regulators who will continue to face ever-emerging challenges. In coming years, as networks proliferate, issues of privacy and intellectual property will come to the fore; the regulatory task will need to extend to the overlap between communications and broadcasting; and efficient methods will be required to allocate scarce airwaves. Regulators thus will require access to the best information, development of new skills, and, most importantly, the institutional flexibility to evolve with the new conditions.

Bibliography

Adonis, Andrew. 1994. "Indonesia's Fixed Cellular Revolution." *Financial Times* August 15, 1994.

Andersen Management International. 1993. *The Future Development of the Telecommunication Sector in Ghana.*

Armstrong, Mark, and Chris Doyle. 1994. "Social Obligations and Access Pricing: Telecommunications and Railways in the UK." Departments of Economics, University of Southampton and University of Cambridge.

Augenblick, Mark, Jill Abehouse Stern, and Jane Sullivan. 1994. "Strategies for Financing Telecommunications Infrastructure Development in the Pacific Rim." Paper for the 16th Annual Pacific Telecommunications Conference. Honolulu, Hawaii.

Banker, Rajiv D., Hsi-hui Chang, and Sumit Majumdar. 1992. "Returns to Scale in Telecommunications: Evidence and Ramifications for the U.S. Local Exchange Sector." Ann Arbor: University of Michigan, School of Business Adminstration.

Baumol, William J., and J. Gregory Sidak. 1994. "The Pricing of Inputs Sold to Competitors." *Yale Journal of Regulation* 11(1): 172–202.

Bell, Alan, and Martin Cave. 1991. "Lessons from the UK Duopoly Review." Paper for CPR Conference in the Netherlands.

bin Isahak, Daud. 1989. "Meeting the Challenges of Privatization in Malaysia" in Bjorn Wellenius and others, eds., *Restructuring and Managing the Telecommunications Sector*. Washington, D.C.: The World Bank.

Boatman, Kara T. 1991. "Telecommunications and Export Performance: An Empirical Investigation of Developing Countries." Ph.D. dissertation. University of Maryland, College Park.

Braeutigam, Ronald, and John Panzar. 1993. "Effects of the Change from Rate-of-Return to Price-Cap Regulation." *American Economic Review Papers and Proceedings* 83(2): 191–98.

Broadman, Harry G., and Carol Balassa. 1993. "Liberalizing International Trade in Telecommunications Services." *Columbia Journal of World Business* Winter: 31-37.

Bruce, Robert, Michael Harrell, and Zsuzsa Kovacs. 1993. "Who Will Win the Battle for Hungary's Telecom Company?" *International Financial Law Review* 7(5): 25–27.

Cave, Martin. 1991. "Regulating Competition in Telecommunications: British Experience and its Lessons." *Economic Analysis and Policy* 21(2): 129–43.

Casasus, Carlos. 1994. "Privatization of Telecommunications: The case of Mexico" in Bjorn Wellenius and Peter Stern, eds., *Implementing Reforms in the Telecommunications Sector: Lessons from Experience*. Washington, D.C.: The World Bank.

Charnes, A., W. W. Cooper, and T. Sueyoshi. 1988. "A Goal Programming/Constrained Regression Review of the Bell System Breakup." *Management Science* 34(1): 1–26.

Cowhey Peter. 1990. "The International Telecommunications Regime: The Political Roots of Regimes for High Technology." *International Organization* 44(2): 169–99.

Crandall, Robert, W. 1989. "Fragmentation of the Telephone Network" in Paula R. Newbury, ed., *New Directions in Telecommunications Policy*. Durham: Duke University Press.

Dougan, Diana Lady, and Susan Bruno, eds. 1991. *Trade, Telecom, and Mexico: The New Bilateral Menu*. Washington, D.C.: CSIS International Communications Studies Program.

Ergas, Henry. 1992. "France Telecommunication: Has the model worked?" Paper for the workshop on International Experiences in Telecommunications Reform and its Relevance to India. New Delhi: Industrial Credit and Investment Corporation of India, Ltd.

Evans, David, and James Heckman. 1984. "A Test for the Subadditivity of the Cost Function with an Application to the Bell System." *American Economic Review* 74(4): 615–23.

Galal, Ahmed, Leroy Jones, Pankaj Tandon, and Ingo Vogelsang. 1994. *Welfare Consequences of Selling Public Enterprises.* New York: Oxford University Press.

Greenstein, Shane, Susan McMaster, and Pablo T. Spiller. 1994. "The Effect of Incentive Regulation on Local Exchange Companies' Deployment of Digital Infrastructure." Paper for the AEI Telecommunications Summit. Washington, D.C.: American Enterprise Institute.

Hill, Alice, and Manuel Angel Abdala. 1993. "Regulation, Institutions, and Commitment: Privatization and Regulation in the Argentine Telecommunications Sector." Policy Research Working Paper 1216. Washington, D.C.: World Bank.

Huber, Peter. W. 1993. "Telecommunications Regulation: The Beginning of the End." *Issues in Science and Technology* (Fall).

International Telecommunications Union (ITU). 1994. *World Telecommunications Development Report.* Geneva: ITU.

Kim, Cae-one, Young Kou Kim, and Chang-bun Yoon. 1992. "Korean Telecommunications Development: Achievements and Cautionary Lessons." *World Development* 20(2): 1829–41.

Mathios, Alan, and Robert Rogers. 1989. "The Impact of Alternative Forms of State Regulation of AT&T on Direct-Dial, Long-Distance Telephone Rates." *Rand Journal of Economics* 20: 437–53.

Mitchell, Bridger. 1994. "Network Interconnection—A Primer." Background note to the *World Development Report 1994*. Washington, D.C.: World Bank.

Mody, Ashoka, and Carl Dahlman. 1992. "Performance and Potential of Information Technology: An International Perspective." *World Development* 20(12): 1703–19.

Mody, Ashoka, and William Reinfeld. 1994. "Advanced Infrastructure for Time Management: The Competitive Edge in East Asia." CFS Discussion Papers. Washington, D.C.: The World Bank.

Mody, Ashoka, and Kamil Yilmaz. 1994. "Is There Persistence in Manufactured Goods Exports?" Policy Research Working Paper 1276. Washington, D.C.: The World Bank.

Mueller, Milton. 1991. "Telecommunications Development Models and Telephone History: A Response to the World Bank." International Center for Telecommunications Management. *ICTM News* 2(2) Omaha: University of Nebraska.

_____. 1993. *On the Frontier of Deregulation: New Zealand Telecommunications and the Problem of Interconnecting Competing Networks.* Los Angeles: The Reason Foundation.

New Zealand Ministry of Commerce. 1992. "Telecommunications Information Leaflet No. 1." Wellington: Ministry of Commerce.

O'Brien, Ross. 1994. "When Pride Holds the Purse Strings." *Communications International* May: 54–57.

Office of Telecommunications (OFTEL). 1993. "Interconnection and Accounting Separation." A consultative document issued by the Director General of Telecommunications, Office of Telecommunications, London.

_____. (OFTEL). 1992. "The Regulation of BT's Price." A consultative document issued by the Director General of Telecommunications, Office of Telecommunications, London.

Oniki, Hajime, Tae H. Oum, and Rodney Stevenson. 1990. "NTT's Productivity Performance." Wisconsin Working Paper 1-90-2, University of Wisconsin, Madison.

Schankerman, Mark. 1994. "Symmetric Regulation for Competitive Challenges." London: London School of Economics.

Shew, William. 1994. "Regulation, Competition, and Prices in Cellular Telephony." AEI Studies in Telecommunications Deregulation Working Paper, Washington, D.C.: American Enterprise Institute.

Sidak, Gregory. 1993. "Telecommunications in Jericho." *California Law Review* 81(5): 1209–39.

Takano, Yoshiro. 1992. *Nippon Telegraph and Telephone Privatization Study: Experience of Japan and Lessons for Developing Countries*. World Bank Discussion Paper 179. Washington, D.C.: The World Bank.

Wellenius, Bjorn. 1991. *Telecommunications: World Bank Experience and Strategy*. World Bank Discussion Paper 192. Washington, D.C.: The World Bank.

Wheeler, David, and Ashoka Mody. 1992. "International Investment Location Decisions: The Case of U.S. Firms." *Journal of International Economics* 33(1/2): 57–76.

Williamson, Maurice. 1993. "Telecommunications Reform in New Zealand." Wellington: Ministry of Communications.

Winston, Clifford. 1993. "Economic Deregulation: Days of Reckoning for Microeconomists." *Journal of Economic Literature* 31: 1263–89.

World Bank. 1991. "Issues in Telecommunications Development: Policy Responses and Sector Strategy for Sub-Saharan Africa." Africa Technical Department, Industry and Energy Division Note 6. Washington, D.C.

_____. 1993. "The United Republic of Tanzania, Third Telecommunications Project." Staff Appraisal Report. Washington, D.C.

3

Principles of Regulatory Policy Design

David E. M. Sappington

*Regulatory goals, social institutions, industry characteristics, and the extent of re-
sources all influence the form, function, and scope of regulatory policy. Regulatory
design is thus a complex undertaking that involves the balance of many influences.
This chapter provides guidelines for policymakers and others trying to strike such a
balance—and find the appropriate regulation for a given environment. A country's
institutional structure, for example, can limit the regulator's potential for commitment, especially if the regulator is unable to deliver proper rewards or penalties. The
scope and function of regulation may also be fairly limited when technological conditions make competition a better discipline for producers. In fact, in such environments, comprehensive command-and-control regulation can be ineffective or debilitating to that industry's growth. Inappropriate relationships between the regulator
and the constituency of the regulated environment can also undermine effective regulation. When the constituency is able to pressure the regulator into maintaining out-
dated policies or when it offers personal rewards for a regulator to enforce policies that
do not protect consumers, regulation no longer serves society's best interests. Finally,
even when regulators are not "captured" by constituencies, their ideas of what is best
for society may differ from those of other government officials or those of the public.
When that happens, the goals pursued largely depend on the autonomy of the regulator and the balance of power among government bodies. This larger context is essential to fully comprehending the form, function, and scope of any regulatory policy.*

Regulatory policies employ different methods of oversight and control that
influence different aspects of the conduct and behavior of individuals and
firms. These differences are seldom arbitrary. Rather, they result from the

ways regulatory goals and resources, social institutions, and industry characteristics influence the form, function, and scope of regulatory policy. The *form of regulation* refers to the procedures used to design and enforce regulatory rules, the nature of these rules, and the locus of decisionmaking authority in the regulatory arena. For example, does the regulator make and enforce all relevant decisions, or is considerable decisionmaking authority delegated to the regulated entities? The function of regulation refers to its basic purpose. Some regulations are designed to ensure safety, others to secure production at minimum cost, and still others to provide information to consumers. The *scope of regulation* refers to the extent of regulatory oversight and control. Regulation can be all-encompassing—imposing strict rules on all relevant activities—or it may merely suggest guidelines for a small subset of relevant activities.

A great variety of regulations are practiced. Price, quality, information disclosure, and compatibility regulations are common examples. Price regulation often places an upper bound on the price of a product. Quality regulation can specify a minimum level of quality to be achieved. Regulation of information disclosure can require producers to accurately describe the key features of their products. Manufacturers of similar or complementary products (computer hardware and software) are forced by compatibility regulations to design their products so that consumers can easily substitute the product of one manufacturer for that of another manufacturer when assembling a good (like a computer system) with multiple component parts.

The variety of regulations arises in part from the many different functions or purposes of regulation. Sometimes product safety is paramount (purity of food products), while other times product price is the central concern (the amount consumers pay for basic telephone service). Even regulations with the same purpose take different forms. The methods employed to ensure reasonable but not exorbitant financial returns to producers of commodities like electricity and telecommunications services differ across countries and across jurisdictions within some countries. Rate-of-return regulation with little or no pricing flexibility is a common form of regulation in these industries. Under this form of regulation prices for all products are set to generate a predetermined return on investment for the producer. Price-cap regulation is another form of regulation that is gaining popularity. Under price-cap regulation, the prices charged by the regulated firm for its services must not exceed a prespecified level on average, but the firm has significant freedom to set individual prices.

The overarching purpose of this chapter is to provide a perspective for policymakers to use when deciding whether regulation is appropriate for their environment and, if so, what form of regulation is most appropriate. The discussion goes beyond the sphere of infrastructure regulation, where necessary, but does not attempt a complete explanation of all relevant differences in regulatory policy across all jurisdictions. Many of the examples refer to "the regulator," defined here as a government official (or body of officials) charged with establishing rules to govern economic activities in one sector of society, such as a public utility commission that sets rules to govern the operation of a regulated firm.

Form: Centralized versus Delegated Decisionmaking

A key concern of regulatory policy is the extent to which the regulator delegates decisionmaking. If the regulator's primary goal is to ensure that a high-quality product is delivered to consumers, the regulator will likely specify a minimum quality level that must be achieved. Under one extreme form—*command-and-control* regulation—the regulator dictates the actions of the regulated firm in great detail. For instance, in water purification and delivery regulation, the regulator might dictate the exact details of the purification process, the rate at which water is purified, the type of pump and conduit used in water delivery, and the exact price at which water is sold to all customers. Similarly, in regulating the provision of taxi service in a large city, the regulator might dictate the number and type of vehicles an authorized supplier of taxi service must own, the number of taxis that must be on the road at each moment in time, each vehicle's service and repair requirements, the type of dispatch system that must be employed, the qualifications of drivers, and the price of taxi service.

Alternatively, the regulator may delegate considerable discretion to the regulated firm. Consider again the regulation of water purification and delivery. The regulator who merely states the level of purity delivered water must achieve and the price at which water must be delivered delegates considerable discretion to the regulated firm. The firm chooses the purification process and the delivery system. Similarly, if the regulator of taxi service only specifies that quick, courteous, and safe transportation must be provided at a specified price, the taxi company can decide the types of vehicles to purchase (or lease), how often to service and repair the vehicles, how many drivers to hire, and so on.

When the firm's final performance is monitored but its exact method of operation is not dictated, decisionmaking authority is delegated to the firm. Most *incentive regulation* operates this way. The firm is rewarded according to its realized performance compared with the goals or targets set under the incentive regulation. Price-cap regulation is one type of incentive regulation that has gained popularity in the telecommunications industries of Great Britain and the United States in recent years. Under *pure* price-cap regulation, the *average* price at which the firm sells its services is restricted, but the firm has considerable latitude in setting individual prices and in determining how to provide services at minimum cost.

Other forms of regulation also delegate considerable discretion to the regulated firm. For example, *potential regulation* places no restrictions on a firm's activities unless its performance falls short of some prespecified criterion. The regulator may allow a firm to provide services and set prices in any way it sees fit, provided the firm's customers are satisfied. However, when a sufficient number of customers complain and ask for regulatory intervention, the regulator investigates and forces the firm to rectify any discovered problems. Thus customers become the primary monitors of a firm's performance, and if they are satisfied, the firm avoids direct regulatory control.

Regulated firms also have more discretion when the regulator conducts *reactive* rather than *proactive* policy. Under reactive policy, the regulated firm first proposes or undertakes an action, and the regulator subsequently approves or disapproves of the action. Under proactive regulatory policy, the regulator states in advance which actions will be approved, and which actions will not be permitted. To illustrate, under reactive policy, a regulator may approve or disapprove of new drugs, but place no restrictions on the types of drugs a firm can research and manufacture. A proactive regulatory policy would restrict the type of research the firm could conduct or would state in advance that drugs with certain characteristics (such as drugs that induce abortions) will not be approved.

Regulators may also delegate rulemaking authority to regulated firms. In such instances, the potential regulator (the government) authorizes a substitute regulator to set rules and regulations, rather than doing so directly. For example, many professions set standards for their members. Medical associations regularly specify licensing requirements, determine which training institutions are accredited, and discipline members who violate the rules or ethics of the association.

One final aspect of regulatory form is the way rules are designed and enforced. Policy design can proceed behind closed doors or in open public hearings. It can also be influenced by formal or informal communication between the regulator and the firm. The regulator may monitor the firm's performance and verify directly that regulatory edicts are being followed. Alternatively, the customers of the regulated firm may be called upon to monitor the firm's performance (as under potential regulation).

Function: Informing versus Enforcing Regulation

Like regulatory form, regulatory function is often intimately linked to the goals and objectives of the regulator. For instance, the primary function or purpose of a regulation might be to protect consumers from unsafe products or it might be to ensure that all customers are treated in a similar fashion. Regulations can also be designed to limit the profits of a monopoly producer or to control various interactions among producers.

One defining characteristic of regulatory function is whether regulations inform consumers about the regulated firm's activities or dictate which activities are allowed. The key distinction between informing and enforcing regulation is the discretion afforded consumers. Informing regulation helps consumers to make well-informed choices. Enforcing regulation makes choices for consumers. The requirement that manufacturers of food products list all the ingredients contained in their products is informing regulation. Enforcing regulation in the food industry might prohibit the use of certain chemicals in foods. In the computer industry, informing regulation might simply require each manufacturer to specify the interfacing capability of its products and to list the compatible products of rival producers. Requiring all manufacturers to adopt standard interface capabilities would be an enforcing regulation. The choice between informing and enforcing regulation depends in part on the relative costs of acquiring and processing information for the regulator and for consumers.

Scope: Comprehensive versus Partial Regulation

The scope of regulation measures its comprehensiveness, or the extent to which it encompasses all of the regulated firm's activities. In some industries, like telecommunications, comprehensive regulation is common. The regulator generally controls the prices charged by the telecommunications provider, limits the firm's earnings, monitors the quality of the firm's products, oversees the firm's major investments, and dictates the markets in which the firm can operate. In other industries, like pharmaceuticals, regulation is often less comprehensive. The safety of drugs is often regulated, but drug prices and pharmaceutical companies' earnings usually are not.

With multiple suppliers of a product, the scope of regulatory control can also vary according to the number of suppliers that are regulated, and the extent to which they are regulated. In such industries as telecommunications and electric power generation, all aspects of the operations of large (dominant) firms are often regulated, while similar activities of smaller firms are either less regulated or not regulated at all. In the United States, for example, the prices charged by AT&T for telecommunications services are regulated by the Federal Communications Commission, but the prices charged by its main competitors (MCI and Sprint) are not regulated.

The Regulator's Objectives

Regulatory goals and objectives vary widely, and so do regulatory policies. The single largest influence on the design of regulatory policies is the regulator's objectives. The following six objectives commonly influence regulatory policy.

FOSTER INDUSTRY DEVELOPMENT AND INVESTMENT. A common goal of regulators is to foster development of the industry they regulate.[1] Often, regulated industries are central to the development of other industries. For instance, a modern, full-service telecommunications system is crucial to the successful operation of the financial sector of a country. Using command-and-control regulation, the regulator can mandate the adoption of operating equipment and techniques (such as nuclear power plants or fiber-optic telephone cable) that have proved successful. Alternatively, the regulator might delegate the choice of technology to the regulated firm, but promise substantial returns for any new investment that improves industry performance.

In the United States' telecommunications industry, states encourage infrastructure development in different ways. Some states mandate that the regulated firm make available to rural customers the same modern services (such as enhanced calling capabilities and features like call waiting and caller identification) that the firm finds profitable in urban settings. Other states are less specific in their mandates, but do require the regulated firm to reinvest a portion of its earnings in infrastructure development. This development commonly takes the form of converting copper transmission lines to fiber lines and replacing analog switches with digital switches.

---

1.   Development can take many forms. For instance, it may involve installing state-of-the-art technology (such as converting from analog to digital switches in the telecommunications industry) or increasing the reliability of the service provided (such as installing back-up transmission facilities that can be employed to carry voice or data traffic in the event of failure of the primary transmission facility in the telecommunications industry).

ENSURE SAFE, HIGH-QUALITY SERVICE. Safety is paramount in many industries. When electricity is generated by nuclear power, for example, it is critical that the generation process proceed safely. High-quality service is also important in many settings. For instance, water supplied in municipal water systems must be purified completely. Command-and-control regulation promotes safety and high-quality service because the regulator dictates operation and performance standards and enforces them. Alternatively, the regulator might set targets for product quality and operational safety, and then penalize or reward the regulated firm according to its performance relative to those targets.

PROMOTE LEAST-COST PRODUCTION. To maintain service at reasonable prices, a regulator will strive to ensure that production occurs as cheaply as possible. Least-cost production can be fostered by careful scrutiny of the operations and financial records of the regulated firm or by providing financial incentives for the firm to reduce operating costs. For example, under price-cap regulation, the prices a firm is allowed to charge for its products are not tied to realized production costs. Consequently, if the firm succeeds at reducing its operating costs, it is not required to pass all of the cost savings on to consumers in the form of lower prices—a strong incentive for least-cost production.

ACHIEVE DESIRED CONSUMPTION LEVELS. Regulators are often concerned with the amount of certain products that are consumed. For instance, a regulator may wish to see increased consumption of commodities, like vaccines against communicable diseases and public (as opposed to private) transportation. The regulator may increase consumption of these goods by subsidizing their provision or by launching advertising campaigns to stress their importance. The regulator may also seek to reduce consumption of products like addictive drugs, pornography, or ozone-depleting chemicals.

PROMOTE MORE EQUITABLE OUTCOMES. Regulators often strive for redistribution of income. Many countries subsidize local telephone service with revenues from long-distance telephone service. Similarly, business customers are often charged more than residential customers for similar telephone service. Such policies effectively redistribute income from individuals with greater wealth (such as owners of business enterprises and citizens who can afford to make long-distance telephone calls) to individuals with less wealth.

LIMIT THE EARNINGS OF PRODUCERS. In industries where technological considerations (such as economies of scale) render production by a single producer most economical, a key charge of regulators is to limit the abuse of monopoly power by the single regulated producer. To redistribute income from producers to consumers and to limit the exercise of monopoly power, a regulator will generally force prices below the levels an unregulated monopolist would charge.

Each of these six goals and objectives affects the form, function, and scope of regulatory policy. Often, these goals conflict. To illustrate, a regulator may wish to limit the earnings of the regulated producer while fostering investment in the regulated industry. Since attractive financial returns must be promised to induce private investment in the regulated industry, the two goals conflict. Similarly, the goals of quality enhancement and cost minimization can also conflict. Often, higher quality service costs more to provide, so the regulator is forced to compromise between high quality and low cost.

When regulatory goals conflict, the resulting compromise depends on the relative importance of each goal. The relative importance of regulatory goals often hinges on the consequences of failing to meet the goals. If the failure to meet a goal would have a substantial, obvious, immediate, and adverse impact, the regulator will likely give that goal a higher priority. For instance, because a malfunction at a nuclear power plant would have a widespread negative impact, a regulator might incur great expense to ensure safe operation of the plant, even though it means higher prices for electricity.

Regulatory policy can also vary over time as various goals achieve different levels of success, even if regulatory goals remain constant. To illustrate, suppose both high-quality service and least-cost production are very important. Initially the regulator might focus on service quality, subsidizing investment and research and development to enhance product quality even though doing so increases operating costs. Once reasonable quality levels are achieved, the regulator might shift efforts towards reducing production costs by implementing regulation (like price-cap regulation) that provides strong incentives for cost reduction. Meeting multiple objectives in sequence in this manner can be particularly effective when progress towards the first goal (such as establishing a modern telecommunications network) enhances progress towards subsequent goals (such as improving the operations of the financial sector of the economy).

Some might argue that this sequential approach to meeting multiple objectives has been pursued in the telecommunications industry in the

United States. In the early 1900s, regulation of the telecommunications industry focused on providing reliable telephone service and interconnection capabilities to as many customers as possible. (Initially, telephone service was provided by different companies and the customers of one company were not able to call or receive calls from the customers of a different company.) By the mid-1900s, interconnection capabilities had been ensured, and regulators had turned their attention toward limiting the profits of the monopoly provider of telecommunications services (Mueller 1993).

A Regulator's Resources

Detailed information about current operating technologies, potential alternative technologies, and consumer preferences is key to designing effective regulatory policy. Substantial information about the performance of the regulated firm (realized earnings, product quality, and customer satisfaction) is also required in many settings to implement and enforce regulatory policy. If regulators have excellent resources—a large, well-trained, and experienced staff to perform research—they are often better able to understand the environment in which they operate and make better policies. Without complete information about the firm's operations, attempts by the regulator to micro-manage production techniques, product offerings, and its pricing decisions through command-and-control regulation can affect the firm's performance adversely.

Therefore, when the regulator's information is limited, regulation that delegates substantial decisionmaking authority to the better-informed regulated firm can make more sense than command-and-control regulation. Furthermore, regulatory goals might be reached more effectively by allowing market forces, rather than regulatory mandate, to govern some dimensions of the firm's operations. To illustrate, consider an industry characterized by rapid technological change, frequent development of new products, and rapidly changing needs of customers. In such an industry (perhaps like the telecommunications industry), it will be difficult for a regulator to determine the least-cost means of operation and the most desired array of products, particularly if the regulator's support staff is limited in number and training. Consequently, an attempt by the regulator to micro-manage the firm's production techniques, its product offerings, and its pricing decisions through command-and-control regulation may result in substantially lower performance than what could be achieved with complete information about the firm's operations.

When the regulator's information is limited, he can sometimes employ the superior information of the regulated firm by delegating some decisionmaking authority to the firm. For example, the regulator might grant the firm pricing flexibility on new services, provided all of the currently offered services remain at existing prices. This ensures that the range of consumption opportunities available to customers is not reduced.[2] Since the regulated firm can use its superior information to determine which products will best serve customers' needs and provide additional net revenues, consumers may benefit. Moreover, the pricing flexibility allows the firm to better cope with competitive pressures.

A regulator with limited knowledge of the firm's capabilities can also allow the firm to use its superior information to choose certain elements of its compensation structure. For instance, suppose the regulator is uncertain of the firm's financial ability to reduce production costs and lower prices. If the regulator guesses incorrectly that the firm's ability is high and forces large price reductions, the financial viability of the firm may be threatened, or high-quality service to customers may be interrupted (perhaps because the firm is forced to declare bankruptcy). However, if the regulator enforces only the small price reductions that the firm can provide even when its ability to reduce cost is low, potential gains for consumers in the regulated industry may be foregone.

To ensure greater gains for consumers where possible and avoid financial distress for the regulated firm, the regulator can offer the firm a choice between two compensation arrangements. The first requires only minor price reductions, but restricts the ability of the firm to earn large profits. The second arrangement requires more substantial price reductions, but allows the firm to retain more of the profits earned from reduced production costs. A pair of such carefully designed compensation arrangements can induce the regulated firm to make larger price reductions when its ability is high, and effect smaller price reductions when its ability is low. The firm will earn higher profits and the firm's customers will benefit from more substantial price reductions implemented when the firm's ability is high. Thus, through well-designed delegation of price-setting authority to the party with superior information, the firm's performance better matches its ability, and all parties benefit.

To illustrate, in 1991, the U.S. Federal Communications Commission, instituted a plan that allows the local exchange carriers (LECs) to choose

---

2.   This policy is discussed in greater detail in Sappington and Sibley (1992). Also see Brown and Sibley (1986), Sibley (1989), and Wilson (1993).

among different methods of compensation for their interstate access charges. If the LECs choose to reduce their average (inflation-adjusted) access charges by 3.3 percent annually, they share with consumers 50 percent of their earnings that constitute a rate of return on capital between 12.25 percent and 16.25 percent. All earnings above 16.25 percent are returned to customers under this plan. If, however, the LEC chooses to guarantee a higher 4.3 percent annual real reduction in average access rates, the firm is only required to share 50 percent of its earnings that represent a rate of return between 13.25 percent and 17.25 percent. Only if earnings rise above a 17.25 percent return are they all awarded to consumers. Thus, a LEC can secure the opportunity to retain more of its earnings by guaranteeing lower prices to its customers (Federal Communications Commission 1990).

In summary, when limited resources result in incomplete information, the regulator may be wise to delegate decisionmaking to the regulated firm in arrangements that induce the firm to further regulatory goals. The scope of activities the regulator can reasonably oversee also depends on its resources.[3]

Institutional Structure

This section explains how the institutional structure of the regulator's environment can influence the design of regulatory policy. Two aspects of institutional structure are emphasized: the ability of the regulator to fulfill his promises and the set of complementary control instruments used in the environment.

A Regulator's Commitment Powers

Regulatory policy is only effective if it influences the activities of the regulated firm. To do so, regulatory policy must create systematic links between the firm's activities and its financial well-being. For instance, if regulatory policy is to ensure high-quality services, the regulated firm must expect to suffer financially if it produces low-quality services. To create meaningful links, regulatory policy must do more than threaten financial penalties for

---

3. For additional thoughts on how a regulator with limited information should design the set of options it offers to a regulated firm, see Baron (1988); Besanko and Sappington (1987); Caillaud and others (1988); Laffont and Tirole (1993); or Sappington (1991).

undesired behavior or performance and promise financial rewards for desired behavior or performance. Regulatory threats and promises must actually be carried out as stated if they are to influence the firm's activities. A regulator's promise to award the regulated firm a higher profit level if it streamlines its operations and substantially reduces cost will only have its desired impact if the promise is credible. If the regulatory environment is such that consumers or other government officials will protest vehemently when the firm's profits surpass a certain level, thus forcing the regulator to rescind the promised increase, announced promises will fall on deaf ears. The firm will anticipate the regulator's inability to fulfill its promises and will not act on the initial promise. Similarly, if the regulator threatens severe penalties for unsafe operating procedures, but then continually gives the firm one more chance to improve its operations when safety violations are detected, the firm's financial integrity is not truly jeopardized by the penalties. The announced regulatory policy will not, then, induce the regulated firm to improve the safety of its operating procedures.

The ability of a regulator to fulfill promises is termed the regulator's *commitment ability*. A regulator's commitment ability is determined by a variety of factors. The political pressures a regulator faces is one important factor. If a regulator can easily be replaced on short notice by his superiors (such as leaders of the executive or legislative branch of government), it may be difficult for the regulator to promise to pursue a policy that differs from the preferred policy of his superiors. For instance, although the regulator might threaten to expose the incumbent producer to competition if the incumbent's performance is judged to be inadequate, the regulator may face great difficulty in allowing new entrants into the marketplace if the country's governing bodies strongly oppose competition.

Similarly, if the regulator is elected directly by citizens at frequent intervals, he may be hard pressed to implement policies that appear contrary to the immediate interests of consumers. For instance, switching to a new technology (like nuclear power generation) that involves large initial investments and substantial price increases for customers may be difficult, even though decreased operating costs in the distant future would more than offset the higher initial costs. If consumers are myopic and have direct control over the regulator's tenure, the regulator may have to adopt a similar outlook if he wishes to retain his position.

A regulator's commitment ability is also affected by the strength and independence of the judicial branch of government. A strong, independent judiciary can uphold and support regulatory decisions that are in the best interest of society, even though those decisions may be unpopular with consumers or legislative leaders.[4] To illustrate, consider again the setting where many of a country's legislators firmly oppose allowing competition in the regulated industry, even though competition is not explicitly forbidden under existing law. If the judiciary functions as an independent body, and its rulings are respected and upheld, the regulator may be able to introduce competition into the regulated industry. On the other hand, if judicial rulings are ignored or if the judiciary only serves to enforce the whims of the legislative or executive branches of government, then the regulator's efforts to increase competition may be futile.

The usual practices and overall stability of the government can also influence a regulator's commitment ability. Consider a setting where the regulator wishes to convince private investors to provide the funds necessary to modernize the production facilities of the regulated firm. Investors must anticipate reasonable returns if they are to provide the desired funds. Substantial returns will not be likely, however, if despite regulatory promises, the government is prone to nationalize successful private operations or otherwise expropriate large returns that result from private investment. And even if the government currently in power has no history of expropriation, when the stability of the government is in doubt because of strong pressure from an opposing government that is known to favor expropriation, investors will be unlikely to believe regulatory promises of large financial returns. Consequently, it may be impossible for the regulator to attract the investment he seeks.

Thus, limited commitment ability can undermine the success of regulatory policy. It can also affect the form, function, and scope of the regulatory policy that is undertaken. For instance, a regulator with limited commitment ability may not solicit construction funds from private investors at all. Any construction that is undertaken may be financed entirely by the government. Similarly, if the regulator cannot credibly promise either to deliver large returns to the regulated firm for outstanding performance or to impose large penalties on the firm for poor performance, the regulator may not develop far-reaching incentive programs in an attempt to influence the firm's behavior. Instead, the regulator may attempt to scrutinize and control directly the limited number of the firm's activities that he can monitor, and allow the firm considerable latitude on other activities. Alternatively, the regulator may adopt more of an informing role than an en-

---

4. For a detailed analysis of the interaction between the properties of a country's institutions (such as the strength of its judiciary) and the design of regulatory policy for the country, see Levy and Spiller (1993, 1994).

forcing role, simply providing information to consumers about the firm's activities and its products, and relying on consumers (and perhaps competitors) to discipline the regulated firm. In extreme cases, where limited commitment ability renders hollow any promises or threats made by the regulator, there is little reason to formulate regulatory policy at all. Hence, the scope of regulation can be restricted severely by limited commitment ability.

To this point, the commitment ability of the regulator has been treated as an exogenous variable. In practice, it is often endogenous to some extent. For instance, recall that it may be difficult for a regulator to solicit funds from private investors because of the threat of government expropriation. This threat can be reduced through careful choice of technology and institutional structure. To illustrate, in the telecommunications industry, long distance telephone service may be provided most inexpensively by laying subterranean fiber-optic cables. However, using satellites may be preferable. Because satellites are readily redeployed for alternative uses, a threat of government expropriation can be reduced by the credible counterthreat of refusing to use the satellites to provide long distance telephone service if the government engages in expropriation.

The threat of government expropriation or nationalization can also be limited by giving many citizens a sizable stake in the profitable operation of the regulated firm. If ownership shares in the regulated firm are widely dispersed, many citizens will be upset and will lobby the government to change policy if any attempt is made to nationalize the regulated firm or unduly restrict its profits. Thus, a widespread distribution of ownership creates a natural constituency for the regulated firm's success, adding credibility to claims that private investment in the firm will not be expropriated.[5]

A regulator's commitment powers can also be enhanced directly. If a regulator is appointed to a relatively long term, rather than elected directly by citizens for a short period of time, the regulator will be insulated to some degree from direct consumer pressure. Similarly, when regulatory appointments are based on training, experience, and credentials rather than party affiliation or political views, an environment of greater autonomy for regulators is fostered.

---

5.   See Levy and Spiller (1993) and Vickers and Yarrow (1988) for additional thoughts on this matter.

Complementary Control Instruments

The design of regulatory policy is also influenced by the set of complementary control instruments in place in a country. The set of complementary instruments includes other governmental rule-making bodies, private rule-making bodies, and the legal system.

Other relevant governmental rule-making bodies in the United States include the Internal Revenue Service (IRS), the Securities and Exchange Commission (SEC), the Federal Trade Commission (FTC), the Consumer Product Safety Commission (CPSC), and the Antitrust Division of The Department of Justice (DOJ). The IRS, the SEC, and comparable bodies in other countries develop rules for calculating and reporting profits, which can free other regulators from this task. Among many other roles, the FTC ensures the veracity of the claims that firms make to their customers. When truthful advertising is enforced, a regulator may be better able to rely on consumers to discipline the regulated firm, allowing the shift from command-and-control regulation to delegated decisionmaking. Because bodies like the CPSC oversee the safety of products that are sold to consumers, other regulators can focus their efforts on different aspects of the firm's operations, such as least-cost production. Similarly, because bodies like the DOJ enforce rules that govern the interactions among firms in an industry, other regulators can focus on other elements of production.

Other rule-making bodies can impinge on a regulator's activities. For instance, suppose a body like the CPSC imposes higher safety standards on the products sold by the regulated firm than the regulator would impose. If the higher safety standards are more costly, then the regulator may have to authorize higher prices for the firm's products than it would otherwise. Similarly, if the DOJ insists that the regulated product be supplied by multiple producers even though the regulator would prefer a single producer, then the regulator may be compelled to consider new aspects of the firms' operations. For instance, the regulator may wish to ensure that consumers can freely switch among the services of different suppliers, and that different products are compatible with each other.[6] Thus, new considerations arise when multiple bodies oversee a firm's operations, including the coordination of policy among the overseers.[7]

---

6.   For an overview of the many regulatory considerations associated with the compatibility issue, see Besen and Saloner (1990).

7.   See Sah and Stiglitz (1986) for additional thoughts on how the arrangement of decisionmaking authority can influence the likelihood of correct social decisions when government decisionmakers make mistakes in judgement because the information at their disposal is imperfect.

Losses to society can result when regulatory policy is not properly coordinated across regulatory agencies. Thus, in addition to designing the
best policy for a particular regulatory body given the policies adopted by
other regulatory bodies, it is important to ensure that the various regulatory policies are optimally coordinated. Such optimal coordination can be
quite subtle. Sometimes, it is best to eliminate the duplication of powers.
For instance, if significant resources and expertise are required to carefully
analyze the social benefits and costs of a proposed merger between two
competitors, then it may be best to conserve these resources by granting a
single regulatory body sole authority to approve or disapprove proposed
mergers. In other instances, intentional duplication of powers can com-
pose part of an optimal system of checks and balances. For example, if
large, powerful firms are thought to have undue influence over
policymakers, it can be best to disperse rulemaking authority, so as to make
it more difficult for the regulated firm to "capture" all relevant regulators
(Baron 1985).

These new considerations will arise even if the "other regulators" are
not official government bodies. The presence of professional governing bodies
(like the rule-making arm of the American Medical Association) that establish accreditation requirements, codes of conduct, and disciplinary measures
for its members can fundamentally alter the regulator's activities. The regulator may only enforce the edicts of the professional governing body, or it
may serve a consultative role when policy is formulated. Or the regulator
may be reactive, vetoing those rules suggested by the professional governing body that do not further the regulator's goals and objectives. For example, a regulator may strike down an industry ban on advertising of prices
when the regulator wishes to enhance the ability of consumers to switch
suppliers and thereby limit the earnings of suppliers.

The ability of consumers to discipline suppliers in a regulated industry largely depends on another aspect of the institutional structure in a
country—consumer access to the legal system. When consumers can easily recover damages for losses suffered due to inappropriate behavior by
the regulated supplier (such as illegal price discrimination, unscheduled
interruption of service, and supply of unsafe products), the regulator can
rely more on consumers to monitor the firm's activities and to discipline
the firm for inappropriate behavior. In contrast, when court fees are very
high relative to consumers' incomes, when cases are slow to be heard, when
the court appears to favor industry over consumer interests, and when
compensation for personal loss is minimal, the regulator will be less likely
to rely on consumers to discipline the regulated firm. Instead, the regula-

tor may monitor the firm's performance directly, or establish an internal complaint and penalty system that encourages consumers to report per- ceived service deficiencies directly to the regulator.[8]

Institutions and complementary control instruments can have profound effects on the form, function, and scope of regulatory policy. If institutions limit a regulator's commitment powers, the regulator's rules will have less effect on the behavior of the regulated firm. This lack of influence can limit the scope of regulatory activity and can restrict the regulator's function to informing consumers rather than enforcing policy. Complementary con- trol instruments affect the scope of regulatory policy by dividing areas of responsibility or necessitating cooperation among regulatory bodies. They can also affect the form and function of regulatory policy by altering the perceived costs and benefits of regulations to consumers.

Production Technology

The production technology reflects the means by which inputs (capital, labor, and raw materials) are transformed into final products and services. The production technology affects the likely number of suppliers of regu- lated services and the rules that govern their interactions. It also influences the number of services that are regulated.

When the production technology exhibits increasing returns to scale (so the unit cost of supplying a regulated product declines as the production level increases) supply by a single producer minimizes production costs. Effective regulatory policy differs for the single supplier and multiple sup- plier settings. With only one supplier, there is no natural benchmark for com- parison of performance. Thus, the regulator's task of determining reason- able performance requirements and compensation levels for the regulated firm becomes more difficult. The regulator often cannot rely as heavily on the discipline provided by consumers either, as they have no alternative sup- plier when one fails to perform adequately. Consequently, when economies of scale dictate supply by a single firm, the regulator may be forced to inves- tigate the firm's operations in lengthy detail before it can fashion reasonable regulatory rulings. Thus, the production technology can impact various as- pects of the form of regulatory policy, including its basic formulation.

---

8. In Great Britain, for example, British Telecom is obligated to compensate its customers directly if the company fails to meet established service requirements. British Telecom must pay a customer five pounds for every day beyond two that an actual repair or installation lags behind the scheduled repair or installation (Rovizzi and Thompson 1992).

The presence of economies of scale, however, does not preclude multiple suppliers in an industry. A regulator may allow two or more producers even when a single producer could serve total demand at a lower cost because the benefits that result from competition among suppliers may outweigh the extra multi-supplier cost. [9] Competition can reduce prices below the levels a regulator would be able to enforce for a monopoly supplier—especially if the supplier's true capabilities are uncertain. Competition can also spur product innovation and induce the supply of higher-quality products.

When there are multiple suppliers of a product the regulator may rely less heavily on command-and-control regulation to dictate the firm's activities. Instead, competition among suppliers may be employed to motivate them to act in the best interests of consumers (such as keeping prices close to minimum possible costs). When competition prevails, the regulator's role may be more to inform consumers about firms' activities and their performance than to dictate specific actions and performance levels directly. For example, when many banks and mortgage companies compete to provide loans to homeowners, a government may not need to regulate mortgage loan rates. However, the government might want to impose standards on how the key terms of the mortgage (the annual rate of interest, the duration of the loan, penalties for premature repayment of the loan, application fees, and other fees) are disclosed to consumers. Standard reporting formats enable consumers to better compare the products of alternative suppliers and can enhance competition among suppliers.

In addition, the regulator may take actions to support the activities of developing firms (such as subsidizing the research and development or the infrastructure development of these firms) to ensure they can ultimately function as viable competitors. In the United States, the Small Business Administration provides low-interest loans and counseling to small businesses, particularly new entrants. In many industries, it is common for governments to regulate the activities of large incumbent suppliers, but to exempt new suppliers from regulatory scrutiny. Following the entry of MCI and Sprint into the long-distance telecommunications industry in the United States, the Federal Communications Commission imposed rules that facilitated the ability of consumers to switch from the incumbent supplier of long-distance service (AT&T) to one of its new competitors. In particular, consumers were permitted (at no charge) to designate a long-distance provider other than AT&T as

---

9.   See Nalebuff and Stiglitz (1983).

their primary carrier, so that their long-distance telephone calls would automatically be carried by the designated carrier.

The regulator can create competitive pressures among suppliers in other ways, too. The regulator may devise compensation programs based on relative performance criteria.[10] The firm that achieves the lowest costs of production in the industry or the highest level of product quality may be permitted to earn higher profits. Of course, the regulator must consider innate differences among suppliers when designing such relative performance policies. If some firms in the electric power industry have more abundant supplies of water power in their operating regions than others, these firms may have a natural cost advantage in generating electricity that must be accounted for. The Mississippi Public Service Commission has implemented a "Performance Evaluation Plan" that bases the allowed rate of return for the Mississippi Power Company (MPC) both on the company's own performance and on the returns earned by other comparable utilities. Under the plan MPC can earn no more than comparable firms earn if MPC's own performance is judged to be poor. However, MPC will be allowed to earn at least what comparable firms earn, and more, if its performance is judged as excellent.

Actual competition is not always necessary to discipline an incumbent supplier. Even the threat of competition can induce a firm to minimize production costs and enhance product quality.[11] Regulatory form can be structured to take full advantage of this threat. For instance, a firm's right to serve as a monopoly supplier may be limited to a prespecified period of time. At the end of that time period, the right to serve consumers may be auctioned off to the highest bidder, or consumers might vote on whether to renew the license of the incumbent supplier or to procure service from a new supplier.[12] The threat of losing one's franchise provides strong motivation for high performance.

There are sound reasons why regulatory policy may not rely on actual or potential competition, however. Recall that one of the many potential goals of regulators is to promote more equitable outcomes. At times, prohibiting production of regulated services by firms other than the incumbent monopoly supplier is the best way to achieve that goal. For example, in some jurisdictions, the policy of setting relatively high prices on long-

---

10. See Shleifer (1985) for a theoretical analysis of how to design relative performance schemes.

11. See Baumol, Panzar, and Willig (1982) for a detailed theoretical treatment of this issue.

12. See Laffont and Tirole (1988) and Williamson (1976) for additional thoughts on how such franchise policies might be designed.

distance telephone calls allows the monopoly supplier to earn a reasonable level of profits while keeping the price of access to the telephone network and the price of local telephone calls relatively low. This policy ensures that even citizens with low income can afford basic telephone service. A policy of using enhanced revenues from one service to offset limited revenues from another service can be undermined by allowing unrestricted entry into the regulated industry. If prices from long-distance telephone service are set in excess of costs while prices for local telephone service are set below cost, an entering competitor may choose to supply only long-distance telephone service at a price that is less than or equal to that charged by the regulated supplier. Such supply may be profitable for the entrant and welcomed by long-distance consumers, but it may leave the incumbent supplier with insufficient revenues to offset the losses incurred by providing local telephone service below cost. Consequently, the regulatory goal of cross-subsidization may be incompatible with unfettered entry into the industry.

Of course, regulatory policy can sometimes be redesigned to take advantage of the benefits of competition while still promoting income redistribution. For instance, in the telecommunications setting just described, new suppliers of long-distance telephone service might be charged a fee for the right to operate. The revenues from these fees could be used to offset some of the incumbent supplier's losses in providing local telephone service at uneconomic rates. Or, new entrants might be required to provide some local telephone service if they wish to supply long-distance service.[13] A third possibility is to restructure regulated prices. When competitors are allowed to supply long-distance service, keeping the price of local telephone service below cost for all customers may not be advisable. Only those customers with particularly low income (those who participate in other government assistance programs) might be eligible for a greatly discounted price for local telephone service.

Exploring alternatives like these is crucial when technology makes competition feasible. Regulators have a complicated choice that goes beyond allowing or prohibiting unfettered competition in the existing regulatory environment. Regulators must determine whether competition coupled with appropriate changes in regulatory policy can better meet regulatory objectives than can the best regulatory policy that prohibits competition.

---

13. In the cable television industry, local municipalities often require the selected supplier of cable service to offer public service channels at no additional cost to subscribers, or to provide special services (such as special broadcast channels) to local schools or community groups.

The production technology also influences the proper scope of regulatory oversight, in part because the service provided by regulated suppliers often has many components. Electric power supply, for example, involves both the generation of electricity and transmission to customers. While a regulator might oversee all elements of production in some circumstances, it might regulate only a subset of the components in certain circumstances. To illustrate, suppose the production technology is such that: (1) different firms producing the different components of a service have the same production costs as a single firm producing all components, and (2) there are limited economies of scale in producing one or more of the components, as in the generation of electricity. The best regulatory policy under these conditions may be to deregulate the components with limited economies of scale (electricity generation) and to maintain regulatory control over the components of service provided by the monopoly supplier that have pronounced economies of scale (electricity transmission). Such a policy takes advantage of both the benefits of competition and the cost savings provided by scale economies.

Of course, new considerations arise when some components of production are regulated and others are not. For example, with electricity, the regulated producer of transmission services must not grant special favors to an unregulated, but affiliated, subsidiary generator of electricity. A policy mandating uniform treatment of all potential input suppliers is often advisable.

Special precautions may also be needed to ensure quality. When all aspects of electricity supply are conducted by a single firm, identifying the exact source of a problem is usually less important. If the single, regulated firm is financially responsible for any breakdown in quality, it has incentive to find the source of quality problems and eliminate it. However, when the regulated firm supplies only one component of the regulated service, the regulator will not want to penalize the firm for quality problems caused by other suppliers. Consequently, the regulator will need to determine whether an unscheduled power outage was caused by failure on the part of the generating firm or the transmission firm. When the different components of a regulated product are supplied by different producers, better monitoring technologies or other measures to avoid quality problems may be required.

Consumer Demand

The nature of the regulated product and its consumers also affect the form, function, and scope of regulatory policy. If the regulated product is a basic commodity considered essential for everyday life, such as clean water and electricity, society may want the product available in abundant supply on reasonable terms to all citizens. Most consumers have an inelastic demand for these essential services, since their consumption is relatively insensitive to changes in prices. Regulation that limits the price a firm can charge for an essential service can avoid expropriation of consumers with inelastic demand. This is particularly true when economies of scale make production by a single firm most economical, eliminating competition's ability to lower prices. In contrast, if the product in question is more a luxury than a necessity, consumers will tend to purchase the product only if they can afford it, which naturally limits expropriation of consumers.

Externalities in consumption also influence regulation. For instance, individuals may have insufficient incentive to consume a vaccine to prevent communicable diseases. Therefore, regulations may require all individuals to get the vaccine. If the true cost of the vaccine is prohibitive for some individuals, the regulator may choose to subsidize its consumption, particularly if income redistribution is an important goal of government. Regulations may also limit activities that involve negative externalities—regulation of polluting emissions from industrial plants is common.

Regulatory policy may also be influenced by consumer characteristics. For example, because children are physically smaller and less experienced than adults, they may warrant special protection. Government agencies designed to limit child abuse are not uncommon, and regulations are often imposed that limit the activities of minors (such as voting, consuming alcohol, and enlisting in the military). Similarly, products purchased mainly by large, sophisticated, well-informed businesses may be less regulated than those whose most common purchaser is a relatively unsophisticated, uninformed household. Sophisticated purchasers can often secure substitutes for products whose announced price is considered to be too high. Furthermore, a purchaser who has the potential to buy many units of the product often has a stronger position from which to bargain for concessions from the supplier.

Information Structure

The information structure in an industry is another important determinant of regulatory policy. When critical information is difficult for consumers to discern, and when there are large economies of scale in information collection and dissemination, a natural role emerges for the regulator as an information provider. For example, consumers may have difficulty evaluating the safety of a product (such as a new drug), but its safety can be ascertained fairly easily by trained experts operating under controlled conditions in a laboratory. In such a setting, social resources can be conserved and the sale of unsafe products can be avoided if a testing facility is established and firms are not allowed to sell products that do not pass the safety tests conducted at the facility. Where a central authority can collect relevant information at a relatively low cost while consumers face prohibitive costs of collecting the information, regulatory policy will often encompass centralized monitoring and enforcement of standards.

In other cases, it may be relatively inexpensive for consumers to discern relevant product information, but far too costly for a central authority (like the government) to do so. For example, consumers can readily observe the courtesy, timeliness, and attention with which services are delivered, while a person outside of the transaction could not observe the delivered service as accurately. Therefore, direct government monitoring would not be cost effective. A more effective policy would use the information that consumers receive naturally at little or no cost by setting up a facility that records consumer complaints and penalizes the regulated supplier based on the number of complaints received. Regulatory policy might also provide consumers with information about potential alternative suppliers, giving them the option to abandon suppliers that provide inadequate service.

In many regulated industries, the punishment for inadequate quality supply is more implicit than explicit. While most state public service commissions in the United States have a long list of quality standards that telecommunications providers are supposed to meet, it is uncommon for explicit monetary penalties to be associated with failure to achieve the standards. There are exceptions to this general rule, however. For instance, in Georgia, the share of its earnings that Southern Bell is permitted to retain depends on its compliance with specific quality standards. As noted, explicit penalties are also imposed on British Telecom for failure to meet service and repair obligations. Recall, also, that under the Performance Evaluation Plan instituted in Mississippi, the allowed earnings of the Mississippi Power Company are closely linked to its measured performance in a variety of dimensions.

The costs of acquiring information affect the form, function, and scope of regulation in other ways. When it is very costly to measure key dimensions of certain activities, policies are often centered on other dimensions. To illustrate, a common goal in industrial settings is to limit the pollutants firms expel during production. In practice it can be very costly, if not impossible, to accurately measure the amount of pollution expelled by a firm. Consequently, regulators commonly dictate the amount and type of pollution abatement equipment that must be installed. For example, electric utilities have been required to install industrial scrubbers to help purify the exhaust released into the air. In addition, restrictions have been placed on the type of inputs (hard coal versus soft coal) used in the production process. These indirect forms of control can be more effective when the costs of monitoring and enforcing direct control are prohibitive.

Information in an industry also affects the nature of the regulatory process. When many people other than the regulator possess relevant information, an open regulatory process can be useful, in which individuals are afforded the opportunity to provide information to the regulator before regulatory policy is set. Most hearings to set prices for public utilities in the United States are open to all interested parties, and consumer groups commonly supply information about consumer preferences while producers supply information about production costs. When all relevant information is known to the regulator, however, the need for open hearings may be less pressing. If little relevant information is revealed during a lengthy, open regulatory process, such a process may serve more to retard than to inform regulatory policy. To illustrate, when a developing country's overriding concern is to begin delivery of a standard, essential service (such as water, electricity, or basic telephone service) rather than to fine tune the pricing structure in a sophisticated delivery system, an open regulatory process may provide little relevant information.

Rapid technological change can make it very difficult for a regulator (particularly one with limited resources, as explained earlier) to remain well-informed about all aspects of the actual and potential activities of the regulated firm. Although lengthy hearings and investigations to inform the regulator can be valuable, they can also be very costly. In particular, they can slow the introduction of new products and new pricing structures that better reflect production costs. Sometimes, unregulated competitors can intentionally prolong hearings in order to suppress the regulated supplier's response to competitive pressures. Consumers can be hurt by this process, and inefficient industry structures can result.

Regulatory form and scope can be structured to avoid such problems. In particular, greater decisionmaking authority can be delegated to the regulated firm. This delegation might allow the firm to choose one compensation plan from a well-structured menu of alternative compensation plans, or to couple less scrutiny of the firm's proposed activities with more severe penalties (such as lower prices or lower allowed rates of return) for marked differences between observed industry performance and the firm's predictions.

In summary, the production technology in an industry can influence regulatory policy in many ways. In particular, it can determine the extent to which competition is feasible, and the extent of competition can profoundly affect policy design. The characteristics of consumers, the products they consume, and the industry's information structure also help determine whether the regulator should perform an informing role or an enforcing role. Information and knowledge about the firm also influences how much decisionmaking authority the regulator should delegate to other parties.

Conclusion

Three key factors influence the form, function, and scope of regulatory policy: (1) regulatory objectives and resources, (2) the institutional structure of the policy environment, and (3) various industry conditions in the regulated environment.

Different regulatory objectives have differing direct effects on the types of regulatory controls used. When very focused, specific objectives are paramount, and the form, function, and scope of regulatory policy may be similarly focused. Limited resources also affect the nature of regulatory activities. They can cause regulation to be more reactive than proactive and can lead to substantial delegation of decisionmaking authority.

The institutional structure of the country in which regulation is imposed affects the regulator's commitment ability. The form, function, and scope of regulatory policy can be severely restricted when the regulator has a limited ability to deliver promised rewards or threatened penalties. The proper scope and function of regulation·may also be decreased when technological conditions allow competition to discipline producers. Sophisticated buyers with economic power often reduce the need for regulatory control, and comprehensive command-and-control regulation is often ineffective or debilitating to sectors undergoing rapid technological change.

For expository purposes, the discussion in this paper has isolated individual influences on regulatory policy. In practice, the effects identified here and many others simultaneously influence the proper formulation of regulatory policy—making regulatory design an intricate and complex undertaking.

In closing, some additional influences on observed regulatory policy are briefly noted. Regulatory controls that served an important purpose at one point often persist after they no longer serve their intended purpose.

They usually persist because they favor a particular group or constituency, and that constituency convinces the regulator to keep the controls in place. For instance, subsidies to firms and tariff protection against competing imports often continue long after they have served the intended purpose of promoting the development of an infant industry. The firms argue for continuance of the policy, even when they are fully capable of competing against foreign producers. When there is limited public outcry against continuing the special treatment, and strong urging by the affected firms for its continuance, the regulator may adapt the course of least resistance and allow the obsolete policy to endure.

Personal ambitions of regulators can also play a role in regulation. Even though a regulator may be charged to protect consumers, he may be diverted by promises of personal rewards for favorable treatment offered by the regulated firm. In this way, the regulator may be controlled by the regulated firm so that his rulings no longer reflect the goals and objectives of society as a whole.[14]

Regulations may also be influenced by personal goals and objectives of regulators that, while differing from perceived social goals, are not motivated by self-interest. Regulators may have genuine differences of opinion with society at large or with other government officials about what is best for society. Where goals and objectives conflict, the goals pursued depend in large part on the autonomy of regulators and on the balance of power among government bodies.

In summary, when attempting to understand the form, function, and scope of regulatory activity, it is important to understand the entire structure of government influence and control. Particular regulations in particular industries are often partial, interdependent components of the overarching governmental structure.

Bibliography

Baron, David. 1985. "Noncooperative Regulation of a Nonlocalized Externality." *Rand Journal of Economics* 16(4): 553–68.

_____. 1988. "Design of Regulatory Mechanisms and Institutions" in R. Schmalensee and R. Willig, eds., *Handbook of Industrial Organization.* Amsterdam: North-Holland.

Baumol, William, John Panzar, and Robert Willig. 1982. *Contestable Markets and the*

---

14. For a more detailed discussion of the capture theory of regulation, see Stigler (1971) and Laffont and Tirole (1993).

Theory of Industry Structure. New York: Harcourt Brace Jovanovich.

Besanko, David, and David Sappington. 1987. *Designing Regulatory Policy with Limited Information.* London: Harwood Academic Publishers.

Besen, Stanley, and Garth Saloner. 1990. "Compatibility Standards and the Market for Telecommunications Services" in R. Crandall and K. Flamm, eds., *Changing the Rules: Technological Change, International Competition, and Regulation in Telecommunications.* Washington, D.C.: The Brookings Institution.

Brown, Stephen, and David Sibley. 1986. *The Theory of Public Utility Pricing.* New York: Cambridge University Press.

Caillaud, B., Roger Guesnerie, Patrick Rey, and Jean Tirole. 1988. "Government Intervention in Production and Incentives Theory: A Review of Recent Contributions." *Rand Journal of Economics* 19(1): 1–26.

Federal Communications Commission. 1990. *News.* Report on Action in Docket Case No. 87-313, September 19.

Laffont, Jean-Jacques, and Jean Tirole. 1988. "Repeated Auctions of Incentive Contracts, Investment, and Bidding Parity with an Application to Takeovers." *Rand Journal of Economics* 19(4): 516–37.

_____. 1993. *A Theory of Incentives in Procurement and Regulation.* Cambridge: The MIT Press.

Levy, Brian, and Pablo Spiller. 1993. "Regulation, Institutions, and Commitment in Telecommunications: A Comparative Analysis of Five Countries." Washington, D.C.: The World Bank, Policy and Research Department.

_____. 1994. *Institutional Foundations of Utility Regulation: Research Results and Their Operational Implications.* Washington, D.C.: The World Bank.

Mueller, Milton. 1993. *Telephone Companies in Paradise: A Case Study in Telecommunications Deregulation.* New Brunswick: Transaction Publishers.

Nalebuff, Barry, and Joseph Stiglitz. 1983. "Information, Competition, and Markets." *American Economic Review* 73(2): 278–83.

Rovizzi, Laura, and David Thompson. 1992. "The Regulation of Product Quality in the Public Utilities and the Citizen's Charter." *Fiscal Studies,* 13(3): 74–95.

Sah, Raaj, and Joseph Stiglitz. 1986. "The Architecture of Economic Systems: Hierarchies and Polyarchies." *American Economic Review* 76(4): 716–27.

Sappington, David. 1991. "Incentives in Principal-Agent Relationships." *Journal of Economic Perspectives* 5(2): 45–66.

Sappington, David, and David Sibley. 1992. "Strategic Nonlinear Pricing Under Price Cap Regulation." *Rand Journal of Economics* 23(1): 1–19.

Shleifer, Andrei. 1985. "A Theory of Yardstick Competition." *Rand Journal of Economics* 16(3): 319–27.

Sibley, David. 1989. "Asymmetric Information, Incentives and Price Cap Regulation." *Rand Journal of Economics* 20(3): 392–404.

Stigler, George. 1971. "The Economic Theory of Regulation." *Bell Journal of Economics* 2(1): 3–21.

Vickers, John, and George Yarrow. 1988. *Privatization: An Economic Analysis.* Cambridge: The MIT Press.

Williamson, Oliver. 1976. "Franchise Bidding for Natural Monopolies—in General and with Respect to CATV." *Bell Journal of Economics* 7(1): 73–104.

Wilson, Robert. 1993. *Nonlinear Pricing.* New York: Oxford University Press.

4

Financing Infrastructure in Developing Countries: Lessons from the Railway Age

Barry Eichengreen

In recent years suggestions for reforming the provision and financing of infrastructure services in developing countries have focused on private participation. This alternative to public financing is seen as a way both to minimize the inefficiencies of public administration and to avoid the need for external borrowing. In fact, for much of the nineteenth century, infrastructure projects were privately financed and built. This approach, however, did not obviate the need for government intervention and foreign capital. Because of the difficulties of assessing projects, investors were reluctant to commit their funds, and governments turned to subsidies and loan guarantees to encourage investment. Often, however, government intervention only replaced one set of problems with another. Investors with government-guaranteed loans had no incentive to monitor the firm's performance—a limitation that led to the diversion of funds , which frustrated the public interest. This article draws out the implications of this experience for policymakers in developing countries today.

For low-income countries, investments in infrastructure have alluring benefits as well as daunting costs. Where transportation, communication, and power generation are inadequate, increased supplies can do much to boost productivity and growth. But where income and productivity are depressed by inadequate infrastructure, the financial resources needed to underwrite investments are difficult to mobilize. Because the lack of infrastructure limits investment and the lack of investment limits infrastructure, low-income countries can find themselves in a low-level equilibrium trap from which it is difficult to escape.

Two potential escape routes—government subsidies and foreign borrowing—are available in principle. If infrastructure is critical for raising productivity and profitability elsewhere in the economy but those who finance the project cannot capture sufficient revenues to repay their costs, the classic efficiency argument for subsidies applies: that a subsidy that closes the gap between private and social benefits will prevent the relevant form of infrastructure from being undersupplied. And even when the returns can be appropriated, investment may still not be attractive if high interest rates make domestic funds costly; investors may then seek finance abroad, where it is cheaper. Not surprisingly, government guarantees and foreign borrowing are prominent features of infrastructure finance in many developing countries.

Increasingly, these arguments for government intervention and foreign borrowing are regarded with skepticism. The costly "white elephants" subsidized by governments have underscored doubts about the efficiency of public finance, and the debt-servicing difficulties of developing countries have raised questions about the efficacy of foreign borrowing. Both observations encourage an interest in proposals to commercialize and privatize infrastructure projects and to fund them by promoting the development of financial markets.

There is nothing new about these arguments or these reservations. Infrastructure projects were privately financed and constructed in virtually all the overseas regions of recent European settlement in the 19th century (which, for the purposes of this article, is assumed to extend to 1914). At the same time, however, government subsidies and external finance were integral to the process of developing infrastructure. Although early U.S. railways, to take a prominent example, were private undertakings, land grants and government guarantees subsidized their construction. Finance was raised abroad, mainly on the London capital market. This history suggests that private initiative should not be viewed as obviating the need for government guarantees and foreign finance.

This chapter elucidates these historical patterns of public intervention and external finance for infrastructure investment, with a particular emphasis on railways. Its premise is that these patterns are consequences of the structure of financial markets in countries in the early stages of economic development. Nineteenth-century infrastructure investments included canals, docks, electric power grids, sanitation systems, telegraph systems, tramways, and turnpikes, but railways—the most prominent and capital intensive of these investments—commanded center stage. Railways forged unified national markets, linked domestic producers to the expanding world economy, facilitated the development of mass-production techniques, and incubated modern management practices.[1] The analysis therefore draws on the literature on 19th century railway investment, focusing most notably on recent contributions such as Baskin (1988) and Carlos and Lewis (1992 and forthcoming).

Government intervention, external finance, and debt-servicing difficulties are correlates of the imperfections in financial markets that impose a heavy burden on governments seeking to finance infrastructure projects. At the same time, government policies to overcome asymmetric information can encourage management to engage in bankruptcy for profit (a problem that Akerlof and Romer 1993 refer to as "looting"). This tradeoff between credit rationing and the risk of bankruptcy for profit is at the heart of this chapter.

The chapter reviews the interaction of asymmetric information, moral hazard, and adverse selection and, in this context, describes the financial and economic environment in which 19th century firms and governments operated. It then considers two arrangements—government guarantees and land grants—used to subsidize infrastructure investment and to attract foreign finance and describes how these arrangements worked to relax credit constraints and weaken the incentive for creditors to monitor management. The chapter concludes by drawing some implications for developing countries today.

Theoretical Considerations

According to the Modigliani-Miller theorem, investors should be indifferent to the composition of a firm's financial structure; if a firm is highly leveraged, investors can offset the risk by adjusting the composition of their portfolios. But in the real world there are several reasons why this strong result does not prevail. The relevant reason here is asymmetric information (Keeton 1979; Stiglitz and Weiss 1981). That is, the entrepreneur knows more about the probability of failure than do external investors. So long as all projects yield the same expected return and investors are risk-neutral (that is, they are willing to accept risk rather

---

1. Fogel (1964), however, concludes that the social savings attributable to railway construction in the United States was small. Given geographical and topographical differences, subsequent studies have yielded larger estimates for other parts of the world. Nor do calculations of social savings attempt to quantify the dynamic effects emphasized by authors as diverse as Chandler (1990), Jenks (1944), and Williamson (1974).

than pay to avoid it), entrepreneurs with riskier projects will be willing to pay more for external funds. Because their information is poor, lenders cannot discriminate among borrowers. To cover their risk, therefore, lenders raise interest rates, prompting entrepreneurs with safer projects to drop out of the pool of potential borrowers. (This is the problem of adverse selection.) Higher interest rates, in turn, encourage the borrower to take on riskier investments. (This is the problem of moral hazard.) Raising interest rates can therefore reduce the lender's expected return. Under these circumstances, lenders may ration credit.

In this model, credit rationing is driven by the riskiness of the underlying environment and the severity of the barriers to the dissemination of accurate information. The more costly it is to sort projects (and the more pervasive the informational asymmetries), the more serious the problems of adverse selection and moral hazard. Many developing countries fit these conditions: they are, for example, subject to terms-of-trade shocks and lack effective regulations requiring financial disclosure.

What pattern of finance is likely to emerge when information is asymmetric and conditions favor adverse selection and moral hazard? Entrepreneurs or promoters with risky but potentially profitable projects will be forced to rely on their own funds. The more limited the lender's information, the more capital promoters will have to subscribe before external finance can be obtained. De Meza and Webb (1987) show that the resulting level of investment will be socially suboptimal. Under ideal conditions (known as first-best equilibrium, in which all markets clear exactly, information is perfect, and there are no distortions), with risk-neutral investors, all projects that yield returns equal to the world rate of return will be undertaken. But when information is distributed asymmetrically, some such projects will not be financed. In such cases, a government interest-rate subsidy or guarantee may effectively relax the credit constraint. The problem is that such an arrangement weakens the incentive for investors to monitor management performance, because bondholders are guaranteed a return. This may allow management to divert resources to nonproductive uses from which it benefits (Jensen and Meckling 1976). In the extreme, promoters may resort to bankruptcy for profit. That is, they compare the returns from the earnings of the firm with those they would receive by taking out funds until they exhaust the resources that are available under the interest guarantee and are forced to declare bankruptcy. Or they inflate accounting rates of return relative to economic returns to appear solvent and acquire additional debt to be invested in activities that provide a high cash flow that the owners can tap. Because the government guarantees set the process in motion by weakening the incentive for investors to monitor management performance, the taxpayer is left holding the bag. This problem is most acute where government guarantees are unconditional, where public oversight is lax (effective surveillance and regulation should prevent promoters from gambling that they can get away with this strategy), and where promoters and their confederates attach the least value to their reputations.

Asymmetric Information and Investment in the Railway Age

Early infrastructure projects in North America posed formidable information problems for investors. Three factors in particular were conducive to informational asymmetries: the novelty of the technologies, the uncertain prospects for local market growth, and the dearth of reputable promoters.

Technology

The lack of familiarity with the technologies and the paucity of experience outside England hindered investors' search for information.[2] Hence, so prominent and profitable a project as the Erie Canal sent a powerful signal to the capital market. The canal was completed in 1825 at a total cost of $11 million—$3 million of which came from current sources and $8 million from long-term loans. The project was able to meet interest payments on the debt in its first year of operation and was fully paid off within ten years. The Erie's success set off a canal-building boom that engulfed the mid-Atlantic and New England coasts. And yet the costs of building the canal were of only limited value to those estimating the costs of building a canal through the higher mountains in western Pennsylvania. It is not entirely surprising that Pennsylvania's canals turned out to be more expensive than anticipated.

Uncertainties

In areas such as the American West that had only recently appeared on maps, not even geography could be taken for granted. At a dinner thrown by the

---

2.   Foreign investors were put off by political uncertainty as well. The disruption caused by the Civil War, for example, lingered into the 1870s.

Lord Mayor of London, an English investor asked an American guest whether Cincinnati or Illinois was the larger city. Even when the location was known, potential profitability was not: the amount of traffic a railway could generate was contingent on the economic development of adjoining regions, which depended on such unknowns as the fertility of the soil, the reliability of the rainfall, and the extent of mineral reserves.[3] Where the volume of traffic ultimately depended on these reserves, uncertainty posed a considerable risk. Construction of many North American railways was based on crude forecasts of coal or silver deposits. Where land had to be settled and cleared before it could be farmed, it took years before the need for transport networks caught up with the investment in railroad infrastructure. In Canada, for example, although railway construction peaked in the final decades of the nineteenth century, significant gains in wheat production and rail traffic did not occur until the second decade of the 20th century (Ankli 1980).

Experience with Promoters

In addition to evaluating the economic prospects of the project, investors had to assess the reputability of the promoter. Recently settled, sparsely populated regions were prime locations for fly-by-night operators who could strike "sweetheart" deals with construction companies that would permit them to siphon off resources, saddling the project with insupportable debts. Typically, the uncertainty was reduced by drawing on the expertise and information of local investors. Where industrial and commercial development was precocious, it was possible to finance infrastructure through limited partnerships of local residents. Because early canals, turnpikes, and railroads had modest capital requirements (by the standards of the long-distance rail lines that followed), a local partnership could raise the requisite capital.

Local Finance

Examples from New England illustrate the point. The region was the center of American textile manufacturing and hence of American industry in the early 19th century, as well as the heart of commerce, ship-

---

3. The same was true elsewhere, of course. Thus, in 1852 the chairman of the Madras Company cited "want of local knowledge" as an obstacle to attracting external finance for railroads in India (MacPherson 1955: 180).

ping, and whaling. A growing number of small industrial towns provided a fertile market for shorthaul railways (Chandler 1954). From the trade with China, Boston merchants learned how to use entrepreneurial and managerial techniques to overcome the long spans of time and distance (Johnson and Supple 1967). Much of New England's railway finance was raised the same way in which the region financed its textile mills, by relying on family, friends, and other personal contacts.

Where contract enforcement was problematic and information was difficult to verify independently, the markets made heavy use of such links. Friends and associates vested their confidence in individual financiers with reputations for honest dealing who signaled their commitment by putting their own funds at risk (Baskin 1988; Lamoreaux 1986). As Johnson and Supple (1967: 338) put it, "investment tended to be a cumulative social process in an environment lacking an impersonal, national money market." Thus, the danger of looting by fly-by-night operators was correspondingly reduced. Local farmers, bankers, merchants, landowners, contractors, and manufacturers subscribed the majority of New England's early railway shares. Not only did such individuals have favored access to information, but they stood to benefit from the transportation links. At the head of many early syndicates were textile producers seeking roads that would serve their mills and Boston merchants looking to railroads as a link with the hinterland market and the Great Lakes (Platt 1984).

That these projects were relatively modest (they connected Boston with nearby Portsmouth, New Hampshire, or Providence, Rhode Island) facilitated the local mobilization of capital. Even a more ambitious line built in the late 1830s and early 1840s, the Western Rail-Road linking Boston with Albany, raised most of its finance locally.[4]

Underdeveloped markets could, however, impede efforts to raise local finance. The attempt to market bonds for Canada's St. Lawrence and Atlantic Railway in the 1840s illustrates these difficulties: farmers who had no cash paid their subscriptions in the form of pork and eggs to feed the construction gangs. Some early U.S. railways similarly took subscriptions in the form of labor and materials (Cleveland and Powell 1912).

---

4.   Although the Western Rail-Road had more than 2,000 shareholders, most of these were located in Boston. Only 17 percent had 100 or more shares as of 1841. To continue the road from the state line to Albany, the city of Albany subscribed the entire capital, paying for it with city bonds (Johnson and Supple 1967).

External Finance

This model of local finance was difficult to generalize because the capital requirements of early railways were more modest than those of subsequent projects, and the funds available in New England exceeded those of other regions. Elsewhere it was necessary to seek external finance.[5] Such funds were not a substitute for local finance; local investors still had to subscribe to indicate their willingness to put their money where their mouths were. If locals put up funds, external investors could be confident that those in the best position to assess the needs of the project and monitor its progress and the actions of its promoters would do so.

When Boston began to invest in the railroads of the U.S. South and West in the 1840s, personal ties played a significant role. Railroad men coming to Boston contacted merchants who had invested in earlier railways. The promoters invested their own money in the project as evidence of their commitment and talked friends and business acquaintances into investing as well. Long-term relations between entrepreneurs from the West and merchants from Boston and between the merchants and their contacts provided a conduit for information about investment projects and individual promoters.

Railway securities tended to be traded in distant markets before such trade developed in manufacturing and commercial concerns. Manufacturing used more exotic technologies, and commercial undertakings had less tangible assets (knowledge of customer requirements, for example), so investing in industry and commerce had to surmount even higher information hurdles. The railways were consequently among the first enterprises to access external finance on a significant scale (Baskin 1988). According to Adler (1970), as early as the 1830s several lines around Philadelphia and in Virginia and North Carolina were able to market securities in London, attracting support from British investors familiar with financing rail networks. The pattern persisted: as late as 1914 railway securities accounted for perhaps half of all outstanding foreign investments in the United States. Foreign financing entailed the intermediation of specialized institutions that had grown up in the principal European financial centers to deal with information problems: issue houses, private banks, bill brokers, and financial investment companies. An illustration of the im-

---

5.   I refer to "external" rather than "foreign" finance for two reasons. First, entities such as Canada and India, which were not fully independent, relied on external finance from the imperial center, Great Britain. Second, regions that were late in developing, such as the western United States, relied on external finance from regions that had developed earlier, such as New England.

portance of these institutions in Britain is shown in table 4.1. British investment houses typically retained American agents familiar with the American economy and railway projects. They specialized in recommending high-
quality foreign bonds, usually those of railroads that were well known and
long established or were backed by the credit of a state government. To
show that they had confidence in the project, these firms often bought the
same bonds for their own portfolios. Most British investors followed their
advice, limiting their purchases to a few large eastern companies that provided adequate information (Adler 1970).

Table 4.1. *The Proportion of Overseas New Issues Introduced by the Main Types of
British Issuing Houses, 1870–1914*

Years	Official and semi-official agencies	Private banks[a]	Joint-stock banks	Overseas banks and agencies	Companies via their bankers	Other media[b]	Total amount issued (£ millions)
1870-74	1.8	53.0	4.4	9.6	18.2	13.0	390.6
1875-79	14.5	36.5	0.8	24.7	13.0	10.5	149.2
1880-84	6.7	38.5	3.3	14.1	26.7	10.7	355.3
1885-89	9.9	43.7	5.3	7.5	26.1	7.5	479.2
1890-94	10.4	46.4	9.0	8.8	19.6	5.8	349.6
1895-99	8.7	25.1	11.2	20.3	25.2	9.5	359.6
1900-04	27.4	19.2	17.8	14.4	16.7	4.5	258.2
1905-09	10.3	32.7	12.2	22.4	18.7	3.7	509.9
1910-14	8.3	35.2	17.4	18.8	17.5	2.8	783.8
1870-1914	9.8	37.2	10.3	15.4	20.5	6.8	100.0
Total issued (£ millions)	355.0	1,354.0	371.0	562.0	746.0	248.0	3,636.0

Note: Figures are percentages unless otherwise specified.

a.   That is, merchant bankers

b.   Investment trust (£23 million); finance, land, and property companies (£18 million);
special purpose syndicates (£41 million); issue house with stock exchange connections (£22
million); companies as their own issuers (£13 million); and miscellaneous issuers (£131
million).

Source: Based on a table prepared by W. A. Brown published in *The Economist* (November
20, 1937) and reprinted in Balough (1947: 233).

Financial institutions were not the only conduits for surmounting information problems. Immigrant communities were another, as were specialized publications such as *The American Railroad Journal* and *Poor's Manual of the Railroads of the United States*. From the 1860s British investors organized themselves as the Council of Foreign Bondholders and the English Association of American Bond and Shareholders to collect information on arrears and to negotiate with debtors (Wilkins 1989; and Eichengreen and Fortes 1989). Protective associations were established in France, Germany, and Holland as well. Some foreign investors traded in the securities of small or obscure railways, which they obtained from jobbers and dealers who purchased blocks of stock in the United States for sale in Europe. But the vast majority of investors concentrated on first class securities issued by the London offices of prominent American railways and endorsed by British issue houses or banks.

The preferred financial instruments varied with economic and geographic distance. Nearby lenders, such as New Englanders lending to the Midwest, purchased common stock, because personal and business contacts provided a reliable flow of information. The short, inexpensive lines of central New York were able to supplement local subscriptions with sales of equity in New York City. (According to Chandler 1954, trading in these shares played a central role in the early development of the New York Stock Exchange.) A group of investors in New York State purchased a substantial block of shares in Canada's Welland Canal, built in the late 1820s and 1830s to circumvent Niagara Falls and open Montreal to the western trade. British investors sometimes purchased common stock as well, although the majority of their—as well as other investors'—holdings were in bonds which, as primary claims, were perceived as less risky (Lewis 1938; Wilkins 1989). Such bonds were secured by mortgages on the railroad's property or were guaranteed by the government. Many lines issued bonds that were convertible into stock at the holder's option, and such bonds eventually became the standard instruments for financing railways and other infrastructure projects (Chandler 1954). A very few railways, such as certain early southern lines, were able to issue stock, but the returns were guaranteed by cities such as Charleston and Savannah.

Normally, the regulations and surveillance of an organized stock market help to attenuate the moral hazard and adverse selection problems caused by poor information. But the institutions of the London market carried out these functions only to a limited extent. The ability of the London Stock Exchange to restrict trading in particular securities was constrained by competition from European and provincial exchanges as well as from outside brokers and so-called bucket shops (the 19th century equivalent of modern discount brokers) (Adler 1970; Wilkins 1989). Paish (1951: 4) notes that "before 1914 the [London] Stock Exchange made no attempt to restrict or control in any way the right to deal in any security, whether British or foreign. ... It was in general more concerned with arrangements to ensure a reasonably free market in the securities than with the intrinsic merits of the company or with the adequacy or accuracy of the information provided."

This meant that the portfolio of projects to be financed grew riskier as interest rates rose. Promoters had an incentive to take on excessive debt because they stood to make huge profits if the venture succeeded but could lose no more than their equity stake if it failed. Contemporaries consequently complained that many worthwhile investment projects were unable to raise external funds, and this inability to obtain credit created an obvious argument for government intervention.

Government Subsidies and Guarantees

"When great schemes of public utility are brought before the country," the editors of *The Economist* wrote in 1858, "it is natural that the Government should extend its aid to such enterprises" (MacPherson 1955: 181). In the case of investments in infrastructure, government aid came in three forms: interest guarantees on bonded debt, subsidies, and aid-in-kind (often financed by a bond issue designated for the purpose or by earmarked revenues). Canadian governments borrowed $20 million to build canals in the 1840s (Jenks 1938). In the United States, state governments spent $121 million of the $195 million allocated to canal construction between 1815 and 1860; private companies spent only $74 million (Cranmer 1960). State and local governments were also key subscribers to the securities of early American railroads. Before 1840 nearly all East-West projects—both railways and canals—were financed by public bonds. Thus, in the 1830s the Commonwealth of Massachusetts took a one-third partnership in the Western Railroad Corporation of Massachusetts, which it financed by floating state paper in London (Platt 1984: 156), and the state of Ohio subscribed one share in its state's railroads for every two shares purchased by private investors (Chandler 1954). Only the early North-South railways and the Pennsylvania coal roads were paid for largely by bonds of private corporations; these lines were shorter and cheaper to build and more certain of regular traffic.

The classic efficiency argument for subsidization rests on externalities: that a project's social returns exceed its private returns. The historical literature supports the proposition that the railways were a source of positive externalities. Fogel's (1960) study of the Union Pacific Railroad in the United States, for example, estimated that the social return averaged 30 percent a year, two-and-a-half times the private return. Yet it is not clear that private entrepreneurs were always unable to capture these returns. In many cases the promoter of an infrastructure project purchased adjoining lands whose productivity and value were enhanced by construction of the turnpike, canal, or railway. In others, textile mills and mercantile enterprises whose profits were boosted by infrastructure investments that moved a steady supply of raw materials to the factory and finished products to the market could be—and often were—owned by those who organized the infrastructure projects. This ability to capitalize on their investment clearly weakened the case for subsidization.[6]

A further justification for government intervention was the need to offset the imperfections in capital markets that resulted from asymmetric information. Even if investors could otherwise capture the social returns, incomplete information that led to credit rationing sometimes prevented them from doing so.

A very different explanation for government intervention is rent-seeking by those who stood to benefit from government subsidies and guarantees. Lewis and McKinnon (1987) argue that the Canadian Northern Railway may have been socially as well as privately unprofitable but those who stood to benefit from its construction succeeded in enlisting government subsidies for the project. Rent-seeking was certainly prevalent, but one need not dismiss it as unimportant in order to acknowledge that at least some government intervention was justified on other grounds.

Government Guarantees

Capital market constraints explain one form of subsidy commonly used for canal and railway construction in the 19th century—interest guarantees on government bonds. In India, for example, if a railway company did not attain a minimum rate of return of, say, 5 percent, the government made up the difference. The interest clause in the bond covenant was backed by the government's full powers of taxation. All of India's early railways were built under the terms of the guarantee.

---

6.   Because many different landowners and merchants typically benefited from the construction of a single railway line, the problems of organizing collective actions by a large number of vaguely interested parties might impede efforts to internalize the externalities, leaving a rationale for subsidization.

Government guarantees were particularly important in attracting foreign investors, who found it difficult to obtain accurate information on railway projects in India. Without guarantees, infrastructure projects were considered impossible to finance. MacPherson (1955: 180) reports that because the North Bengal Company was refused a guarantee, it was unable to begin construction and was forced to return all deposits to shareholders. Once the guarantee was provided, however, India's railways had no difficulty raising funds abroad. "The motives of the British investors can be explained almost entirely in terms of the 5 percent guarantee of interest offered by the Indian Government. Indian bonds were regarded as perfectly safe; investors included widows, barristers, clergymen, bankers, and retired army officers."

Canal projects in Canada in the first half of the 19th century received government guarantees under the aegis of the British Colonial Office. Before 1849 attempts to build railways in Canada had foundered on the difficulty of raising capital. That year legislation was passed guaranteeing interest at no more than 6 percent on half of the bonds of any railway more than 75 miles long, provided that half of the line was already built (Easterbrook and Aitken 1956).[7] The guarantee, which covered the principal as well as the interest, enabled Canadian railways to attract significant amounts of foreign finance (tables 4.2 and 4.3).[8] Funds for the Grand Trunk line were raised from individuals, municipalities, and contractors, but roughly half of its bonds were guaranteed and were heavily subscribed by British investors. The Canadian Pacific and the Grand Trunk Pacific also enjoyed public support. Glazebrook (1938) concluded that not one of these lines could have been built without government guarantees.

---

7.   In 1851 the guarantee was restricted to railroads that formed part of a main, or trunk, line. This legislation was passed partly in response to pressure from the Canadian government's British bankers, Baring Brothers and Glyn, Mills and Company, who worried that an unlimited guarantee would encourage excessive building and result in an unsupportable debt. Another act, in 1852, liberalized this condition somewhat, allowing individual municipalities to borrow from a provincial fund to help establish branch and feeder lines (Currie 1957: 9).

8.   An exception was the Great Western Railway, which obtained initial capital from merchants in Detroit and from New York investors who had financed the New York Central. Completion, however, required floating a bond in London in 1852. Other major railways initiated after the passage of the Guarantee Act relied almost entirely on British finance (Carlos and Lewis, forthcoming).

Table 4.2. *Distribution of Total Flow of Capital to Canada 1900–1914,*
(millions of dollars)

Recipient	All countries	Great Britain	United States	Other countries
Dominion and provincial governments	179	175	4	...
Municipal governments	260	200	60	...
Railroads	767	670	50	47
Industrial	630	420	180	30
Land and timber	305	80	145	80
Mining	125	65	60	...
Insurance	82	32	50	...
Other	198	111	81	6
Total	2,546	1,753	630	163

... Negligible.
Source: Buckley (1955: 90).

Although the guarantees helped railway promoters to surmount credit rationing, they also weakened the incentive for investors to hold management accountable. Investors no longer stood to lose—or to lose as much—if promoters and their confederates diverted resources from productive uses, because the government promised to bail them out. In the extreme, this might encourage the construction of railway lines where there was no hope of generating sufficient traffic to service the debt that was incurred. More generally, it gave promoters an incentive to negotiate sweetheart deals with contractors that made it possible to channel cash into their own accounts. Such practices were difficult to detect because reasonable costs for idiosyncratic projects such as railways and canals are intrinsically difficult to ascertain. And because construction generated an abundant cash flow, the diversion of resources into the pockets of the promoters was relatively easy to arrange. Moreover, many partnerships were temporary, so promoters had little reason to be deterred by considerations of reputation. Only those ultimately responsible for the financial liability—or more precisely, their elected representatives—had an incentive to monitor the accounts.

Thus the potential for looting was created. Bondholders, whose rate of return was guaranteed by the government, had little incentive to expend resources to determine whether promoters had identified a project capable of generating an adequate net revenue stream or whether contractors were siphoning off the project's resources. Only if government authorities monitored the actions of promoters and contractors and threatened them with legal sanctions did the latter have reason to be deterred. Although the problem of quantifying minimum construction costs makes the prevalence of looting difficult to establish, the qualitative evidence is suggestive. Of Canada's Great Western Railway, Jenks (1938) wrote that its directors, who enjoyed a government guarantee, sought not to minimize construction costs, but to finance the contractor and share in his profits. The history of Canada's Grand Trunk Railway provides additional gory details. Almost immediately upon floating government-guaranteed bonds, as Easterbrook and Aitken (1956: 309) noted, the company found itself unable to pay interest. To a large degree, its problems reflected "unanticipated costs of construction," as contractors pressed for new links to the railways of New York and Michigan rather than using existing lines. In 1851 Gzowski and Company, a contracting firm run by former directors of railways with connections to the Grand Trunk, was awarded the contract for the construction of these lines. The contractors were paid in cash, "and the individual members of the firm realized sizable fortunes" (Easterbrook and Aiken 1956: 301). The British group of Peto, Brassey, Betts, and Jackson, itself deeply entangled in Canadian politics, was "helped . . . over every difficulty" by "a complaisant legislature and a winning governor-general" (Jenks 1938: 204). Existing lines were added to the network for "inflated" purchase prices. Operating expenses in the first ten years ran between 58 and 85 percent of gross receipts—far above the 40 percent that had been forecast and was typical of other railways.

Table 4.3. Gross Construction Outlays in Major Transport Fields in Canada, 1901–1930

Years	Railways	Highways	Canals and harbors	Total
Values (millions of dollars)				
1901-05	124.3	3.3	32.1	159.7
1906-10	380.7	11.7	48.0	440.4
1911-15	537.4	38.5	93.7	669.6
1916-20	252.5	39.4	59.7	351.6
1921-25	253.2	100.4	109.8	463.4
1926-30	389.4	172.4	138.2	700.0
Percentage distribution				
1901-05	77.8	2.1	20.1	100.0
1906-10	86.4	2.7	10.1	100.0
1911-15	80.3	5.7	14.0	100.0
1916-20	71.8	11.2	16.9	100.0
1921-25	54.6	21.7	23.7	100.0
1926-30	55.5	24.6	19.7	100.0

Source: Buckley (1955: 32).

This type of fraud is consistent with the predictions of the Akerlof-Romer model—that government guarantees extended to relax credit-rationing constraints weaken the effectiveness of corporate control if they are not accompanied by effective public sector oversight and regulation. Currie (1957: 9) summarized the situation: "As the Government would guarantee bonds up to one-half the cost of the road, hard-pressed promoters were tempted to inflate their costs, to effectively force the Government to assume responsibility for more than its proper share of the actual expenditure, and to reduce the real value of the assets against which, under the Guarantee Act, the Government held a first mortgage."

In India there were layers of principal-agent problems: the taxpayers underwrote the guarantee, but the government that extended it was responsible not to them, but to the British Crown; Jenks (1938) attributes failed projects such as the Madras Canal, which was completed but could not be filled with water, to the lack of monitoring encouraged by this weak structure. Of the railways, he reports that an Indian finance minister testified, "All the money came from the English capitalist, and so long as he was guaranteed 5 percent on the revenues of India, it was immaterial to him whether the funds that he lent were thrown into the Hooghly River or converted into brick and mortar" (Jenks 1938: 221-22).

Land Grants

Land grants, which served to correct capital market imperfections by providing collateral, were another prevalent form of government subsidy. Approximately 150 million acres of land were granted to western U.S. railways between 1850 and 1870. Legislation authorizing the use of land grants was adopted in Canada in 1852, although it was not used until the 1870s. Land grants were attractive on several counts. First, because the prairies in both countries were unsettled and the land remained in government hands, such grants obviated problems of assembling parcels for right-of-ways. Second, a land grant tended to confront less political resistance than did government financial subsidies and interest guarantees, which implied the imposition of distortionary taxes. Arguably, ceding land adjoining railways and canals to the promoters of those projects also allowed promoters to recover at least some of the externalities that were thrown off by their investments. Third, compared with other bonds, those backed by mortgages on land had minimal bankruptcy costs; the interest and principal due to the primary creditors could be paid off, at least in part, through the sale of the land if the project failed. The loan was collateralized, thus mitigating the moral hazard and adverse selection problems that otherwise constrain credit.[9] Adler (1970) notes that the importance of this support is reflected in the fact that only American railroads receiving land grants were able to issue regular bonds (as opposed to convertible issues). Alternatively, receipts from the sales of land, known as "land income" bonds, could be mortgaged. In the case of the Atchison, Topeka, and Santa Fe Railroad, this backing was attractive to foreign investors, who had limited opportunities for monitoring the project.

In principle, these land grants collateralized only a portion of an enterprise's bonded debt. Compared with an unlimited guarantee, this should have encouraged closer monitoring by outside investors. But in fact, railways that ran into difficulties were frequently offered additional guarantees and subsidies. In practice, it is questionable that the negative side effects of land grants were less pronounced than those of bond guarantees.

Fishlow (1965) estimates that the land subsidy amounted to roughly 5 percent of total railroad investment between 1850 and 1880; Mercer (1969, 1972) arrives at smaller numbers. The small size of these estimates suggests that land grants only partially collateralized the railways' liabilities. Land grants were not uniformly distributed, however; they were concentrated in the period 1865 to 1870 and were awarded disproportionately to certain risky investments, such as the first transcontinental lines. Mercer concludes that many land grants were wasted on railroads that would have been built in any case. He bases his view on the finding that the private rate of return exceeded the return on alternative uses of funds. In other words, the railways still would have wished to borrow at the prevailing rate. An asymmetric information perspective casts doubt on this conclusion, however, because it implies that, without land grants, some railways might not have been able to obtain external finance at any price.

Policy Implications

Recent suggestions for reforming the ways infrastructure in developing countries is provided and financed include encouraging private provision as a way to avoid the inefficiencies of public administration and tapping local savings as a way to avoid excessive reliance on external borrowing. These suggestions have a back-to-the-future quality: private provision and

9. This was true at least of early mortgage bonds. Subsequently, some promoters issued "collateral trust mortgage bonds" that were secured not by real property, but by the stocks and bonds of other companies. See Bryant (1971) for details.

local finance were characteristic of infrastructure investments in many countries—notably the North American case considered here—for much of the 19th century. Consequently, the historical record is a potentially rich source of information on the circumstances under which these approaches are workable and on their limitations.

What the record reveals is that government intervention continued to be important. The ability of domestic financial markets to underwrite the construction of ports, canals, and railways was constrained, in part because of informational asymmetries characteristic of markets in the early stages of development. To help with these problems and to attract private investment, lenders turned to financial institutions that specialized in assessing projects and monitoring management. These were typically foreign institutions with foreign clienteles whose experience with privately financed projects had given them a head start in raising capital and judging risk. This approach relieved—but did not eliminate—concerns about inadequate information. Nor did private investment and local capital reduce the government's involvement or the need for foreign borrowing.

All too often, however, government intervention simply replaced one set of problems with another. Investors, assured of a guaranteed return, had less incentive to hold management accountable. Management, freed of investor scrutiny and provided with access to capital markets, courtesy of the government, arranged deals with construction companies that left taxpayers holding the bag. Guaranteed loans encouraged investors to finance infrastructure projects, but without built-in mechanisms to monitor spending and protect the public interest, it was impossible to ensure that resources were allocated efficiently.

These failings imply that exploiting nontraditional approaches to financing infrastructure requires two further policy initiatives. First, efforts should be made to enhance the effectiveness of public administration. Government agencies or departments should be responsible for monitoring the efficiency and performance of the enterprise and should be backed by a credible threat of sanctions against managers who are tempted to enrich themselves. Second, policymakers need to encourage the development of financial institutions and instruments such as banks, mutual funds, and bond-rating agencies that can surmount information problems and relieve the government of the need to provide subsidies and interest guarantees.[10]

---

10. The case for subsidization may only be reduced, rather than eliminated, insofar as infrastructure investments continue to throw off positive externalities that private agents cannot internalize fully. This distinguishes the problem of financing infrastructure investments from general problems of financing enterprises in developing countries.

These are essential tasks for governments in any setting. Idealistic strategies for privatizing the provision of infrastructure notwithstanding, it seems likely that government's traditional role—and the traditional problems associated with government intervention—will necessarily remain.

Acknowledgments. The author would like to thank Ashoka Mody for guidance, Ann Carlos, Michael Edelstein, Frank Lewis, Richard Sylla, and Mira Wilkins for comments, and Lisa Ortiz and Andrea Cu for research assistance. This chapter first appeared in the *World Bank Research Observer* 10(1): 75–91

Bibliography

Adler, Dorothy. 1970. *British Investment in American Railways, 1834–1838.* Charlottesville: University of Virginia Press.

Akerlof, George, and Paul Romer. 1993. "Looting: The Economic Underworld of Bankruptcy for Profit." *Brookings Papers on Economic Activity* 2: 1–73.

Ankli, Robert E. 1980. "The Growth of the Canadian Economy," 1896–1920. *Explorations in Economic History* 17: 251–74.

Balough, Thomas. 1947. *Studies in Financial Organization.* Cambridge, U.K.: Cambridge University Press.

Baskin, Jonathan B. 1988. "The Development of Corporate Financial Markets in Britain and the United States, 1600–1914: Overcoming Asymmetric Information." *Business History Review* 62: 199–237.

Bryant, Keith L. 1971. *Arthur E. Stilwell.* Nashville: Vanderbilt University Press.

Buckley, K. A. H. 1955. *Capital Formation in Canada 1896–1930.* Toronto: University of Toronto Press.

Carlos, Ann M., and Frank D. Lewis. 1992. "The Profitability of Early Canadian Railroads: Evidence from the Grand Trunk and Great Western Railway Companies" in Claudia Goldin and Hugh Rockoff, eds., *Strategic Factors in Nineteenth Century American Economic History.* Chicago: University of Chicago Press.

_____. Forthcoming. "Foreign Financing of Canadian Railroads: The Role of Information" in Michael D. Bordo and Richard Sylla, eds., *Anglo-American Financial Systems: Institutions and Markets in the Twentieth-Century.* Burr Ridge: Irwin.

Chandler, Alfred. 1954. "Patterns of American Railroad Finance." *Business History Review* 28: 248–63.

_____. 1990. *Scale and Scope.* Cambridge: Harvard University Press.

Cleveland, Frederick A., and Fred Wilbur Powell. 1912. *Railroad Finance.* New York: D. Appleton.

Cranmer, H. Jerome. 1960. "Canal Investment, 1815–1861" in *Trends in the American Economy in the 19th Century.* Princeton: Princeton University Press for the National Bureau of Economic Research.

Currie, A. W. 1957. *The Grand Trunk Railway of Canada.* Toronto: University of Toronto Press.

De Meza, David, and David C. Webb. 1987. "Too Much Investment: A Problem of Asymmetric Information." *Quarterly Journal of Economics* 102: 281–91.

Easterbrook, W. T., and G. J. Aitken. 1956. *Canadian Economic History.* Toronto: University of Toronto Press.

Eichengreen, Barry, and Richard Fortes. 1989. "After the Deluge: Default, Negotiation, and Readjustment on Defaulted Foreign Bonds during the Interwar Years" in Barry Eichengreen and Peter Lindert, eds., *The International Debt Crisis in Historical Perspective.* Cambridge: The MIT Press.

Fishlow, Albert. 1965. *American Railroads and the Transformation of the Antebellum Economy.* Cambridge: Harvard University Press.

_____. 1986. "Lessons from the Past: Capital Markets and Foreign Lending During the 19th Century and the Interwar Period" in Miles Kahler, ed., *The Politics of International Debt.* Ithaca: Cornell University Press.

Fogel, Robert. 1960. *The Union Pacific Railroad: A Case of Premature Enterprise.* Baltimore: Johns Hopkins University Press.

_____. 1964. *Railroads and American Economic Growth.* Baltimore: Johns Hopkins University Press.

Glazebrook, G. P. 1938. *A History of Transportation in Canada.* Toronto: McClelland and Stewart.

Jenks, Leland J. 1938. *The Migration of British Capital to 1875.* New York: Knopf.

_____. 1944. "Railroads as an Economic Force in American Development." *Journal of Economic History* 4:1–20.

Jensen, Michael C., and William H. Meckling. 1976. "Theory of the Firm: Managerial Behavior, Agency Costs and Ownership Structure." *Journal of Financial Economics* 3: 305-60.

Johnson, Arthur H., and Barry E. Supple. 1967. *Boston Capitalists and Western Railways.* Cambridge: Harvard University Press.

Keeton, William. 1979. *Equilibrium Credit Rationing.* New York: Garland Press.

Lamoreaux, Naomi. 1986. "Banks, Kinship, and Economic Development: The New England Case." *Journal of Economic History* 46: 647–68.

Lewis, Cleona. 1938. *America's Stake in International Investments.* Washington, D.C.: The Brookings Institution.

Lewis, Frank, and Mary McKinnon. 1987. "Government Loan Guarantees and the Failure of the Canadian Northern Railway." *Journal of Economic History* 47: 175–96.

MacPherson, W. J. 1955. "Investment in Indian Railways, 1845–1875." *Economic History Review* 8: 177–86.

Mercer, Lloyd. 1969. "Land Grants to American Railroads: Social Cost or Social Benefit?" *Business History Review* 43: 134–51.

_____. 1972. "Taxpayers or Investors: Who Paid for the Land Grant Railroads?" *Business History Review* 46: 279–94.

Paish, F. W. 1951. "The London New Issue Market." *Economica* 18: 117.

Platt, D. C. M. 1984. *Foreign Finance in Continental Europe and the United States 1815–1870.* London: Allen & Unwin.

Stiglitz, Joseph, and Andrew Weiss. 1981. "Credit Rationing in Markets with Imperfect Information." *American Economic Review* 71: 393–410.

Wilkins, Mira. 1989. *The History of Foreign Investment in the United States to 1914.* Cambridge: Harvard University Press.

Williamson, Jeffrey G. 1974. *Late Nineteenth-Century Economic Development: A General Equilibrium Approach.* New York: Cambridge University Press.

5

The Public Finance of Infrastructure: Issues and Options

Vinaya Swaroop

This chapter analyzes the role of government as the provider of infrastructure. Using economic principles, it provides criteria for financing infrastructure services where consumption-related user charges can be effectively levied. In light of the suggested criteria it examines the experience of developing countries in financing the publicly provided infrastructure services in transport (road), water, telecommunications, and power sectors. The paper draws lessons on where the "optimal" financing rules need to be modified in light of this experience.

What is the rationale for public provision of infrastructure services? How have technological developments changed the role of government as provider of these services over time? How should the publicly provided infrastructure services be financed? In taking on these questions, examples from a few developing countries prove useful. Beginning with a brief analysis of the role of government as the provider of infrastructure, this chapter then develops a framework using economic principles to assess government's role in financing infrastructure services. In light of this framework, the chapter reviews the experience of developing countries in financing road transport, water, telecommunications, and power sectors and concludes that the principles have rarely been applied, causing a large drain on public funds.

Public Provision of Infrastructure Services

Private sector production of goods and services crucially depends on an adequate, well-maintained and efficient infrastructure of roads, electricity, telecommunications, water, waste disposal, and other similar facilities.[1] Electricity and water are essential to the production process. Transport and communications enhance the mobility of goods and services, and sanitary services are needed for waste disposal.

An important rationale for public provision of (or intervention in) infrastructure activities is economies of scale in production. The production and distribution of water, for example, may allow for substantial decreases in average cost when the scale of production increases. In telecommunications, transport, and power, fixed costs are high because these sectors require a few large investments. Once the systems are set up, output can be increased at declining average cost until the capacity limit becomes binding. Therefore, such cases suggest a monopoly of production. And the easiest monopoly to regulate is a public one. Another rationale for public provision may be nonexclusively and/or metering costs. These present a second set of problems for technology to overcome.

An unregulated private monopolist providing infrastructure services would charge monopoly prices (often based on cost overrun) to maximize profits. These monopoly prices are not only inequitable, but they usually decrease efficiency when compared with outcomes in the competitive market. Thus, government emerges as a producer that is relatively easy to monitor. In many cases, however, the government does not produce the services but regulates the sector's prices and market entry. Infrastructure services such as electric power, telecommunications, transportation, and water and gas are either publicly provided or regulated (if privately produced), under the assumption that the government as producer or regulator will maximize social welfare.

Technological advancements over the years, however, have gradually reduced the need for a single supplier in many of these services and have created conditions for competition. For example, in telecommunications new technologies such as cable-based telephone access, cellular radio, and

---

1. Evidence on the link between infrastructure and economic growth, however, remains sketchy. There is a lack of empirical consensus regarding the magnitude and the direction of the effect. The size of infrastructure, the efficiency of provision, and the appropriate public-private balance in its provision appear to be the major issues of contention. See Barro (1991), Easterly and Rebelo (1993), and Devarajan, Swaroop, and Zou (forthcoming).

direct microwave links to local or long-distance switching nodes have reduced the natural monopoly of the industry. Local telephone exchange service still justifies a single supplier because unit costs typically fall over a large range as capacity increases. But new microwave technology and satellites in the interexchange markets have made it possible for several different providers to transmit calls on many routes without significantly reducing unit costs, thereby increasing the potential for competition.

Similarly, while electricity transmission and distribution continue to justify a single supplier, competition can now be introduced for power generation because advanced steam-driven turbines and combined-cycle technologies have reduced the scale economies. Some developing countries are now encouraging the private sector to construct and operate power plants through build-operate-transfer (BOT) or build-own-operate (BOO) schemes. Further, to increase choice and competition in transport and water supply, some countries enhance efficiency by contracting services for operations and maintenance.

The bulk of the service provision in developing countries continues to be in the public domain, even though the private sector has been playing an increasing role in recent years. First, with a few exceptions, electric power continues to be provided by a single, publicly owned utility. In the Philippines, for example, while power distribution is largely handled by the private sector, the National Power Corporation accounts for the bulk of power generation and transmission. Second, in the telecommunications sector of most developing countries the main institutional feature (as in Brazil) is a network operated by a protected state monopolist. Domestic private enterprises provide telecommunications equipment and act as contractors for some projects. Third, water and sewerage services are still largely centralized in the government hands. In Indonesia they are jointly managed by the central and local governments. In Swaziland, the Water and Sewerage Board undertakes all transactions relating to the management, operation, maintenance, and development of public water supplies and water-borne sewerage facilities. Fourth, in the road sector, schemes range from the use of private contractors to collect bridge tolls (as in Pakistan) to BOT schemes where the private sector builds and operates a toll road (as in Malaysia and Thailand) while management and provision of roads remains essentially with the government.

Although future technological developments will continue to open up markets for competition and further reduce the public sector's share of infrastructure services, any amount of publicly provided service must be kept efficient. Here the role of financing is critical.

Principles of Public Finance of Infrastructure

How should publicly provided infrastructure of roads, telecommunications, power, water systems, and other similar services be financed to ensure adequate, continuous, and efficient provision? Should such public enterprises be required to have full cost recovery?[2] Alternatively, should there be a flexible approach to cost recovery that incorporates efficiency and fiscal and distributional considerations? What is the role of borrowing in infrastructure finance? Should revenues generated from a sector be linked to its expenditures?

Cost Recovery

Given that most of these services are provided at the local level and can be subject to user charges, the cost should arguably be recovered from the beneficiaries. Fairness based on the benefit principle requires consumers of a publicly provided service to pay for it, especially when user charges can be effectively levied. User charges can be levied in proportion to actual consumption, and when it is difficult to measure individual consumption (say due to high metering costs), a benefit-related betterment levy can be designed to recover the cost of infrastructure development.

Production of infrastructure services is typically characterized by decreasing cost in the long-run, which implies that average cost falls as production is increased up to a level often referred to as the minimum efficient scale. Beyond that point, cost per unit is roughly constant until the capacity constraint becomes binding. The principle of marginal cost pricing, also known as efficient pricing, is used to price many infrastructure services.[3] While a financing plan based on short-run marginal cost (SRMC) pricing would imply efficient allocation of resources, there are a few drawbacks.

---

2.   If such a service were to be provided by a regulated private monopolist there would need to be at least a zero, if not positive, profit constraint; otherwise there would not be private provision of these services without subsidy.

3.   The efficient production argument in this context, however, needs qualification. In the absence of a pure profit motive for these public (or regulated private monopoly) enterprises, some amount of freedom is introduced in the choice of production method. The marginal cost pricing argument implicitly assumes that the chosen output combination will be produced at minimum cost. This is true in profit maximizing situations. In regulated enterprises, however, there may be very little incentive for the managers to minimize costs, possibly leading to an inefficient operation. Effective regulatory supervision and internal controls are needed to ensure that infrastructure enterprises produce at minimum cost.

First, this policy could lead to price volatility. For example, if electric utility rates were strictly tied to SRMC, they would be quite volatile.[4] Second, it would most likely be insufficient to cover total costs. In the road sector, for instance, it is unlikely that the pricing principle based on SRMC (usually defined as variable road maintenance, traffic congestion, and pollution costs) will generate enough revenue to cover total costs.[5]

In a study of road sector charges in Tunisia, Heggie and Fon (1990) found that nearly 45 percent of the total costs were fixed. Similarly, tele-communications, power, and water systems periodically require large in-vestments and this often results in marginal cost being lower than average cost for a small scale of output. In such cases user charges based on SRMC pricing would result in deficits and, therefore, budgetary transfers would be required to subsidize the enterprise. Any tax revenue the government needs to collect—to either make up a deficit resulting from a marginal cost pricing arrangement or for any other purpose—involves some price dis-tortion somewhere in the economy.[6]

In place of SRMC, long-run marginal cost (LRMC) has been suggested as the logical surrogate for marginal cost as it provides a more stable ap-proximation of marginal cost. A more practical measure of cost, LRMC is defined as the cost of producing an extra unit when capacity adjustments can be made over time. Using LRMC, a well-managed public enterprise in most cases should be able to cover all of its operating expenses and debt service and still contribute substantially to its investment program.

In some cases, a two-part tariff can be designed that is based on effi-cient prices and yet covers total cost. The simplest version of such a tariff scheme involves charging the users a constant price per unit—purchased equal to the SRMC and a fixed annual access charge—to buy any positive amount of the service (Feldstein 1972). The total cost of the enterprise is thus recovered by a nondistortionary lump sum access charge on the us-ers, who are then induced to consume in efficient quantities. The pursuit of marginal cost pricing via a two-part tariff, however, is an imperfect solu-tion for two main reasons: first, the resulting allocation of resources is eco-nomically efficient only if the fixed charge does not cause any potential

---

4.   Though in principle, contacts-for-differences can be used to control volatility.

5.   Few exceptions exist, especially in urban areas where roads are extremely congested.

6.   This argument assumes that nondistortionary lump sum taxes are unavail-able.

consumers to drop out of the market and refuse the service; and second, it is appropriate only if distribution considerations are unimportant, because the fixed part of the tariff is essentially a regressive head tax.

Electricity provision in the white municipalities in South Africa illustrates that this financing principle can be successful when distributional issues are not of concern (Swaroop 1993). Roodeport, a white municipality located in the Central Witwaterstand Region, purchases electricity in bulk from Eskom (South Africa's national electric utility) and distributes it to customers. Each year at budget time tariff rates on electricity are determined based on projected expenditures. The structure of the tariff is based on the following charges: a connection charge based on actual cost of connection, a basic charge designed as a fixed monthly charge to recover capital costs (both principal repayment and interest), and a per-unit consumption charge that is closely related to marginal cost. There are no *poor* in Roodeport who cannot pay the regular rates for electricity, therefore the tariff has no equity features.[7] Electricity provides the most revenue for the municipality, and any surplus generated in the process is used to subsidize other municipal services.

In many developing countries, however, the distributional aspect of infrastructure finance is an important policy consideration. A two-part tariff mechanism that is based on efficiency prices and that covers total cost is likely to conflict with social objectives. Not only is the fixed part of the tariff regressive and thus insensitive to the needs of the poor, but social concerns also make it necessary to apply a *lifeline charge* for services such as water and electricity. This allows a subsidized charge up to a threshold amount (generally considered a minimum) with charges at marginal cost thereafter. A financing plan based on efficiency prices that adjusts for equitable coverage (for example, the lifeline charges) would almost certainly require subsidies to cover total costs. The interesting issue then becomes whether these funds should be generated by a mark-up over marginal cost— a second-best pricing rule—or through general tax revenues.

If economic efficiency is the criterion, then the decision on self-financing of the sector should be based on the costs (both administrative and efficiency) of raising the marginal unit of revenue from each of these sources. It is estimated that the efficiency cost of a 1 percent increase in all existing tax rates in the United States in the early 1980s would have been between 17 and 56 cents for each dollar of extra revenue raised (Ballard, Shoven,

---

7.   In the new structure of local government in South Africa, it is expected that equity features would be part of the user charge mechanism.

and Whalley 1985). Although reliable estimates for developing countries are rare, the cost of mobilizing extra tax revenue is likely to be significantly higher for developing countries because they have narrower tax bases and weaker tax administrations than developed countries. This situation suggests that public enterprises in developing countries—water, electricity, highway authorities, and telecommunication systems—should not be subsidized by budgetary sources and should be required to cover a major portion of costs, if not the total, through charges on beneficiaries. The equity features should be carefully designed and properly targeted.

Borrowing

Expansion or asset replacement in sectors such as power, telecommunication, and irrigation requires periodic large investments (Pyle: chapter 7). Often this results in temporary increases in the spending of infrastructure enterprises. According to economic theory it is more efficient to finance a temporary increase in spending by borrowing (after funds have been exhausted from retained earnings) than to increase the charges. Charges over time should be designed to include not only interest payments but also depreciation. Such a financing scheme allows the enterprise to carry a cash surplus over the sum required to meet the debt repayment installment. This cash surplus can be used to smooth the investment cost when expansion is needed or assets need replacement.

Earmarking

When should an infrastructure financing policy include earmarking of funds? Say the telecommunications sector is a net contributor to the treasury. Should a portion of this sector's revenue be earmarked to cover expansion? Similarly, should a percentage of the municipal government revenue obtained from taxing the ownership and use of motor vehicles (for example, license fees, fuel, and vehicle purchase charges) be earmarked for road sector spending? Economic theory says that if economic growth is the objective of the government, the marginal unit of public revenue should be allocated to finance items that yield the highest economic rates of return.

In light of this principle, earmarking is not an efficient expenditure allocation policy. In practice, however, countries do not always allocate expenditure according to this principle even when economic growth is their principal objective. Particularly during fiscal crisis, developing countries often cut expenditures on nonwage operations and maintenance, which usually have high rates of return, instead of reducing the public sector wage bill. In the Philippines, the poor state of infrastructure maintenance—deteriorating roads, bridges, ports, and public facilities, and a number of power plant breakdowns—shows the overall decline in real terms in nonwage operations and maintenance expenditures in the early 1980s (since the fiscal adjustment program). Similarly, in Côte d'Ivoire, while the proportion of the budget devoted to the wage bill was substantially higher during 1981-86 than in 1975-80, the share devoted to nonwage operations and maintenance fell from 28 to 19 percent (Pradhan and Swaroop 1993). This pattern of expenditure restructuring results mainly because a reduction in funding operations and maintenance expenditures has a lower set of political costs than a reduction in the public sector wage bill. In such situations, earmarking can help preserve critical expenditures and bridge the gap between economic benefits and political indifference. Thus, while there is no unique prescription for earmarking, funds generally could be earmarked for expenditure items that are associated with high economic rates of return. Experience from developing countries suggests that funds could be earmarked for spending on operations and maintenance in general and on the maintenance of roads and irrigation and drainage systems in particular. The Road Fund in Tanzania is a good example of earmarking funds for road maintenance.

While earmarking gives some assurance of continuous funding, it is by no means a guarantee. In tight fiscal situations governments often divert earmarked revenues to cover other needs. For example, since 1973 the government of Brazil has been earmarking a portion of telecommunications revenue into the National Telecommunications Fund to support telecommunications expansion into the country's less profitable, poorer regions. The telecommunications sector is highly profitable and pays a corporate income tax. Due to the country's macroeconomic crisis since the late 1970s, part of these earmarked revenues has been diverted to finance other governmental activities. Although this diversion of funds has deprived the telecommunications sector of valuable resources and has affected its investment program, the action can be justified if the resources are allocated to higher priority activities or to areas with a higher rate of return.

Based on the principles discussed above, the following framework could be used for financing infrastructure services when consumption-related charges can be effectively levied. Pricing for efficient provision of infrastructure services involves several elements:

- Before devising a financing plan it is important to ensure that infrastructure services are produced efficiently. The cost of provision should be kept at a minimum, and the regulatory system should be able to effectively counter any supply inefficiencies.
- In general, user charges should be flexible enough to provide a balance among efficiency, distributional equity, and cost recovery objectives. Such a balance of objectives is likely to vary from sector to sector.
- An optimal revenue generation policy requires that the costs (administrative and efficiency) of raising the marginal unit of revenue be equal through each fiscal instrument. If the financing plan based on efficiency prices with adjustments made for distributional considerations cannot cover total costs of the infrastructure enterprises, the cost of raising additional tax revenues should be compared with the cost of increasing prices above marginal cost.
- The experience of developing countries suggests that public enterprises such as highway authorities, electricity, telecommunications, and water systems should be required to cover a major portion of costs, if not the total.
- Full cost recovery in itself is not an indicator of successful financing policy, especially if key expenditure items have been reduced.
- The equity features of the charging system should properly target the intended beneficiaries.
- User charges should be designed to include operations, maintenance, depreciation and interest payments. Given the nature of economic infrastructure investment needs, funds could be borrowed at market rates to finance capital expenditures.
- Whether infrastructure enterprises should be subject to income taxes and whether services such as telecommunications and electricity should be included in a broad-based tax on goods and services are issues that are difficult to generalize. After a careful examination of each country's tax system, these issues should be decided as part of the country's tax reform process.
- Earmarking of funds should be restricted to expenditure items that are generally associated with high rates of return, are politically less visible, and are likely to be cut during tight fiscal periods.

Infrastructure Services Sap Public Funds

In most developing countries public enterprises such as highway authorities, electricity, water, and telecommunication systems are expected to operate commercially without financial support from the government. Except for telecommunication services, this practice is generally the exception rather than the rule. Low and improperly designed user charges, infrequent inflation adjustments, and poor enforcement often lead to major revenue shortfalls, with the resulting budgetary transfers increasing the overall fiscal deficit of the government.

Road Transport

In many Sub-Saharan African countries the public enterprise deficits are often the primary source of general fiscal budget deficits. In Zambia, for example, the budgetary transfers to the transport sector in fiscal 1991 exceeded *K* five billion (nearly $100 million), roughly equivalent to 12 percent of the government's total current revenues. Three public sector agencies—roads, railways, and the airline—were responsible for the majority of this financial drain. In the road sub-sector the shortage of finance was caused mainly by road users paying negligible sums for the use of the road network. License fees had not kept up with inflation and were low by regional standards, and fuel had only a standard excise designed as a general tax, with no explicit user fee added to the price. The specific road user charges—mainly license fees, transit fees paid by foreign vehicles, and road tolls—only financed 10 percent of total expenditures on roads. In fact, the road subsector budget has been in deficit during the entire 1980s. The transport sector in Tanzania was plagued with similar problems. In 1986-87, it showed a deficit of Tanzania Schilling 2,405 million (over $46 million), or roughly 7.3 percent of the government's current revenues. In both Zambia and Tanzania, the transport sector would have required even more transfers from the government had the allocations for road maintenance not been woefully low.

In Indonesia, the total revenue gained by government from road users—import duties on vehicles and parts, indirect taxes on vehicles, parts, and fuel—and from provincial governments' fees for vehicle registration and ownership transfer—has been in line with spending on the public road network in recent years (Swaroop 1991). However, it is unclear whether all the indirect taxes levied were designed to recover the costs of road usage. Some of these taxes, such as value added tax, import duties, and luxury import tax, are levied to generate revenue to support overall government expenditure plans or as part of its trade and industrial policies. Until the two functions of the taxes are clearly defined, it is unclear what part of them is the price of road use. Charges related to vehicle usage (charges added to the fuel tax, tolls, and weight distance charges) and vehicle ownership (vehicle licenses, registration fees, vehicle inspection fees, and vehicle transfer tax) can be defined as road-specific user charges.

In Indonesia, the current structure of annual vehicle registration tax is based on vehicle type, age, and engine capacity. Not only is the level of the annual registration tax low, but the amount charged does not reflect the road-damaging power of the vehicles. The vehicle ownership transfer tax is applied at a rate of 10 percent for new vehicle sales and 5 percent for subsequent ownership transfers. There is a widespread evasion of this tax for second and subsequent transfers of ownership. Clearly, these provisions prevent efficient use of roads by sending the wrong signals to commercial vehicle owners, who in turn make decisions that increase the cost to society.

It is useful to repeat that recovering full cost and contributing to general revenue alone does not indicate a successful financing policy for the sector. This is especially true if key expenditure items have been reduced. For example, the deterioration of road infrastructure in the Philippines has been caused in large part by the decline in road expenditures in real terms, especially for maintenance, during the 1980s. Revenue raised from user charges, however, has more than offset road expenditures during this period; in fact, the road sector has consistently made significant net contributions to the general budget.

In a study of eight developing countries, Heggie (1991) found that road user charges were significantly lower than total expenditures on roads and in some cases were even lower than recurrent expenditures on roads (table 5.1).

Water

IRRIGATION. In many developing countries irrigation charges are so low and collection attempts to collect them so feeble that cost recovery has fallen far short of even modest targets such as recovery of operations maintenance costs. Charges do not reflect the cost of production, consumption increases beyond the optimum level, and the subsidies disproportionately serve the better-off. While total cost recovery for an irrigation district of any size is virtually without precedent, it is even difficult to find cases where irrigation charges even recover operating and maintenance expenses. For example, irrigation charges in India recover roughly 8 percent of operations and maintenance costs; in Bangladesh the range is 10 to 15 percent; in Indonesia it is 8 to 10 percent; in Pakistan between 40 and 50 percent; and in Mexico and in the Philippines it is nearly 80 percent. Consequently, public

Table 5.1. *Road User Taxes and Charges*
(local currencies at current prices)

Country	Overall government tax revenue	Road sector revenue/spending				
		Total taxes	General taxes (percentage of total taxes)	Road user charges (percentage of total taxes)	Total road spending [recurrent]	Ratio of charges to spending [percent]
Argentina 1987 (austral, millions)	29,584	2,922 [a]	81	19	1,209 [a] [...]	47 [...]
Bangladesh 1984/85 (taka, millions)	32,900	1,600	75	25	2,088 [416]	19 [96]
Bolivia 1987 (bolivianos, millions)	613	177	79	21	141 [23]	26 [161]
China 1986 (yuan, billions)	244	11	0	100	9 [2]	119 [470]
Indonesia 1987/88 (rupiah, billions)	25,308	1,495 [b]	44	56	1,707 [b] [1,128]	49 [75]
Mexico 1988 (pesos, billions)	69,214	7,158 [a]	39	5	831 [a] [307]	42 [113]
Tanzania 1985/86 (shilling, millions)	19,776	2,016	88	12	1,267 [672]	19 [35]
Turkey 1983 (lira, millions)	1,938	268	13	94	115 [43]	217 [584]

... Not available.

a. Central government only.

b. Central, provincial and local government road user charges have been separated from the total revenue of the road sector by crediting the user charge with any taxes that were higher than those of similar groups in the tax structure: fuel taxes were ignored unless fuel prices were higher than border prices.

Source: Heggie (1991).

irrigation schemes have become an enormous drain on government budgets, depriving other sectors (where user charges are infeasible) of budgetary resources.[8] Evidence indicates that these subsidies do not even serve the purpose of distributional equity, because they are granted mostly to better-off farmers (Repetto 1986).

This pattern of financing has created a vicious cycle: financial difficulties cause irrigation departments to defer maintenance (or allocate insufficient funds for maintenance) to the detriment of the water system, while farmers complain about the poor services and have little incentive to pay for it. This cycle occurs despite the fact that most irrigation departments in developing countries have a mandate to recover operations and maintenance costs and at least part of the capital cost. India's National Water Policy of 1987, for example, clearly stipulates that charges on water should be designed to cover the annual operations and maintenance charges and a part of the fixed costs. Yet, revenues from irrigation charges were enough to recover only 7.5 percent of operations and maintenance expenditures in 1988-89 (down from 22 percent in 1980-81).

During the 1980s, revenues from water charges increased by 29 percent in real terms, while operations and maintenance expenditures increased by 280 percent during the same period. A number of supply inefficiencies exist in the service, but the slow growth of revenue from water charges has largely been due to infrequent revision in the rates (resulting in substantial erosion over time in real values) and to poor collection rates.[9] Water charges have not been revised since the mid-1980s in most states and not since the mid-1970s in the states of Punjab, Haryana, Tamil Nadu, and West Bengal. The low rates and poor collection are mainly caused by politicians who succumb to the intense farmer lobbying and continue to favor subsidies. Attempts to revise water rates are often aborted and amnesty for nonpayment of charges are frequent. Studies of India have shown that even if irrigation charges are raised to cover operations and maintenance and at least

---

8.   In examining the financial sustainability of irrigation schemes, one argument is to include irrigation sector-based revenues stemming from nonwater charge sources (such as direct taxation of irrigated farmers). Such taxes, however, are designed as part of the general revenue taxes to be used for government services, which are mainly public goods.

9.   The steep rise in operations and maintenance expenditures primarily resulted from growth in irrigation department wage bills burgeoning staff members. In the state of Bihar, establishment (personnel) costs increased by 148 percent in just four years (1980–81 to 1984–85), while expenditures on maintenance of water systems declined slightly. This pattern of expenditure does not produce the services efficiently.

25 percent of capital costs, the value of water delivered to farmers would still far exceed the fee they pay for it (Bhatia 1989).

Irrigation agencies in Pakistan suffer from a similar fate. In the not too distant past, part of the capital costs of irrigation development were recovered from users in Pakistan. Revenue receipts were higher than total operations and maintenance expenditures by 13 and 25 percent in 1972–73 and 1973–74, respectively. In recent years, however, cost recovery has lapsed mainly because of inadequate increases in water charges. The cost recovery was 56 percent in fiscal 1992 and would fall to 43 percent if actual operations and maintenance expenditures were replaced by more realistic operations and maintenance requirements. The irrigation and drainage systems are now in dire straits due to scarce maintenance funds. Current water charges are only 5 percent of farm income. It is estimated that full recovery of current operations and maintenance charges would require a doubling of the water rates, which would amount to less than 10 percent of farm income (Mulk and Mohtadullah 1992).

In Indonesia, public irrigation facilities supply over 80 percent of the total irrigated area. Irrigation water supply—a main agriculture support service provided to farmers—has substantially drained public resources. Although indirect cost recovery exists in the form of a small land tax, farmers are not required to pay directly for irrigation facilities. The estimated total subsidy for irrigation water during the country's fourth five-year plan (1984–89) was Rupiah 4.8 trillion, an amount that even exceeded the subsidy for fertilizer (Varley 1989). Realizing this concern, the government has instituted a pilot irrigation service fee related to cropping patterns and systems in a few provinces to improve operations and maintenance. The starting level of the irrigation service fees is at least 50 percent of the estimated operations and maintenance requirements. As part of the reform process, farmers are also being asked to provide labor services and pay water association user fees.

There is evidence that cost recovery is higher with institutional arrangements that gives users control over irrigation distribution systems. Farmers can control water distribution in these arrangements and reduce the risk of supply shortages at critical growing periods. Such service increases the farmers' willingness to pay for water. In the Philippines, farmers participate in communal programs by operating the irrigation distribution facilities. As part of the Irrigation Associations they are also responsible for maintaining the water systems and collecting the irrigation service fee. Cost recovery as a percentage of operations and maintenance expenditures averaged 80 percent in the 1979–89 period. Relatively high cost-recovery rates for operations and maintenance and capital costs are also captured in the United States, particularly in districts where local irrigation associations own and operate water distribution facilities.

WATER FOR NONAGRICULTURAL USE. The Water and Sewerage Board in urban Swaziland provides treated water to over 80 percent of the urban population and manages four major sewerage schemes that serve 25 percent. The board is expected to operate on a commercial and self-financed basis, but it has been experiencing financial difficulties since mid-1985—due to inadequate tariff adjustment and poor collection—and has relied on government budgetary transfers. Estimates suggest that if the board improves its billing and collection procedures and gets an adequate tariff increase, it will recover its operating expenses and will contribute a significant portion of capital expenditure.

The water supply system in the urban areas of Nigeria has almost completely broken down. Safe water supply is limited to 50 percent of the urban population (an even smaller segment of the population has access to sanitation facilities). It is extremely inefficient (almost half the water output unaccounted for in some areas), and the cost of service is high. Due to low levels of water tariffs, most water authorities depend on federal and state subventions for part of their operating costs and practically all their debt service charges. Since the government transfers have been limited, maintenance is poor, investments are few, and the debt of water authorities increases.

In such cases, partial reforms will not suffice. For example, a rate increase in water tariffs alone would be met with strong opposition from consumers—as demonstrated by recent experience. Such cases require a complete restructuring of the system along the fundamentals of water provision and financing. The objectives of the reform process should give enhanced autonomy to water agencies for staffing and salaries and for periodic tariff adjustment (with appropriate regulatory supervision). If water agencies are permitted to devise a tariff system they could recover operating costs, depreciation charges, and interest payments, and that would enable them to partially self-finance future capital equipment. In turn, they would be able to provide better service. In addition, the option of private sector management of water agencies should also be explored.

Côte d'Ivoire's urban water supply exemplifies an efficient infrastructure service. Sodeci, a private company, has supplied piped water to urban areas for the past 30 years. By operating the state-owned water supply systems within the framework of a lease contract, the company has achieved full cost recovery (user charges cover capital costs and operations and maintenance) for many years. Moreover, Sodeci has paid taxes to the government since its inception and has paid dividends to its shareholders. The water connection ratio in 1992 was 70 percent and increasing, with unaccounted water lower than 15 percent in the last 15 years—a level of service close to Western standards. The efficiency of service in Côte d'Ivoire is further illustrated by the average water tariff being equal to those in neighboring countries where the level of service is lower and full cost recovery is not achieved.

Telecommunications

In developing countries, telecommunications is perhaps the only publicly provided infrastructure service that is profitable (Bishop, Mody, and Schankerman: chapter 2). The sector is a net contributor to the treasury. Unlike electricity and water services, residential telephone service is essentially a luxury in developing countries, so lifeline rates or similar subsidy schemes are unnecessary. With little justification for political intervention, tariff rates are often set at a level that allows both full cost recovery and a significant contribution to general fiscal revenue. Although telecommunications is highly profitable in developing countries, quality and efficient service is far from guaranteed. The Indonesian telecommunication sector and particularly its telephone service, TELEKOM, is one example.

Indonesia's telephone density of roughly 0.5 percent is the lowest among the Association of Southeast Asian Nations. The network remains inadequate, with significant unmet demand, congestion, and high rates of call failure and fault incidence. While the tariff policy of TELEKOM is properly geared towards efficient demand management and more rapid network development, supply efficiency needs improvement. Raising productivity and reducing production costs would improve efficiency and financial performance, enabling the agency to raise its own contribution to an expanded investment program.

Appropriate tariff policy has allowed TELEKOM to achieve full cost recovery and also self-finance a sizable part of its investment program. At the same time, TELEKOM has been making a notable net contribution to the public treasury through income tax payments (it is subject to a 35 percent corporate income tax) and dividends on government equity. Fifty-five percent of its net of tax income goes to the Government of Indonesia Development Fund that is used to finance other governmental activities (Swaroop 1991).

A similar story emerges from Brazil where, despite problems in the quality of service (relative to other comparable countries) and structural inefficiencies in the tariff system, the national telecommunications company, TELEBRAS, has been one of the strongest of all Brazilian state-owned companies. In size and profitability, it is second only to PETROBRAS, the national oil company (Hobday 1991). TELEBRAS financed its substantial expansion in the late-1970s largely from its own funds, and it has been a net contributor to the treasury. Despite its high profitability, service provision needs improvement. A high policy priority is rebalancing the structure of tariffs to improve service quality and to generate funds for capital investment.

Electric Power

The power sector is heavily capital intensive and in most developing countries it requires by far the most resources. Lack of appropriate new investment and inefficient use of existing facilities in the power sector can have a ripple effect on the economy in terms of low productivity, lost sales, and income erosion, as illustrated in the Philippines (Pradhan and Swaroop 1993). The National Power Corporation, the country's source of power generation and transmission, has received the most funds under the public investment program, but service and maintenance have been poor. No new power plants were completed during 1986-92, despite an approximate 10 percent per year increase in demand.

The corporation has also paid inadequate attention to operations and maintenance of its existing facilities, causing reduced plant availability and premature plant aging. As a result, power shortages and frequent brownouts (load-shedding) have taken a toll on the country's commercial and industrial activities. While fiscal constraints have limited the government's capacity to make new investments in the power sector, insufficient levels and inadequate structuring of tariffs have been the main reasons for the National Power Corporation's lack of spending on operations and maintenance for existing facilities. The corporation has not been earning enough cash to finance its investments in recent years (something a well-managed power utility generally can do), but a new set of tariffs recently approved by the government will likely improve the corporation's finances.

Financial performance of a utility could be misleading if financial cost understates economic cost. For example, until recently, Perum Listrik Negara (PLN)—a single, publicly owned electric utility in Indonesia—was able to generate enough revenue to meet its operating costs and finance part of its investment program (Swaroop 1991). One reason why PLN was able to achieve its financial targets was the substantial below-market financing it received from the government for all of its borrowing. Further,

PLN was getting large production facilities as equity to promote region-ally balanced development (basically a social objective) without having to pay any dividends to the government. These provisions understated the true cost of capital. While PLN's borrowing has been at market rates for the last three years, there is still little transparency in the flow of subsidies designed to promote regional development. What is needed is compensa-tion on a transparent basis for any losses incurred by PLN for meeting the government's social objectives.

Often the sector's investment requirements are so high that the re-sources needed exceed the aggregate of the sector's capacity to generate cash from its operations and the government's capacity to finance from budgetary allocations. To cope with such situations, long-term debt instru-ments are needed with terms appropriate for the long construction and payback periods normally associated with power sector investments.

Conclusion

In developing countries the bulk of infrastructure provision continues to be in the public domain, though the private sector share has risen in recent years. The difficulty in raising funds through general taxes has made self-financing of these services a second-best policy endorsed by nearly all coun-tries. Experience suggests, however, that full cost recovery is more of an exception than a rule, except in the telecommunications sector. Financing remains inadequate, and the political economy of setting tariffs contrib-utes to low and improperly designed user charges, infrequent inflation ad-justments, and poor enforcement. Sectors such as water, power, and trans-port continue to drain funds from the treasury, though the impact varies from sector to sector. When budgetary transfers are difficult to make, espe-cially during a fiscal crisis, nonwage operations and maintenance expendi-tures often decrease, resulting in deterioration of services.

Private provision could reduce the financing requirement for the pub-lic sector. A market system where technological advances spur competi-tion could improve the efficiency and quality of infrastructure services. However, for services that still require a single provider because of scale economies or other reasons, private provision would not occur without an appropriate rate of return. User charges that reflect cost would be one ma-jor requirement for private provision.

Acknowledgment. An earlier version of this paper appeared in *World Development* 22(12): 1909–19.

Bibliography

Anderson, David. 1989. "Infrastructure Pricing Policies and the Public Revenue in African Countries." *World Development* 17(4): 525–42.

Aschauer, D. A. 1989. "Is Public Expenditure Productive?" *Journal of Monetary Economics* 23: 177–200.

Ballard, Charles L., John B. Shoven, and John Whalley. 1985. "General Equilibrium Computations of the Marginal Welfare Costs of Taxes in the United States." *American Economics Review* 75: 128–38.

Barro, Robert J. 1991. "Economic Growth in a Cross Section of Countries." *Quarterly Journal of Economics* 106: 407–44.

Bagchi, A., J. L. Bajaj, and W. A. Byrd. 1989. *State Finances in India.* New Delhi: Vikas Publishing House Private Ltd.

Bhatia, Ramesh. 1989. "Financing Irrigation Services in India: A Case Study of Bihar and Haryana States." New Delhi: Institute of Economic Growth.

Churchill, Anthony. 1972. "Road User Charges in Central America." World Bank Staff Occasional Paper No. 15. Baltimore: Johns Hopkins University Press.

Devarajan, Shantayana, Vinaya Swaroop, and Heng-Fu Zou. Forthcoming. "The Composition of Public Expenditure and Economic Growth." *Journal of Monetary Economics.*

Easterly, William, and Sergio Rebelo. 1993. "How Much Do Distortions Affect Growth?" *Journal of Monetary Economics* 32:187–212.

Faulhaber, Gerald R. 1982. "A Public Enterprise Pricing Primer" in Jorg Finsinger, ed., *Public Sector Economics.* Berlin: Macmillan.

Feldstein, Martin S. 1972. "Equity and Efficiency in Public Sector Pricing: The Optimal Two-Part Tariff." *Quarterly Journal of Economics* 86(2): 175–87.

Heggie, Ian G. 1991. "Improving Management and Charging Policies for Roads: An Agenda for Reform." Report INU 92, Infrastructure and Urban Development Department. Washington, D.C.: The World Bank.

_____.1994. "Management and Financing of Roads: An Agenda for Reform." SSATP Working Paper No. 8, Africa Region. Washington, D.C.: The World Bank.

Heggie, Ian G., and V. Fon. 1991. "Optimal User Charges and Cost Recovery for Roads." Manuscript prepared for *Pricing, Cost Recovery and Efficient Resource Use in Transport Projects.* Washington, D.C.: The World Bank.

Hobday, Michael. 1990. *Telecommunications in Developing Countries: The Challenges from Brazil.* London: Routlege.

Mulk, S. U., and K. Mohtadullah. 1992. "Water Resources Management Policies in Pakistan." Paper for the International Workshop on Water Resources Management. Washington, D.C.: The World Bank.

Newberry, D. M., G. A. Hughes, W. D. O. Paterson, and E. Bennathan. 1988. *Road Transport Taxation in Developing Countries: The Design of User Charges and Taxes for Tunisia.* Discussion Paper 26. Washington, D.C.: The World Bank.

Pradhan, Sanjay, and Vinaya Swaroop. 1993. "Public Spending and Adjustment." *Finance and Development* 30(3): 28–31.

Repetto, Robert. 1986. "Skimming the Water: Rent-Seeking and the Performance of Public Irrigation Systems." Research Report No. 4. Washington, D.C.: World Resources Institute.

Shah, Anwar, and John Baffes. 1993. "Productivity of Public Spending, Sectoral

Allocation Choices, and Economic Growth." Policy Research Working Papers, WPS 1178. Washington, D.C.: The World Bank.

Swaroop, Vinaya. 1991. "Pricing Policies for Efficient Provision and Use of Economic Infrastructure: A Case Study of Indonesia." Public Economics Division, Country Economics Department. Washington, D.C.: The World Bank.

_____. 1993. "Financing Electricity and Water in the New Structure of Local Government: A Case Study of the Central Witwaterstand Region." Final Report, Policy Research Department. Washington, D.C.: The World Bank.

Varley, R. 1989. "Irrigation Issues and Policy in Indonesia: 1966–88." Development Discussion Paper No. 322. Cambridge: Harvard Institute for International Development.

Walters, A. A. 1983. "Cost of Using Roads" in G. M. Meir, ed., *Pricing Policy for Development Management*. Baltimore: Johns Hopkins University Press.

Weiss, Leonard W., and Allyn D. Strickland. 1982. *Regulation: A Case Approach*. New York: McGraw-Hill.

World Bank. 1992. *Adjustment Lending and Mobilization of Private and Public Resources for Growth*. Washington, D.C.

_____. 1991. *Lessons of Tax Reform*. Washington, D.C.

_____. 1990. *Review of Electricity Tariffs in Developing Countries during the 1980s*. *Energy Development Information* Note 24. Washington, D.C.

_____. 1988. *The World Development Report 1988*. New York: Oxford University Press.

6

The Role of Export Credit Agencies in the Foreign Financing of Infrastructure in Developing Countries

Ning S. Zhu

A growing number of developing countries are faced with learning how to arrange the necessary foreign exchange financing for infrastructure investment, including the large requirements of imported capital equipment. Traditionally, export credit agencies (ECAs) of industrialized economies have been a major source of support—through direct loans and guarantees. ECAs today are more aware of the risks involved in underwriting cross-border financing of large infrastructure projects, largely due to the losses incurred during the debt crisis of the 1980s. As a result, premium rates have been raised gradually over time and have become differentiated across countries to reflect underlying risks. With the increasing application of project—or limited recourse—finance to infrastructure projects (in the form of build-operate-transfer concessions and their variants), ECAs have increasingly emphasized support of the private sector in developing countries. Two factors have contributed to this changing trend. First, an increasing number of developing countries envisage a larger role for the private sector in their economic growth and so have provided an opening to private sector involvement in infrastructure projects. Second, ECAs have sought additional securities from project cash-flows. The chapter also briefly describes other official and private sources of guarantees to support foreign capital flows to developing country infrastructure.

Large infrastructure projects in developing countries are usually complex, with long and uncertain project periods. As a consequence, the projects are vulnerable to volatile costs and revenues and to other risks such as political disruption or an undesirable change in the country's external payment position. These economic and political risks limit access of developing countries to direct credits as well as credit enhancements—or guarantees. To mitigate their risks, equipment suppliers to the project, private project sponsors, and private lenders seek the presence of ECAs and multilateral development banks (MDBs) in the financing of infrastructure projects. Traditionally, ECAs have been a major source of support—through direct loans and guarantees.

The losses incurred during the debt crisis of the 1980s have made ECAs more aware of the risks involved in underwriting cross-border financing of large infrastructure projects. The portfolio of ECAs was then very concentrated, but now it has shifted in relative exposure across countries—mostly to economies in transition. Premium rates have been raised gradually over time and have become differentiated across countries to reflect underlying risks.

ECAs are also paying more attention to individual project risk analysis. Until very recently, ECAs have provided guarantees on long-term export credits to government undertakings or to other public sector borrowers. With the increasing application of project—or limited recourse—finance to infrastructure projects (in the form of build-operate-transfer (BOT) concessions and their variants), ECAs have begun placing increased emphasis on supporting the private sector in developing countries. Two factors have contributed to this changing trend. First, an increasing number of developing countries envisage a larger role for the private sector in their economic growth and so have provided an opening to private sector involvement in infrastructure projects. Second, ECAs have sought additional securities from project cash-flows.

In examining the role of ECAs in project finance, certain general lessons on the viability and effectiveness of project finance also emerge. Investor perceptions of risk can be addressed by dealing with general country and political risks as well as by sector reform and attention to project design. A stable economic environment with prudent fiscal and monetary policies is the most effective inducement for foreign investment in infrastructure projects. Removal of exchange controls and the development of currency markets for spot and future transactions would greatly help mitigate currency convertibility risk and reduce the need for government-sponsored, project-specific guarantees.

The chapter explains the role of ECAs as important underwriters of developing country long-term credit risks in importing capital goods. The changing attitude of ECAs toward developing country credit risks is re-vealed by reviewing past trends in the volume, concentration, and terms of long-term export credit flows to developing country infrastructure in-vestment. Also highlighted are recent ECA policy changes regarding higher credit guarantee premiums. The chapter then shifts to case-studies of project finance where ECAs play their traditional roles as underwriters for sover-eign risk; some ECAs are willing to underwrite a well-structured project financing without a host country counter-guarantee. Finally, other (non-ECA) risk mitigation services are briefly described. The chapter concludes with observations on policy lessons for developing countries.

Export Credit Agencies as Traditional Guarantors/Financiers

The external financing of developing country infrastructure projects has involved ECAs, multilateral development banks (including the World Bank and regional development banks), and such private sources as equipment suppliers, commercial banks, and capital markets. Since infrastructure in-vestment often requires import of capital equipment, trade credit from ECAs or guaranteed by ECAs is central to most financing packages.

Trade credit includes credit extended by suppliers (exporters) and credits granted by financial institutions to importers. Trade credits of short dura-tion (say, up to six months) for exports to more creditworthy countries are often arranged through normal banking channels. Credits of longer dura-tion (appropriate for export of capital goods and major project equipment) or credits to importers in less creditworthy countries are usually extended by exporters or banks based on guarantees provided by ECAs or other similar agencies supported by the government of the exporting country. The focus here is on the long-term credit activities of these officially supported agen-cies as they pertain to developing country infrastructure investments.

The Export Credit Guarantee Department (ECGD) of the United King-dom, established in 1919, marks the beginning of official support for ex-port credits. It was part of the new British credit insurance scheme, which was set up to support industry (and thus employment) and to meet com-petition. It was expected to operate, on average, at no cost to the taxpayer, balancing its premium income with administrative expenses and settle-ment of claims. Many other governments also established ECAs in the late 1920s and 1930s with similar objectives. For example, the Export Insurance Department of the Japanese Ministry of International Trade and Industry commenced in 1930, and the Export-Import Bank of the United States (Eximbank) was chartered in 1934.

An ECA guarantees a national exporter or a banker against risks of nonpayment when extending credit to an overseas borrower for the export of goods and services.[1] In its most restricted form, such a guarantee or insurance cover may be extended by the ECA only against sovereign risks, leaving the financier responsible for nonpayment resulting from commercial risks. In most cases, the cover of ECAs is extended against both types of risk, partly because of the difficulty in distinguishing between political and commercial risks. Unlike short-term trade finance that may cover repeated transactions through a line of credit, the coverage for medium-term and long-term businesses is normally extended to exporters on an individual contract basis.

ECAs have been under pressure by domestic constituents to justify their existence. They have been criticized as an example of "corporate welfare" and mere contribution to increased exports is not considered enough. Why then do governments support their ECAs? First, a narrow economic justification is that export promotion offsets the protection from imports: the exporting sectors draw resources away from inefficient import substituting sectors. Thus, in the imperfect world of restricted trade, some level of export subsidy (through credit enhancement) is desirable.[2] Second, because of government support, ECAs have a comparative advantage in negotiating with rescheduling debtor countries.

Volume of Official and Officially Supported Export Credits

The importance of official export credits to developing country finance is evident. The latest World Bank statistics show that officially supported export credits (either guaranteed or directly financed or refinanced) accounted for 19 percent of the $1,912 billion total developing country external debt outstanding at the end of 1994. Export credits represent 37 percent of developing country debt to all official creditors, which exceeds debt to multilateral creditors by a significant margin (IMF 1994). In terms of flows, long-term export credits (defined as credits with a maturity longer than five years) to developing countries averaged $8 billion per year in 1984-92, compared with $52 billion total bilateral and multilateral official disbursement in the same period.

In the debt crisis of the early 1980s, many major developing country borrowers defaulted on their external obligations, including ECA-guaranteed

1.   See Tambe and Zhu (1993) for an overview of export credit agencies.
2.   See Eaton (1986) for more discussion.

export credits. The response of ECAs was to immediately stop providing credit support to countries that fell into arrears or asked for rescheduling of official debt. The resumption of guarantees or direct lending would only be considered after a multilateral agreement had been reached with most ECAs. Such resumption of medium-term and long-term credit guarantees was, however, generally on a very restricted basis, given the fragile economic condition of debtor countries and the continuing risk perceptions of the ECAs. As a consequence, net export credit flows to developing countries declined sharply and finally turned negative in the late 1980s. Recent years have shown a modest revival.

The Creditor Reporting System of the Organization for Economic Cooperation and Development (OECD) tracks officially supported export credits with a longer than five-year maturity (for major capital plant and equipment) on a loan-by-loan basis. Such relatively long-maturity credit is especially relevant to infrastructure financing. These data, therefore, provide the basis for our discussion of ECAs' credit support of developing country infrastructure. This rich dataset apparently has not been explored in the academic literature or in policy discussions of export credits.

The volume of new commitment on long-term credits to all recipient countries exhibited a similar trend to overall flow from $7 billion at the beginning of the sample period in 1984 to $4 billion through 1987 (figure 6.1). Following 1987, the volume of export credits increased. It was not until 1991 that long-term export credits recovered in nominal terms to 1984 levels. The volume of infrastructure export credits to low-income and middle-income countries has a similar trend to that of aggregate export credits (figure 6.2).

Infrastructure sector export credits were important during this period. They averaged more than 60 percent of total long-term export credits from 1984 to 1992 (table 6.1). Some sectors consistently attract more export credits than others. In particular, power averages 36 percent per year, telecommunications 17 percent per year, and air transportation 21 percent per year (table 6.2). In 1984 and 1985, export credits for railroads were at their highest in terms of share and volume. The sanitation sector received no export credits until 1988. Its share of export credits was still quite small at the end of the sample, less than 2 percent. This share figure, however, obscures this sector's large increase in volume of export credits. In 1988, the sanitation sector received less than $1 million in export credits. This figure increased to $17 million in 1991 and $169 million in 1992.

Figure 6.1. *Annual Export Credits, Actual and Trend*

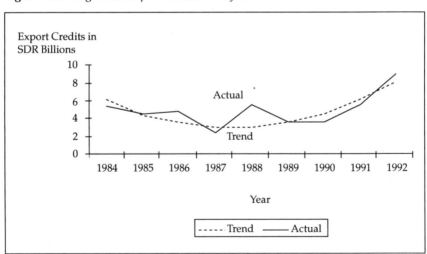

Source: OECD and author's calculations.

Figure 6.2. *Long-Term Export Credits to Infrastructure Sectors*

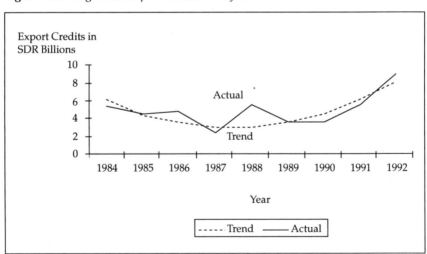

Source: OECD and author's calculations.

Table 6.1. *Long-Term Export Credits*
(SDR billions and percent)

	1984	1985	1986	1987	1988	1989	1990	1991	1992
Total	9.3	7.3	7.1	4.6	8.1	6.4	6.7	9.3	12.9
Infrastructure									
volume	5.5	4.5	4.9	2.4	5.5	3.5	3.6	5.6	9.0
Share in total	58.6	61.4	68.7	53.2	68.1	55.5	54.3	59.8	69.4

Note: Low- and middle-income countries only.

Source: OECD CRS Form1C database.

Table 6.2. *Long-Term Export Credits to Infrastructure Sectors*

	1984	1985	1986	1987	1988	1989	1990	1991	1992
Volume in									
SDR millions									
Infrastructure	5,477	4,472	4,869	2,436	5,528	3,542	3,634	5,557	8,967
Power	2,158	937	1,815	632	3,394	988	1,015	2,901	2,815
Transportation	2,403	2,851	2,118	1,221	1,441	1,525	1,534	1,262	4,767
Railroad	720	966	435	207	243	103	400	89	552
Highway/road	16	121	293	39	209	76	151	100	387
Water	287	616	263	473	132	136	131	491	1,223
Air	1,373	911	951	461	774	1,164	755	432	2,438
Oil/others	7	237	176	41	83	45	96	151	167
Telecomm.	838	654	513	507	621	802	1,021	1,084	1,121
Water supply	78	30	423	75	71	224	55	293	96
Sanitation	0	0	0	0	1	3	9	17	169
Share in									
percentage									
Power	39.4	20.9	37.3	26.0	61.4	27.9	27.9	52.2	31.4
Transportation	43.9	63.8	43.5	50.1	26.1	43.0	42.2	22.7	53.2
Railroad	13.1	21.6	8.9	8.5	4.4	2.9	11.0	1.6	6.2
Highway/road	0.3	2.7	6.0	1.6	3.8	2.1	4.2	1.8	4.3
Water	5.2	13.8	5.4	19.4	2.4	3.8	3.6	8.8	13.6
Air	25.1	20.4	19.5	18.9	14.0	32.9	20.8	7.8	27.2
Oil/others	0.1	5.3	3.6	1.7	1.5	1.3	2.7	2.7	1.9
Telecomm.	15.3	14.6	10.5	20.8	11.2	22.6	28.1	19.5	12.5
Water supply	1.4	0.7	8.7	3.1	1.3	6.3	1.5	5.3	1.1
Sanitation	0.0	0.0	0.0	0.0	0.0	0.1	0.3	0.3	1.9

Note: Low- and middle-income recipient countries only.

Source: OECD CRS Form1C database.

Concentration of Export Credit Flows

In addition to high-risk developing countries, ECAs provide direct credit and credit enhancement to developed countries (those in the category I of the OECD Development Assistance Committee income classification). Shares of long-term export credits by the three income groups have remained relatively stable (except in 1988), indicating that credit enhancement is widespread in cross-border trade.

An important principle of insurance is risk pooling, which requires that third-party guarantors have a well-diversified portfolio of borrowing countries. As shown in table 6.3, most recipients are middle-income countries. Risk diversification does not seem to be an important factor for ECAs in providing credits to low-income and middle-income countries. Of the more than 100 developing countries, nearly half the volume of export credits went to the top five recipients each year. Table 6.4 provides the share and volume of export credits to the top five and top ten recipients each year. The composition of the top recipients changes slightly from year to year, but the share remained fairly constant at about 50 percent for the top five recipients and about 70 percent for the top ten recipients. Figure 6.3 illustrates the concentration of export credits to the top recipient countries over time.

Figure 6.3. *Share of Long-Term Export Credits to Top Recipient Countries*

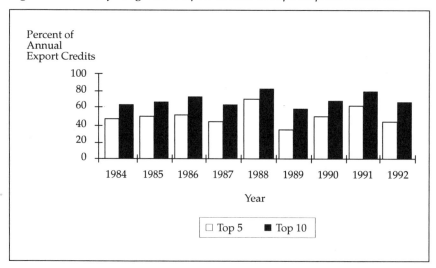

Source: OECD and author's calculations.

Table 6.3. Long-Term Export Credits to Countries by Income Categories

	Volume in SDR millions			Share in percent		
Year	High	Middle	Low	High	Middle	Low
1984	1,446	3,908	1,569	20.9	56.5	22.7
1985	605	3,055	1,418	11.9	60.2	27.9
1986	624	2,799	2,070	11.4	51.0	37.7
1987	1,160	1,379	1,056	32.3	38.4	29.4
1988	433	1,812	3,716	7.3	30.4	62.3
1989	1,200	2,368	1,174	25.3	49.9	24.8
1990	409	2,233	1,401	10.1	55.2	34.7
1991	1,556	3,102	2,455	21.9	43.6	34.5
1992	1,713	5,624	3,344	16.0	52.7	31.3

Source: OECD CRS Form1C database.

Table 6.4. Long-Term Infrastructure Export Credits for the Major Recipients

	1984	1985	1986	1987	1988	1989	1990	1991	1992
Volume in SDR millions									
Total	5,477	4,472	4,869	2,436	5,528	3,542	3,634	5,557	8,967
Top 5	2,562	2,240	2,490	1,082	3,903	1,253	1,812	3,433	3,894
Top 10	3,594	3,030	3,592	1,599	4,572	2,088	2,533	4,472	6,105
Share in percentage									
Top 5	46.8	50.1	51.1	44.4	70.6	35.4	49.9	61.8	43.4
Top 10	65.6	67.7	73.8	65.7	82.7	58.9	69.7	80.5	68.1

Note: Low- and middle-income country recipients only.
Source: OECD CRS Form1C database.

Interest Rates and Maturities

Over time, the average interest rate on long-term export credits (including those for infrastructure financing) has declined, reflecting the downward trend of international interest rates in the late 1980s (table 6.5). The coefficient of variation of interest rates for individual credits is an indicator of the dispersion in credit terms. The increase in the coefficient of variation over the period 1984–91 shows that as interest rates decreased, the rates varied more across countries and individual projects over time.

Table 6.5. Interest Rates and Maturities for Long-Term Export Credits
(percent and number of years)

	1984	1985	1986	1987	1988	1989	1990	1991	1992
Averages									
Interest rates	9.5	9.2	9.0	8.4	7.3	7.9	7.8	7.6	n.a.
Maturities	8.8	8.6	9.1	9.2	9.4	9.6	9.6	9.5	9.3
Coefficient of variation									
Interest rates	17.2	25.0	26.8	23.1	29.1	30.4	37.1	42.0	n.a.
Maturities	21.0	17.1	30.2	19.9	21.8	21.3	27.8	29.9	21.4

n.a. Not applicable.

Note: Low- and middle-income recipient countries only.

Source: OECD CRS Form1C database.

Average maturities (second part of table 6.5) slightly increased over the period. The coefficient of variation fluctuated over time, but not substantially and not in any systematic way. This is largely because the maximum 10-year maturity stipulated by the OECD Consensus agreement is usually binding for most infrastructure projects.

Finance versus Guarantee

Most ECAs have co-insurance in the sense that they cover less than 100 percent of credit risks (between 80-85 percent for commercial risks and 90-95 percent for political risks). In addition to guarantees, many ECAs also make direct lending to developing country importers. For instance, the United States and Japanese export-import banks provide substantial direct financing and refinancing of export credits. Daniel Bond, chief economist of U.S. Eximbank, has proposed that OECD governments look increasingly towards export credit guarantees rather than financing to extend support to reforming economies. This way, governments limit their exposures and hence their budgetary stress.

Direct export credits by official agencies, as distinct from guarantees provided to private creditors, averaged a quarter of their total long-term export credit support in 1984-92 (table 6.6). Direct ECA financing became increasingly important in the second half of the 1980s, accounting for more than 40 percent of ECAs' total long-term activities. This share fell to between 20 and 30 percent in the early 1990s. Looking just at infrastructure financing, we see similar trends.

Table 6.6. Share of Export Credits Financed or Refinanced by ECAs

	1984	1985	1986	1987	1988	1989	1990	1991	1992
Volume in SDR millions									
All sectors	1,314	818	781	882	1,619	2,380	2,823	3,089	3,479
Infrastructure	994	428	495	464	1,133	1,266	1,379	2,368	2,056
Share in total long-term export credits (percent)									
All sectors	14.1	11.2	11.0	19.2	19.9	37.3	42.2	33.2	26.9
Infrastructure	18.1	9.6	10.1	18.8	20.5	35.7	37.9	42.6	22.9

Note: Low- and middle-income countries only.

Source: OECD CRS Form1C database.

One possible explanation is that from 1985 through 1990 private sector provision of export credits decreased in the aftermath of the debt crisis. Even though their overall scale of lending shrank, ECAs continued providing a substantial amount of export credits to delinquent debtors once a Paris Club rescheduling agreement was reached and a cutoff date was established and respected. As the perceived risk of export credits decreased for many emerging economies in the late 1980s, financing by private financial institutions rebounded and ECAs reverted their focus to guarantees.

Premium Rates of Guarantees

To offset the contingent liabilities arising from guarantee operations, ECAs have traditionally charged premiums or guarantee fees on creditors to compensate potential loss claims. As there is no international coordination on premium setting policies, the practice of premium pricing varies greatly across ECAs. The basis on which to calculate premiums ranges from eligible contract value to principal loan value. In order to price varying country risks, ECAs have sharpened their differentiation of premiums. Consequently, the disparities between the premiums charged by different ECAs for providing cover for export to any individual market have also widened. The highest premium charged for several developing country markets by an ECA can currently be three or even four times the premium charged by another ECA in the same markets and may be equivalent to 10 to 15 percent of the credit value, or more. These premiums are generally payable by the suppliers or exporters to the ECAs (and are not directly a cost of the credit). The wide disparities in premiums that have now developed can thus place some of these suppliers at a great competitive disadvantage.

Since the ECAs' losses during the past decade stemmed mainly from their medium-term and long-term credit guarantees against sovereign risks, attention has focused on developing approaches for setting premium rates for covering sovereign risks in medium-term and long-term business. The levels and structure of premiums on medium-term and long-term export credits have recently become the subject of an intense debate in the movements towards harmony in the European Union and in the OECD export credit group (IMF 1994).

Some ECAs have already upwardly revised their premium structures. For example, the United Kingdom's ECGD has adopted the Portfolio Management System, which determines sovereign risk premium rates based on probabilities of default and expected loss for each specific market. Two main components of the system are the borrower country's projected debt ratios for estimating default probability and the Bank of England matrix for sovereign debt recoverability (Lunn-Rockliffe 1992). The U.S. Eximbank has also developed a market-based risk assessment system that classifies countries into 11 categories according to a graded scale of payment problems based on conditions expected to prevail over the next five years. Another correlation has been developed between the first 8 of the 11 categories and Moody's and Standard & Poor's long-term bond classification. On the budgetary side, U.S. Eximbank's appropriations have been affected by the new system (Bond 1992; Mody and Patro: chapter 8).

Export Credit Agencies and Project Finance

ECAs have been increasingly supporting exports to the private sector in developing countries. Until recent years, most infrastructure projects in developing countries were undertaken by governments or public sector enterprises. Mounting fiscal deficits and efficiency concerns in many countries have provided an opening to private sector involvement in infrastructure projects. Many borrowing countries now see a larger role for the private sector in their economic growth. Private sector project sponsors and their creditors are expected to mobilize a large part of the substantial finance required on a nonrecourse basis.

At the same time, in light of the declining creditworthiness of many importing countries after the debt crisis, ECA support of export financing has increasingly relied on unconventional security arrangements in addition to sovereign counter-guarantees. ECAs are increasingly relying on and obtaining security from project profitability and assets. Where ECAs have participated in limited recourse project financing, the agencies have expected the commercial lenders or project sponsors to be prepared to assume some, if not all, of the related commercial risks.

Capital Structure and Financial Risks

Capital structures used for financing projects vary (Shah and Thakor 1987). A project sponsor may finance a new project using existing projects—and hence his total assets—as collateral to secure the financing. Thus, any outstanding financial claim against the new project is a claim on the sponsor's total cash flow. With this structure (referred to by Shah and Thakor as conventional financing), lenders look at the overall creditworthiness of the project sponsor and are less concerned with the profitability of an individual project. This way, creditors fund firms, and firms fund projects.

An alternative is for creditors to fund projects directly (Pyle: chapter 7). A special purpose corporation dedicated to a project is incorporated as a distinct legal entity with limited liability. For example, an electric utility may finance a capacity addition, not by relying on its balance-sheet, but by using for security the cash-flows of the independent, power producer constituted as a special-purpose corporation.

Project finance is one of the oldest forms of investment financing, with roots tracing back to a mining venture in England about 700 years ago. In 1299, the English Crown financed the development of the risky Devon silver mines largely with loans from a leading Italian merchant bank, Frescobaldi. Debt repayments were to be silver from the mines, for which the Italians had full control under a one-year lease (Kensinger and Martin 1988).

In the purest form of project financing, creditors have no recourse against project sponsors' assets other than the cash flow of the project. This type of pure project finance is uncommon because lenders typically insist on some support from sponsors—at least in the project development phase. A completion guarantee by the sponsors or their parent companies is typically obtained. As a result, even in industrialized countries, project financing on a wholly nonrecourse basis has worked only in a limited number of cases with one or more of the following characteristics: (1) the project sponsors were internationally established with credible contractors or multinationals; (2) the products were robustly profitable; and (3) the revenue stream could be initially directed to an escrow account and made available for debt service on a preferential basis.

In project financing, the various risks need to be carefully evaluated with satisfactory measures for their containment laid out in contractual arrangements among all those involved, including each party's rights, obligations, and liabilities. Measures for risk containment, such as insurance, must also be put in place. Guarantees enable promoters to shift the financial risk of a project to one or more third parties. Investors thus seek to transfer risks from their balance sheets to those of the guarantors. This is particularly essential when substantial nonrecourse debt finance is involved, as the project balance sheet is unlikely to be able to withstand a major loss for several years until the project is generating a sustainable stream of revenue. As guarantors and providers of direct credits, ECAs have an evidently important role in project financing. All major ECAs have established strong project finance groups.

An Anatomy of Risks

Pinpointing the risks of greatest concern to project sponsors and creditors is the first step in managing and containing risks in any project financing arrangement. The ability of a sponsor to shift risks to lenders and the extent to which lenders retain some risks and transfer other risks to guarantors both depend on the nature of the risk, the timing of the risk, and the contractual arrangement among different parties. In other words, some risks may be laid off from the outset, others may only be shed once the project has been completed and become operational, and with others, continuous recourse to a sponsor may remain. The challenge lies in structuring those risks which are of greatest concern while offering sufficient credit support to lenders. Notwithstanding sovereign risks prevalent in cross-border lending, a commercially viable project financing helps reduce the likelihood of sovereign default.

Sovereign (or Country) Risk

Sovereign (or country) risks include the risk of abrogation of agreements with the host government, outright or creeping expropriation (through nationalization, for example), and the risk of damage to property or the inability to operate due to war, civil strife, or political violence. Also, public sector utilities or enterprises can also fail to provide contracted inputs such as fuel or water, or fail to pay for the off-take of the project production, say, of electric power. Invariably, the successful operation of infrastructure facilities also crucially depends on government policies—especially those relating to legal, regulatory, and taxation systems. The possibility that revenues earned in local currency may not be convertible into an internationally acceptable currency is also typically classified under country risk (this is discussed in the following section).

In many of the early project finance deals (primarily for the power sector) in the Philippines and in Pakistan, for example, ECAs sought and obtained host government guarantees to back their direct lending or assurances to private lenders. However, since the debt crisis of the 1980s, ECAs and many other creditors have learned that governments sometimes fail to honor their commitments. Commercial banks and ECAs now see sovereign guarantees offering less than perfect security for new credits, and, as a result, they are more willing to support private sector investment in developing countries without government guarantees. Moreover, the large infrastructure projects that ECAs traditionally financed are now increasingly sponsored by private companies. Some ECAs, such as U.S. Eximbank and EXIM Japan, are prepared to provide financing under such sponsorship. However, ECAs providing political risk coverage expect lenders to take the commercial risks (Rodriguez 1993-94).

The recent Paiton I power project in Indonesia exemplifies this typical financing arrangement. It is a 30-year BOT project for a 1,230 MW, coal-fired complex on the north coast of East Java, near the city of Surabaya. Once commissioned, the power station will add significantly to the national utility's existing power-generating capacity of 9,700 MW. The Indonesian government is strongly committed to the project, and the national electricity utility will purchase the electricity at a guaranteed price. Total cost of the project is estimated at $2.5 billion. The majority of the equity (85 percent) is held by three Japanese and U.S. power-generating companies, and a local company takes up the remaining 15 percent share. EXIM Japan ($900 million), U.S. Eximbank ($540 million), the Overseas Private Investment Corporation (OPIC) ($200 million loan and $200 million insurance), and commercial banks ($180 million) combined to supply $1.8 billion debt finance of the project. The project reached financial closing in May 1995. In this project there was no full faith and credit guarantee of the government of Indonesia. The government did provide a "comfort letter," which stated that the government would "cause" the national electric utility to "discharge its payment obligations."

The follow-up project, Paiton II, has signed a 30-year power purchase agreement and is expected to reach financial closing in late 1995. Total cost is estimated at $1.6 billion, of which $1.3 billion will be debt. U.S. Eximbank and Hermes, a German ECA, are expected to guarantee the debt finance.

Some ECAs have been willing to underwrite project financing with a local government as opposed to a central government guarantee. An international consortium including Siemens of Germany and PowerGen of the United Kingdom has secured a deal for a 650 MW power plant in the Indian state of Gujarat. Bayerische Landesbank and Kreditanstalt fur Wiederaufbau (KfW), Germany's official financing agency (which, like Hermes, also facilitates German exports), arranged a DM 400 million (US$272 million), 16-year loan package to finance the total cost of the project (US$750 million). The financing is backed by state government guarantees of payment for the power produced and there are no central government counter-guarantees.

A similar financing arrangement involving Siemens and KfW has been signed for a US$625 million power project to build two 350 MW power units at Rizhao on the coast of Shandong province, China. Total debt financing amounted to US$350 million arranged by KfW and Banco Central Hispano of Spain with risk insurance being provided by Hermes and CESCE, a Spanish ECA. Concerned about a build-up of its sovereign debt, the central government has stopped providing bank guarantees for most infrastructure projects. The Rizhao project has no Chinese bank guarantee and the funding arrangements, including export credit guarantees, were based on a strong power sales contract with the local Shandong electric power authorities, who have agreed to pay "come what may."

Finally, the Mamonal 100 MW, gas-fired independent power station in Columbia does not rely at all on government involvement, other than gaining its permission. The project is an "enclave" investment since the sponsors sell electricity to an industry estate composed of 24 exporting enterprises. Excess electricity is sold to the local utility. Inter-American Leasing Company, an affiliate of K&M Engineering and Consulting Corporation, signed a 15-year power purchase agreement with local electric utilities (30 percent) and the 24-enterprise industry estate (70 percent). K&M and Scudder Latin America Trust for Independent Power, an infrastructure investment fund, contributed to the $14 million equity financing. Debt financing, arranged by Chase Manhattan, amounted to $56 million, of which $35 million was provided by OPIC. OPIC also covered political risk of the project. OPIC supports U.S. investors rather than exporters, but effectively plays a role similar to that of U.S. Eximbank. It has extensive infrastructure interests.

Currency Transfer Risk

The transfer risk—the chance that the host country central bank is unable or unwilling to sell investors the equivalent foreign exchange in return for nonconvertible local currency earnings—is a major consideration for external lenders. In addition to requiring a sovereign guarantee from host countries, external investors will also select projects in sectors that generate revenue in foreign exchange rather than in local currencies. For this reason, project financing first became popular with enclave-type mining and extractive activities. Because proceeds of these projects—oil and gas—are usually for sale abroad, revenues would not be limited to host country currency. Another sector that earns foreign exchange and is relatively easy to finance is telecommunications (Bishop, Mody, Schankerman: chapter 2).

The public infrastructure utility services in developing countries usually do not generate revenues in foreign currency directly. The risk of local currency depreciation is usually covered by denominating the tariff in a hard currency, such as the U.S. dollar. But a satisfactory arrangement for repatriation of equity dividend and debt servicing is a key concern of investors and lenders. The establishment of off-shore escrow accounts has been viewed as a necessity in many cases to provide adequate security for the ECAs and other external creditors. Escrow accounts can address transfer risks by credibly committing a project's future foreign exchange earnings to claimants. An early example of a project relying on an escrow account is the Navotas 200 MW gas turbine 12-year BOT facility in Manila, the Philippines, developed by Hopewell Holding Ltd. of Hong Kong.[3]

Earlier, Hopewell developed the successful Shajiao-B project, a 2x350 MW, coal-fired power station in Guangdong, China, through a joint-venture arrangement (60-40 partnership). The total cost of the project, $540 million, was financed through $55 million equity, $131 million syndicated loan, $92 million local capital, and $262 million EXIM Japan supplier credit. Foreign exchange convertibility guarantees were provided by Provincial Government Agencies.[4] (Pyle discusses the follow-up Shajiao-C project in chapter 7.)

The $875 million debt financing for a major gas pipeline, Cogasco, across central Argentina also required convertibility assurance. Lloyd's Bank International and Amsterdam Rotterdam Bank lead-managed the project in

---

3.   Hopewell is a major shareholder (60 percent), as well as operator of the facility. Other shareholders for the $11 million equity investment include Citicorp (20 percent), Asian Development Bank (10 percent), and International Finance Corporation (10 percent). Debt financing of $30 million was provided by IFC ($10 million), ADB ($10 million), and cofinancing ($10 million) under ADB's Complementary Financing Scheme. In addition to an off-shore escrow account to be used for debt servicing, the government agreed to provide the site, transmission facilities, and all fuel for generation of electricity at no cost to the project company. The estimated cost of these services totaled $4.5 million. The project construction started in 1990 and the facility is now fully operational.

4.   For more information see Euromoney (1992: 121–22).

1989 and received a convertibility guarantee from the government. The project managers were able to obtain $715 million of Dutch export credits with 95 percent insurance cover. The pipeline is scheduled to be transferred back to the government after the completion of pipeline construction in 1996 (Hooke 1992).

Commercial Risks

Commercial risks cover all the technical, economic, and market risks inherent in any major infrastructure project, regardless of location. They relate primarily to pre- and post-commissioning period of projects. Cost risks typically include completion delay and operating cost escalation, and revenue risks usually refer to output price volatility and market demand deficiency, to name a few.

New projects and expansions usually involve substantial civil construction works. They are considered more risky to finance because of construction hazards and completion delay. In the past, project construction risk was carried by contractors. In many cases, investors preferred turnkey projects or a performance bond provided by the project sponsors to reduce this type of risk. Now there is a growing demand to further unbundle construction risk and use insurance mechanisms to contain it, including the use of ECA guarantees. Traditionally ECAs have limited themselves to covering export credit business after a project's construction phase. As they get further into project financing, however, ECAs have been asked to provide comprehensive coverage for project development—including construction risks.

In a recently signed Hopewell Pagbilao 2x350 MW, coal-fired power project in Quezon, the Philippines, EXIM Japan assumed completion risk of the project on a nonrecourse basis for the first time. U.S. Eximbank covered the political risk in the construction period, aiding a Citibank-led syndicated loan financing. Once construction is completed on time—within cost and to specification—the risk reduces substantially, proved by U.S. Eximbank's willingness to refinance on a fully nonrecourse basis at this stage (Nameth 1994).

Third-Party Underwriters Other Than Export Credit Agencies

The expansion of the private insurance market can be an alternative to officially supported credit guarantees and insurance. Private insurance companies that offer guarantees against commercial risks such as construction hazards include American International Group (AIG), Citicorp International

Trade Indemnity, and Lloyd's of London. But the private market for political risk insurance is thin, with a high premium rate and limited coverage. Generally, private markets are not currently in a position to extend insurance against the kind of risks covered by officially supported ECAs for medium-term and long-term export credits to most developing country markets. For this reason, continuing official support to medium-term and long-term credits is necessary.

To attract international private capital to developing countries, several multilateral development banks—including the World Bank, the ADB, and the Inter-American Development Bank (IDB)—developed guarantee schemes in addition to their standard lending instruments. Under its recently mainstreamed Guarantee Program—building on the earlier Expanded Co-financing Operation program—the World Bank issues guarantees for project financing to cover sovereign risks or risks related to later maturities of commercial bank lending. The Bank's partial risk guarantee supports specific government undertakings promised to sponsors, thus catalyzing private financing for the project on a limited recourse basis. The partial risk guarantee (covering sovereign contractual risks, such as payment obligations under a power purchase agreement, tariff setting, and currency convertibility) was used for Pakistan's Hub Power Project, which recently reached financial closing. Total project cost was $1.9 billion, of which commercial lending of $240 million was guaranteed by the Bank; EXIM Japan provided an identical guarantee on $120 million of commercial lending. In the Yangzhou thermal power project in China, the Bank's partial credit guarantee was used for a $120 million syndicated commercial bank loan; the guarantee covered repayment of the loan from years 10.5 to 15, substantially lengthening the maturity compared with maturities available to China without credit enhancement at the time.

In supporting private sector projects on a limited recourse basis, the World Bank Guarantee program helps mobilize term finance from private sources to complement the export credits supported by ECAs. Since export credits may not be available on suitable terms for many elements of a project—such as civil works, construction materials (steel or cement), and know-how fees—this program can push the completion of total financing packages on appropriate terms.

On the part of ECAs, there is a greater interest in exchange of information with the World Bank and of cofinancing Bank-supported projects where possible. Planned export credit cofinancing with the World Bank declined from a peak of $1.9 billion in fiscal year 1983 to $0.3 billion in fiscal year 1986. It has since revived, reaching (on average) the earlier peak level of

$1.9 billion for fiscal years 1991-93. It is interesting to note that cofinancing amounts, which have come up to the level of pre-debt crisis years, now represent a much higher proportion of the new long-term export credits committed by OECD ECAs—a commitment that has declined from a level of SDR 18 billion in 1982 to approximately SDR 8 billion in 1991.

Multilateral Investment Guarantee Agency (MIGA), also a member of the World Bank group, provides political risk insurance. During fiscal year 1993, MIGA guarantees totaled about $302 million, covering largely mining, manufacturing, and banking sector investment. One telecommunications project in Argentina had $15 million in coverage by MIGA. Recently MIGA has reinsured the total risks of some projects underwritten by the Export Development Corporation, a Canadian ECA, ($50 million) and OPIC ($30 million).

More exchange of information and better coordination among third-party guarantors and financiers concerning individual projects, host government policies, and appropriate development priorities, will result in more efficient use of project financing.

Conclusion

The increasing demand for infrastructure financing in many developing countries occurs at a time when commercial banks and their national export credit agencies are consolidating their balance sheets and, to some extent, still cutting their losses from sovereign lending made in the early 1980s. Export credit agencies—as essential underwriters of developing country long-term credit risks—are using project financing or limited recourse techniques for privately sponsored infrastructure projects. Given the importance of infrastructure in economic development, success of project financing in infrastructure investment will not only bring much-needed infrastructure, but it is also likely to improve a developing country's overall creditworthiness in international capital markets.

To a large extent, the evolving role of ECAs in financing developing country infrastructure projects reflects two things: the economic environment inside developing countries and the changes in global financial markets. The future success of ECAs would mean less use of official and officially guaranteed credits as more developing country borrowers become creditworthy in the international capital market. As developing countries become more mature borrowers supported by stable macroeconomic environments, private capacity to raise resources from domestic and foreign sources will grow. Some countries already have made good progress in that direction.

For example, despite perceived risk, Guatemala has organized sizable flows of foreign direct investment without any escrow accounts because there exists a working market for foreign exchange. Arbitrary price and tax policies increase the uncertainty of project success and often deter foreign investors. Investors in the power sector, for instance, seek long-term power purchase agreements partly because of pricing and tax uncertainties, but also because the government has reserved for itself a monopoly in retailing power. Where that is not the case, as in Colombia and Chile, private-private deals are made without much government support. Similarly, fuel supply risk is passed back to the government in countries with national energy monopolies. Given transparent and stable policies, commercial risks—especially of construction and operation, but increasingly of market uncertainties—should be allocated to project sponsors, equity investors, and commercial lenders, all of which are better able to field such risks.

Bibliography

Bond, Daniel 1992. "From Ordinal to Cardinal Measures of Country Risk." Washington, D.C. U.S. Eximbank.

Eaton, Jonathan. 1986. "Credit Policy and International Competition" in *Strategic Trade Policy and the New International Economics*, Paul Krugman, ed., Cambridge: The MIT Press.

Euromoney. 1992. *Project Finance Yearbook 1991/92*. London

Hooke, Jeffrey. 1992. "Dynamics in Project Financing," *Project Financing in Latin America* 4–14.

International Monetary Fund (IMF). 1994. "Officially Supported Export Credits: Recent Developments and Prospects." Washington, D.C.: IMF.

Kensinger, John, and John Martin. 1988. "Project Finance: Raising Money the Old-Fashioned Way." *Journal of Applied Corporate Finance* August: 69–81.

Lunn-Rockliffe, V. 1992. "Portfolio Management System." ECGD paper presented at the Berne Union Workshop on Country Underwriting and Treatment of Sovereign Debt, Capetown, April 13–16.

Nameth, Louise. 1994. "Who Will Cover Construction Risk." *Infrastructure Finance* February/March: 31–33.

Rodriguez, Rita. 1993-94. "Eximbank: A Partner to Latin American Business in the 1990s." *Latin America Trade Finance, a Latin Finance Special Projects Supplement*:34–38.

Shah, Salman, and Anjan Thakor. 1987. "Optimal Capital Structure and Project Financing." *Journal of Economic Theory* 42: 209–243.

Tambe, Waman, and Ning S. Zhu. 1993. "Export Credits: Review and Prospects." World Bank Cofinancing Discussion Paper No. 102. Washington, D.C.: The World Bank, Cofinancing and Financial Advisory Services.

World Bank. 1994. *World Development Report 1994*. New York.: Oxford University Press.

7

Project Finance in Practice: The Case Studies

Thomas H. Pyle

Project financing allows sponsors of infrastructure projects to raise funds from private sponsors, other equity holders, and lenders using as security primarily a project's cashflows, with secondary support from the project's assets. Project financing is a transitional response to new financial needs, but it also complements the discipline of regulation and competition. Working in partnership, public and private entities can each work to attract the other. For the private investor, benefits are achieved from secured project cash-flows as well as sizable early completion bonuses and other incentives tied to efficient performance. For the government, shifting the financial burden of infrastructure provision onto the private sector is the major benefit. As infrastructure projects continue to unfold, norms and standards for project investments will evolve that can be modified and replicated. Moreover, evolution in local currency markets, bidding processes, infrastructure planning, and the legal and regulatory systems of developing countries will greatly reduce risks and free the flow of financing.

Increasing demand for infrastructure worldwide calls for a transitional form of financing that includes the private sector. Investment of public funds has been substantial, but has fallen short—and will continue to fall shorter (Swaroop: chapter 5). Approximately $450 billion is the infrastructure requirement for power generation alone in developing countries for the next ten years. Since the multilateral development banks can provide at best 10 to 15 percent of the financial requirement, hopes for fulfilling demands

rest on new ways of funding infrastructure that tap private financial resources and entrepreneurship, such as project financing.

Project financing allows sponsors of infrastructure projects to raise
funds from private sponsors, other equity holders, and lenders using the
security provided by the project's cashflows, backed up by the project's
assets. The lack of, or limited, recourse to the credit of the sponsor or other
collateral is chosen especially where projects are big and complex, and sponsors wish to limit their liabilities. Lenders incur more risk in these projects
than in traditional public projects or in projects backed by the credit of
project sponsors. But new safeguards and conventions are evolving to deal
with the often complex process of risk allocation.

Project financing is a transitional response to new financial needs, but it
also complements the discipline of regulation and competition. Privately
sponsored and financed projects measure their success against contractually agreed targets for new capacity, construction costs, and time overruns
and against indicators of service quality. Such investment provides an initial
footing for private investors in developing economies. In early financings,
recourse to private parties is strictly limited, but eventually project company credit histories will grow, allowing the financing of new projects.

Working in partnership, public and private entities can each work to
attract the other. For the private investor, benefits are achieved from secured project cash-flows as well as sizable early completion bonuses and
other incentives tied to efficient performance. For the government, shifting
the financial burden of infrastructure provision onto the private sector can
provide major benefits. But a government must still ensure that public policy
goals—regional imbalances, consumer protection, and the needs of the
poor—are met. The government in many cases may therefore provide economic support to projects, either through guarantees or subsidies, such as
land grants in association with toll road construction.

This chapter illustrates project financing through case studies of power
plants and toll roads, the two significant sectors currently using project financing. These case studies are not comprehensive but are intended to tell individual project financing stories, highlighting such innovative sources as the
use of local bank and bond markets and the tapping of international capital
markets. Some of the case studies also describe the kinds of risk analyses conducted by bankers—at the economy level and the project level. As the case
studies show, power stations are slightly better investments because they generally have support at the highest levels of host governments and factor first in
most government development plans. Furthermore, economic returns are generally ensured—and can be substantial—because the buyer is typically a single

government-owned entity whose credit is assured by the government. By contrast, toll roads are more often characterized by uncertainties in construction costs, traffic risk, and several political and administrative processes that can undermine financing of projects.

As infrastructure projects continue to unfold, norms and standards for project investments will evolve that can be modified and replicated. Moreover, evolution in local currency markets, bidding processes, infrastructure planning, and the legal and regulatory systems of developing countries will greatly reduce risks and free the flow of financing.

Case Studies in Power Generation

The private sector has become significantly involved in power generation, as opposed to transmission and distribution, because of the self-contained nature of generation. The revenue stream comes from one buyer, which allows for long-term contracts and lower risks. This characteristic is completely distinct from toll roads, where the consumer base is diverse and the revenue stream far less predictable. A well-established structure for a BOT power generation project is illustrated in figure 7.1.

Figure 7.1. *Asian Power Generation Projects: Model Financial Structure*

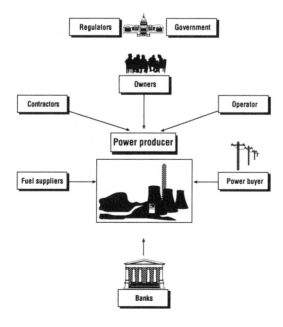

Sources for Financing Power in Asia

Starting with a relatively small capacity base, Asia is projected for dramatic growth in its energy generation and consumption.[1] Of all the world's power generation additions in the next decade, Asia is projected to demand up to 40 percent. Asia's largest demands will be in China, India, Korea, and Indonesia. Even if such investments materialize, developing Asian economies will still have relatively low per capita use by 2000—only about 18 percent of that for more developed countries.

How will such investments be financed? The first task in many countries will be to raise tariffs and improve operational efficiency. Committing to private investment is one way to ensure that tariffs reflect costs and that operations are conducted efficiently. Average real power tariffs have declined along with quality of service in many developing countries. Transmission and distribution losses alone are two to four times higher than in OECD countries, and the older generation plants consume 20-40 percent more fuel per kwh than the more efficient OECD utilities.

Turning to the structure of a power plant financing, and assuming currently achievable project leveraging of three parts debt to one part equity, a $500 million project will have about $125 million in equity. Foreign party participation will likely range from 30 to 60 percent of project equity. Technical majority control will generally be maintained by local partners, though effective control will remain with the foreign contractor.

Commercial bank debt is generally provided by large, international banks acting through syndicates. A project can attract as many as 15 to 20 banks, each funding between $5 million and $20 million for 6 to 12 years. Smaller "club deals" are usually handled among five to seven banks.

The investment requirements in Asia alone are likely to outstrip the cumulative country limits of banks prepared to lend to the power generating sector. At the same time, funding problems and declining reserves valuations for certain banks, notably Japanese, have further diminished sources of funding. The share of commercial bank debt in Asian power stations has, therefore, tended to fall. This has provided an opportunity for mezzanine debt providers. Private placements, for example, provide long-term debt support beyond what might be available from commercial banks.

---

1.   Projects under consideration in Asia range from 30 MW power barges for marginal supplemental capacity in the Philippines and 50 MW module jet-engine stations for municipalities in Southern China to 1,300 MW coal-fired thermal stations for strategic national projects in China, Indonesia, and Pakistan. Project costs vary from tens of millions to $1 billion.

Local bank debt helps cover local project costs and working capital. Although large and prestigious local projects can usually attract local bank financing for at least as long as foreign commercial debt (8 to 10 years), local currency lenders are sometimes limited by the lack of depth in their local funding markets, and so they accept only shorter tenors (5 to 8 years). Due to high local interest rates, local currency loans at the moment are also more expensive than foreign currency loans.

Foreign export credits can provide up to 85 percent of equipment cost (and in some cases up to 85 percent of project costs, including local costs) for as long as 15 years at slightly concessionary rates (Zhu: chapter 6). Multilateral agency credit from institutions like International Finance Corporation (IFC) and Asian Development Bank (ADB) can provide loans with grace periods and repayment periods far longer than commercial sources, depending on the project's credit factors. Multilateral agencies can also provide lending support via cofinancing facilities. With the multilateral agency acting as the technical lender of record, commercial banks are under an umbrella that allows them to enjoy the benefits of the multilateral agency, including relatively stronger assurance against sovereign rescheduling and exemption from local withholding taxes. Guarantees to lenders against political risk and those for late maturity payments are other forms of multilateral support.

Hopewell Energy Philippines

By 1987, the Philippines had begun to show the effects of over a decade of insufficient investment in the power sector. Power outages became a daily occurrence, especially in Metro Manila, disrupting local business and crimping the country's investment promotion efforts. A rapid solution was needed, and the National Power Corporation (NAPOCOR) invited bids to develop and supply a 200 MW peak-lopping gas turbine facility on a build-operate-transfer (BOT) basis.

Hopewell Holdings Ltd., a Hong Kong property development company with previous power station experience in China, was the only bidder to submit an offer on the BOT basis requested. All other vendors only proposed to supply equipment. Not only did Hopewell respond to the BOT request, it presented a comprehensive financing plan to cover the development cost. NAPOCOR was expected to deliver the land and certain infrastructure.

Hopewell submitted its bid with two important conditions. First, if Hopewell were to arrange bridge financing for the equipment and construction cost, the Philippines government would have to agree to

Hopewell's subsequent arrangement of long-term refinancing. Second, all payments from NAPOCOR would have to be in U.S. dollars, unless otherwise agreed, and all payment obligations would have to be guaranteed by the Republic of the Philippines. Based on this understanding, a project agreement was signed in November 1988, and Hopewell Holdings formed a wholly owned subsidiary, Hopewell Energy (Philippines) Corporation (HEPC) to run the project under a 12-year concession.

In the project contract, the specific obligations were laid out. NAPOCOR was to supply the site, access roads, and certain infrastructure; provide all necessary utilities at site for the construction, testing, and commissioning of the power station; supply all fuel for the electricity generation at no cost to the project; and accept and pay for all electricity produced.

In turn, Hopewell was to: (1) deliver gas turbines capable of 200 MW; (2) deliver all auxiliary equipment including control center and switchyard for connection to NAPOCOR's existing 115 KV system; (3) deliver all buildings, roads, landscaping, drainage, fire protection, lighting, and security; (4) raise all funds for the Hopewell portion of the contract ($41 million); and (5) provide all insurance policies as required for construction and development. The breakdown of the project costs and the financing plan are described in table 7.1.

During the twelve-year concession NAPOCOR was to pay HEPC three fees:

- A monthly capacity fee based on certified available capacity
- An energy fee for the amount of electricity produced and taken by NAPOCOR
- A start-up fee for electricity consumed during the start-up process.

To ensure the project's profitability and bankability, HEPC required specific approvals:

- "Pioneer" status for the project, allowing exemptions from tax for six years and from customs duties on imported equipment and supplies
- Certification from the National Economic and Development Authority confirming that the project had "high national priority"
- Receipt of all government approvals including permission to remit foreign exchange
- Receipt of a performance undertaking from the Republic of the Philippines for NAPOCOR's payment obligations, including an "Accession Undertaking."

Table 7.1. *Hopewell Energy (Philippines) Corporation Project: Costs and Financing*

Project costs ($ 000)

Supply of gas turbine power station	23,600
Refurbishment and modifications	1,165
Dismantling, inspecting, packing, shipping, re-installing, commissioning, testing	4,450
Electrical switch-gear and installation	1,300
Ancillary power station equipment and installation	1,750
Spare parts	100
	32,365
Civil engineering	2,057
Project supervision and engineering	800
Insurance	700
Financing, professional and legal fees	700
Interest, start-up expenses, working capital	3,378
	7,635
Total	41,000

Financing plan ($ 000)

Shareholder funds	11,000
of which:	
Hopewell Holdings	60.1%
Citicorp	19.9%
International Financial Corporation	10.0%
Asian Development Bank	10.0%
Term loans:	
International Financial Corporation	10,000
Asian Development Bank	10,000
Commercial banks (under ADB complimentary cofinancings)	10,000
Total project cost	41,000

The Accession Undertaking was a vital and unique feature of this BOT financing. Hopewell may require NAPOCOR to buy out, or NAPOCOR may require Hopewell to sell out: (1) if any approval, consent, law, or regulation required for the project is withdrawn, rescinded, or amended; (2) if the power station is unable to operate within its parameters due to subsequent environmental laws or regulations; (3) if Hopewell's economic returns are affected by changes in laws or regulations; (4) if certain events of *force majeure* occur; (5) NAPOCOR fails to pay sums due within three months of due date; and (6) if not less than five years after completion NAPOCOR gives Hopewell not less than 90 days' notice of its intention to relocate the plant.

Three gas turbines were purchased from Tri-State Generation and Transmission Association, a private power generation cooperative in Denver, Colorado. The units were the same Westinghouse W501B gas turbine generators in operation at Tri-State's facility in Wray, Colorado. Originally installed in 1975, the units had very low running hours and numbers of starts.

Thus, despite thorough planning, project completion was delayed by three events. Delays were encountered in obtaining certain governmental consents—in particular the Accession Undertaking by the Department of Finance in support of NAPOCOR's payment obligations. A further delay occurred in securing a registered title for the land at Navotas, which was to be leased by NAPOCOR from another government authority. Pending satisfaction of these conditions, Hopewell delayed its purchase of the equipment from Tri-State. After these problems were solved, Hopewell concluded its equipment purchase and had it shipped to Manila. During the ocean voyage to the Philippines the vessel encountered severe weather, which damaged the units. An inspection in Hong Kong determined that two units occasioned only superficial damage, but the third unit required substantial repair. Remedial work was undertaken in Hong Kong.

Despite these delays early on, the project has proved very successful. Hopewell completed a profitable project and established a framework for future BOT power generation projects. The Philippines government received a reliable supply of much needed power. The Navotas plant was originally intended as a peak-lopping plant to run three hours per day. It currently averages 13 hours daily, with plant availability running at 98 percent.

YTL Malaysia

A building contractor founded nearly 40 years ago in Malaysia has become Asia's second most successful indigenous power generation development company. YTL Corporation Berhad, listed on the Kuala Lumpur Stock Exchange with a market capitalization of approximately $1 billion, now is engaged in two power station projects in Malaysia.

The impetus for YTL's power generation efforts lies in the strategic development policy of the Malaysian government. Although well ahead of most developing nations, Malaysia's GNP currently lags behind those of the so-called Asian Tigers. Thus it has established the year 2020 as the goal (the "20/20 Vision") for full economic parity with its neighbors. To achieve this goal, Malaysia must grow at an annual compounded rate of 7 percent until that time. Local businessmen believe the goal is achievable, since the country for the past 20 years has achieved an average annual growth rate of 6.8 percent.

Because of this rapid past and projected growth, there has also developed a burgeoning need for more electricity capacity. The Malaysian government views privatization as the chief means for accomplishing this objective. Malaysia is now in its twelfth year of privatization.

For a construction company like YTL, power generation was a logical extension of its other activities. The company's plans call for it to own and operate two power stations of combined capacity of 1,207 MW. One plant is in Paka, on Malaysia's central eastern coast, while the other is near the distribution center in Pasir Gudong in the southern state of Johore. The sites were selected by the government and are located next to existing power stations and transmission facilities.

Total cost of the project will be in the range of 3.5 billion ringgit (US$1.4 billion). YTL has arranged to sell the load power to Tenaga, the national utility, of which the government currently owns 77 percent. YTL has also established a long-term natural gas fuel supply with Petronas, the government-owned national oil company. The power purchase agreement with Tenaga is denominated in ringgit, and the fuel—to be supplied from Malaysia's extensive reserves—will also be purchased in ringgit.

Under a BOT scheme similar to Hopewell's in the Philippines, the project concession period extends 21 years, the current maximum period for a power generating license in Malaysia. According to YTL officials, however, the project license will likely be extended at the end of the period, making the power plant a build-own-operate (BOO) project, instead of a classic BOT.

The project's financing scheme has broken new ground in several areas. The project was financed entirely in ringgit to eliminate foreign exchange risks, and it has achieved the largest domestic financing to date—2.66 billion ringgit. Floating rate commercial bank loans provided by Malaysian banks totaled 1.16 billion ringgit. The project also claimed the largest ever local bond issue—1.5 billion ringgit. It was the first time that Malaysia's Employee Provident Fund, provider of the long-term debt funds, took on a nonrecourse project risk. All previous loans extended by the Fund required guarantees from local banks. The bond issue received a AA rating by Malaysia's rating agency—another first for a greenfield project—and this further encouraged the Fund's participation. Shareholders' equity was 750 million ringgit.

With equipment supplied by Siemens of Germany, the role of Kreditanstalt fur Wiederaufbau (KfW) was pivotal. KfW provided bridge financing of DM 712 million until the domestic financing could be arranged. A deutsche mark forward exchange contract (from Deutsche Bank) was arranged to hedge the bridge financing against currency fluctuation risk.

Shajiao C

Following its success with Shajiao B in Dongguan, China, Hopewell Holdings went on to develop a second and larger BOT project in China called Shajiao C. Located on the same site just to the east of the B station, the project is a joint venture company called Guanghope Power Co. Ltd., organized under the framework of China's joint venture law—60 percent owned by Party A and 40 percent by Party B. Party A is a Chinese registered company established for the project and owned by Guangdong General Power Company, a People's Republic of China state-owned corporation, to deal with foreign parties in connection with the management of the electricity in Guangdong Province. Party B is a Hong Kong-registered company currently wholly owned by Hopewell Holdings Ltd.

Pursuant to the joint venture contract, Party A and Party B have entered into a power station development contract under which Party B will be responsible for appointing contractors to complete the project on a turnkey fixed price basis by or before a contract completion date. Party B is also responsible for procuring bank facilities to fund the construction and operation of the project. Part B will then on-lend the proceeds from the bank facilities to the joint venture company under an on-lending agreement.

Under the project's turnkey contract, the project contractor is a joint venture comprising three companies: GEC Alstrom, Combustion Engineering, and Slipform Engineer (a subsidiary of Hopewell). Under the project's operation and offtake agreement, Party A and its shareholder jointly operate the plant, while the Chinese shareholder purchases the electricity produced. The operator is responsible to ensure that electricity is generated in a steady pattern to enable the payment obligations of the joint venture company under the on-lending agreement to be met when due.

The purchaser is obliged to purchase a minimum offtake quantity of electricity per year from the joint venture company. The electricity price payable by the purchaser to the joint venture company is also calculated based on the kwh of electricity generated and made available by the C station. The operation fee is deducted from the electricity price when the purchaser makes payment under the operation and offtake agreement.

The almost $2 billion financing and supporting guarantees are described in table 7.2. The portion of payment obligations denominated in U.S. dollars are guaranteed by the Guangdong International Trust and Investment Corporation. The joint venture company shareholders provide a shortfall guarantee of up to $250 million. Party A's shortfall obligations are guaranteed by Guangdong General Power Company. In addition, the Guangdong Provincial People's Government has pledged its support of the project by way of a comfort letter.

This large financing was significant for its conservative leverage ratio and its relatively short tenor. The debt/equity ratio of the project was conservatively set at 1:1. Flush with cash from several rights issues, Hopewell elected to contribute a substantial amount of funds—directly and by shareholders' loans—to the project's equity. The consensus among Hong Kong bankers was that Hopewell could have achieved financing with 25 percent equity, but it would have taken longer than Hopewell wished.

Syndication of the facilities among banks in Hong Kong was reasonably successful. It was fully underwritten by 20 underwriters, achieving Hopewell's goal of financing, although the underwriting commitments were sold down by only 30 percent, a relatively low percentage.

Case Studies in Transportation

Infrastructure projects in transportation are often associated with large construction outlays and uncertain revenue flows. They also involve coordination among numerous agencies and municipalities with differing objectives and regulatory requirements—which can delay time schedules. Success in private financing of toll roads, therefore, has been difficult to achieve. The lesson is that adequate preparation, including contract terms that specifically pin responsibility for construction time and costs on the private project sponsors, can preclude the shift of cost increases to the consumer or government.

Table 7.2. *Shajiao C: Costs, Financing, and Guarantees*

Project costs($ million)

Shareholders equity	375
Shareholders loans and capitalized interest	444
Shareholders shortfall finance and capitalized interest	214
EGB loans and accrued interest	183
Bank loans	750
Total	1,966

Summary terms
  and conditions
  of the bank facilities

Borrower	Hopewell Energy Limited
Facilities	Tranche A: A term loan of $650 million
	Tranche B: A revolving letter of credit facility of up to $100 million.
Interest rates	Both Tranches: Pre-completion: 1.375 % over LIBOR.
	Post-completion: 1.0% over LIBOR.
Commitment fees	0.375% per year

Guarantors and Other Sources of Comfort

1. GITIC, of the joint venture company's and the Borrower's U.S. dollar obligations under the operation and offtake agreement.
2. Guangdong Provincial People's Government, with a comfort letter to the Borrower.
3. State Administration of Exchange Control, for approvals of the:
   • Joint venture's obligations under the on-lending agreement
   • GITIC's obligations under its guarantee
   • Joint venture's payments of advances to security accounts
   • Conversion of RMB funds at swap centers and remittance of FX by joint venture company
   • Opening by joint venture company of bank accounts in Hong Kong.
4. Guangdong General Power Corporation, Hopewell Holdings, and Party A to guarantee the joint venture and Borrower for shortfall funds up to $250 million.

Tate's Cairn Tunnel

In February 1988, the Hong Kong Government passed a special ordinance to grant a 30-year franchise to a private sector consortium led by the Japanese construction firm Nishimatsu. The mandate was to finance, construct, and operate a road tunnel under Tate's Ridge linking Shatin and the northwest New Territories with East Kowloon. Completed two months ahead of schedule in June 1991, the tunnel is the longest road in Hong Kong, a four kilometer twin-tube tunnel with four lanes and approach roads. The tunnel provides an additional strategic highway link between northeast Kowloon and Shatin, which leads directly to a principal border crossing to the PRC. Total project cost was HK$2.15 billion ($276.5 million).

Tate's Cairn was financed completely by the private sector. Its shareholders were Nishimatsu Construction (37 percent), China Resources (24 percent), New World Development (24 percent), C. Itoh (5 percent), Jardine Matheson (5 percent), Trafalgar House (5 percent).

Bankers took comfort from the fact that shareholders had contributed equity of HK$600 million, which translated to a relatively conservative debt-equity ratio of 2.6:1. Vehicle traffic growth projections for all of Hong Kong were then conservatively estimated to grow at 8.5 percent per year until 1991 and 5.0 percent per year from then until 1996. Tunnel traffic growth was estimated to be only 4.7 percent per year.

The project's financing structure adequately addressed major risks. First, precompletion risks ran for the relatively short 18-month construction period. The construction risk was low, since the tunnel had already been started and the method used was well known. The contractor risk was mitigated first by the good reputation of the contractors, then by a delay penalty of HK$400,000 per day. The cost overrun risk was overcome by several guarantees from the shareholders, whose financial strength was adequate. To ensure the quality of workmanship, the performance risk was addressed by a 10-year performance bond put up by the contractors.

The postcompletion risks ran for the rest of the 12-year loan period. Interest rate risk was tackled with an interest rate cap purchased by the shareholders. Traffic volume risk was satisfactorily addressed by traffic experts, MVA Consultants, who were experienced in other Asian road projects and well known by the bankers. Cash flow risk (which depended on toll rates) was nailed down by in-principle preapprovals from the Hong Kong Government to increase tolls over time. Since the project extends well beyond the 1997 deadline, political risks were considered to be mitigated by the large participation in the project of shareholders from the People's Republic of China.

Bangkok Second Stage Expressway

The Bangkok Second Stage Expressway is a private sector BOT infrastructure project encumbered by changes in national policy and delays in land acquisition. The $800 million project involves construction of a 37-kilometer elevated expressway with two sections, Sector A and Sector B. Under a 30-year concession agreement, the project was awarded to the Bangkok Expressway Company Limited (BECL), headed by Japanese construction giant Kumagai Gumi. Financed by Thai and international banks, the 19-kilometer Sector A is almost completed. Disagreement over contracted tolls has delayed work on Sector B.

Under the terms of the contracts, the Expressway and Rapid Transit Authority (ETA), the concessioning agency, was responsible for acquiring and paying for the right-of-way for the Second Stage Expressway. For acquired land BECL had agreed to make periodic payments to ETA over the contract period. As it became apparent that ETA would not be able to complete land acquisition by the contracted delivery date, the two parties together determined certain land plots to be priority portions to be delivered by a newly agreed date, upon which the government would be obliged to raise tolls for the road from 15 baht to 30 baht (US$0.60 to 1.20).

The implementation date for the revised agreement was based on construction completion and not the road opening, so that even though the ETA did not deliver the rest of the land until a year later, BECL would be able to continue work on the project. Construction was officially completed in November 1992, but the ETA held the view that the toll could not be increased until the priority components were operational.

As private toll road (and other private transportation) projects have unfolded, the Thai government has been faced with new challenges. Both the government and the private parties were, in effect, engaged in a learning process on the capacity of various administrative units to deliver on the arrangements required—as well as consumer acceptability of toll costs—in the initial plans. To its credit, the government has charted a difficult course with sensitivity to the various interests and concerns. For example, to resolve the disagreement over the toll increase to 30 baht, the government proposed to increase the toll to 20 baht, with 18 baht of the new toll directed to BECL—the same amount BECL stood to receive if the toll were raised to 30 baht. While at first the proposal seemed to soothe the project's financiers, soon it was clear that too little toll revenue would be available to the ETA, which still had extensive land acquisitions to complete and fund (Bardacke 1995; World Bank 1994).

ETA also held the view that BECL could not share toll revenues until Sector B was completed, posing the prospect of considerable cash flow trouble for BECL. Sector B was considered an important component of the entire project. Although located in an area of relatively less traffic, its construction would relieve bottlenecks at both ends of Sector A and increase the capacity of the entire system. But land acquisition was again a problem. ETA was to complete land acquisition for Sector B by August 1992. As of June 1993, however, it had only delivered 60 percent, hindering sufficient capacity for generating revenues.

Adding to these problems was a dispute over legal authority. Under the ETA Act, only ETA has rights to collect tolls on public roads in Bangkok. To finesse this requirement, ETA issued terms of reference in 1987, when the project was being planned, which stated that the Second Stage Expressway was a BOT project in which the concessionaire would have the right to operate the toll road, including the right to collect all tolls. Realizing that the terms of reference constituted a private contract (whereas the ETA Act was a sovereign law) bankers to the project required BECL to seek written confirmation of the contract's legal efficacy from Thailand's Attorney General. Although this was achieved, five subsequent changes in government caused the confirmation to be less than secure. Indeed, when completion neared and BECL prepared to hire toll collectors, ETA objected and contested the action.

Finally, the two groups reached an impasse, and in 1994 BECL and a consortium of international banks were bought out by a local group of financiers. It remains to be seen how this development will affect the success of the project.

Don Muang Tollway

Don Muang Tollway is a private sector highway project that will connect the Don Muang Airport to the Bangkok Second Stage Expressway. The 15.4 kilometer elevated road uses new technology and operates under a government concession for 25 years. The structure of this loan involved both local and foreign currency facilities of a direct and a contingent nature. Project size was THB10.4 billion (US$400 million), of which equity was THB2.4 billion. The project owner is Don Muang Tollway Company Limited, owned by a large consortium led by a construction company headed by Dywidag of Germany. Total foreign debt amounted to $130 million, repayable in eight years.

Extensive risk analysis was conducted in preparation for financing. The country risk of Thailand was deemed by bankers as acceptable.

Thailand's economic risk was then considered, including its sensitivity to oil price changes—since most of the country's petrol is derived from imported sources—and its sensitivity to the demand of export markets for its goods. The demand of export markets influences the national GDP growth rate and, by association, traffic growth assumptions. The Thai economy's sensitivity to world interest rates—for the projects' non-baht funding—and Thai baht currency risk were also considered.

Also important was the construction risk. Cost overruns were covered by lump-sum turnkey contracts from companies considered strong enough to back them up. Project delays were addressed by provisions for liquidated damages from the contractors. Performance risk was considered acceptable in light of Dywidag's experience with similar technology in Germany and in Singapore. A 10 percent performance bond was also offered. Next were the legal risks, which involved the regulatory framework under which the concession was granted, as well as the actual provisions of the concession agreement. Finally there was traffic risk, and this broke down into four parts: reliability of demand estimates (a concern since traffic development in Bangkok has been episodic), toll sensitivity, the project road's capacity, and alternative road capacity.

The Don Muang Tollway opened in December 1994, but traffic flow is light because the untolled flyovers, which the government had agreed to dismantle as part of a concession agreement signed in 1989, have not been torn down. Revenue projections depended on the flyovers being removed so that motorists would have little choice but to use the tollway. The Thai government has all but ruled out tearing down the flyways. Instead, it is discussing other incentives, including soft loans and a longer concession period.

Toluca Tollway

To stimulate private-sector investment in Mexico and to promote the development of Mexico's infrastructure without burdening the public sector, the Mexican government began in 1989 to pursue a policy of granting concessions to private parties for the construction, maintenance, and operation of highways, bridges, and tunnels. Between 1989 and 1991 the Mexican Government awarded concessions for approximately 3,810 kilometers of toll highways.

As of May 1992, 30 concessions had been awarded, pursuant to which about 2,540 kilometers were put under construction and about 1,270 kilometers of toll highways were made operational. Then the Mexican Ministry of Communications and Transport announced that it would award concessions for approximately 2,230 additional kilometers of toll highways by 1994. Short concession periods raised toll rates to high levels, severely limiting traffic on many roads. Much of the toll road program is being reassessed and refinanced currently (World Bank 1994).

Among the few successful roads is the Mexico City-Toluca Toll Road. The 22-kilometer, limited-access expressway connects the western suburbs of Mexico City with the principal east-west highway that runs from Mexico City to Toluca, the capital of the State of Mexico. The traffic capacity of the road is over 4,000 vehicles per hour in each direction. Tolls are collected at an across-the-road plaza configured with 15 booths and 16 traffic lanes. The toll collection equipment is supplied by Companie de Signaux et D'Equipements Electroniques, a French company specializing in this type of installation.

The concessionaire is PACSA, a Mexican corporation jointly owned by two of the largest construction companies in Mexico. In addition to the road itself, PACSA holds the titles to two other toll roads in the Mexico city area. PACSA is 70 percent owned by Tribasa and 30 percent owned by CIESA.

Given the strong traffic flow, securities were issued, backed by the assurance of further revenues. The $207.5 million for the Toluca highway was raised by an innovative structure called Toll Revenue Indexed Participation Securities (TRIPS), issued in June 1992 through Global Depository Units (GDU) in the United States. Each GDU represented 31,702 ten-year, 11 percent Amortizable Ordinary Participation Certificates (due May 19, 2002) issued by Nacional Financiera, SNC Trust Department, as Trustee of a Mexican trust in respect of the toll collection rights for a portion of the Toluca Toll road. The face amount of the issue is to be amortized over the term in quarterly installments. Such access to foreign capital markets allows the concessionaire to refinance existing debt and hence lengthen debt maturity to stretch out payments and apply the proceeds to financially weaker roads.

Guangzhou-Shenzhen Superhighway

The Guangdong-Shenzhen-Zhuhai Superhighway in China is one of Asia's classic private infrastructure projects. It is a 122.8-kilometer dual three-lane tollway accommodating vehicles up to 120 tons traveling up to 120 kilometers per hour. With 15 interchanges, the highway will run the length of the eastern corridor of the Pearl River Delta, connecting its final stage with primary roads east of Guangzhou and, ultimately, with a proposed Guangzhou ring road. Operating under a 30-year concession, it is to become the transportation aorta of Guangdong Province. Total project cost was planned at $1.2 billion.

The project is a joint venture between the promoter, Hopewell Holdings in Hong Kong, and Guangdong Provincial Highway Construction Company, representing the Guangdong provincial government. Also distinctive was the strong support for the project operating company offered by Hopewell and Guangdong International Trust and Investment Corporation, an investment arm of the Guangdong provincial government.

Although Guangdong Superhighway's technology was much simpler than that of the Don Muang Tollway, the more complicated political and economic environment of China made credit assessment more problematic for the bankers. Negotiations on the project concept were carried out off and on between Hopewell and the Guangdong government over an eight-year period.

The country risk of China was, of course, paramount. The bankers were reassured about political risk by a project guarantee offered by GITIC and the project approval from China's State Council. On top of that, political risk insurance was arranged. The economic risk was considered low due to the considerable migration of factories from Hong Kong already occurring at the time. In Dongguan City alone, through which the road passes, there are an estimated 5,000 joint venture factories exporting products for hard currency. Renminbi risk was an important factor, since about 60 percent of the highway's revenues would be denominated in local currency. Bankers found comfort in the project's projected ability to absorb a 15 percent per year renminbi devaluation against the dollar and still turn a profit.

Cost overruns due to construction risk, as in Don Muang's case, were covered by a lump-sum turnkey contract, backed by the guarantees of the construction consortium partners, GITIC and Hopewell Holdings. Cost overruns have occurred and are currently a source of contention between Hopewell Corporation and the Guangdong Government. Project delays were addressed by budgeting into the projections a construction period two years longer than what was actually expected. Coverage for the legal risks was found in the regulatory framework and the concession agreement and a toll adjustment formula flexibly based on investment payback requirements, construction costs, reasonable profits, and management and maintenance expenses.

The reliability of demand estimates proved acceptable to the bankers on the strength and performance of the experts, MVA Consultants, who also worked on the Tate's Cairn Tunnel project. Looking at toll sensitivity, the bankers determined that the project's revenues could decline by 40 percent against projections and still manage to service its debt on time. As to alternative road capacity, the practical maximum capacity of the current road system was estimated to be 25,000 vehicles per day. Recent calculations concluded that current usage is already at 17,000 vehicles, leaving little available road room in one of the fastest growing regions in Asia.

Mitigating Risk

For long-term development of private finance in infrastructure, three institutional fronts require attention. First, experts agree that the next frontiers of project finance banking will include local currency financing. Economic development must thus achieve broader and deeper local capital markets. Thailand, Indonesia, Malaysia, the Philippines, and China all urgently need—and appear ripe for—capital market mechanisms for debt and equity instruments that can help project developers sell and refinance large indivisible assets of infrastructure. For local debt markets, long-term public bond markets must be built in developing countries. And long-term publicly owned debt can help set benchmarks for private transactions.

Second, even though laws that regulate BOT-type projects have progressed in many countries, the evolution of legal systems must be further advanced. In most countries too many infrastructure projects are arranged case-by-case, while lenders and investors can only wonder how contracts and agreements will be enforced in a legal environment lacking experience. Third, once projects are operational, a predictable and rational regulatory framework is essential to ensure consistency and project success.

In cases where the strengthening of these three fronts is not enough, credit support or guarantees may be necessary to offset project-related risks. For example export credit agencies (ECAs) can mitigate risks in cross-border financing with guarantees. ECAs have been placing increasing emphasis on supporting exports to the private sector in developing countries, including some major power sector projects in East Asia and Latin America (Zhu: chapter 6). An ECA guarantees a national exporter or a banker against risks of non-payment when extending credit to an overseas borrower for the export of goods and services. In most cases, the cover of ECAs is extended against both political and commercial risks, partly because distinguishing between the two can be difficult. Additional credit support may also be necessary. The Multinational Investment Guarantee Authority (MIGA), the World Bank Group's recently formed affiliate, supports promoters against political risks. The World Bank's new partial guarantee program provides another instrument for risk mitigation (Zhu: chapter 6).

Finally, the sophistication demanded for financing infrastructure extends to managing these projects. Many developing countries are learning fast, but need to practice greater sophistication in setting incentives for bidding processes and choosing tolling and pricing mechanisms. Also, two closely related policy areas—privatization and permitting—will need further development. Simple but rigorous and transparent permitting policies may be a developing country's best guarantee of effective private sector infrastructure development.

Bibliography

Bardacke, Ted. 1995. "Bangkok in second tollway contract row." *Financial Times*, September 6.

World Bank. 1994. *World Development Report 1994.* New York: Oxford University Press.

8

Methods of Loan Guarantee Valuation and Accounting

Ashoka Mody and Dilip Kumar Patro

Partial government guarantees of private financing can be an effective tool for maintaining public-private partnerships. Loan guarantees that cover some or all of the risk of repayment are frequently used by governments to pursue policy objectives such as supporting priority infrastructure projects or corporations in financial distress. Studies show that guarantees are extremely valuable—the value of a guarantee increases with the risk of the underlying asset or credit, the size of the investment, and the time to maturity. The flip side of a guarantee's value to a lender is a cost to the government. Such a cost is not explicit, but is nevertheless real. When providing guarantees, governments, therefore, require place risk sharing, valuation, and accounting mechanisms to set in place. This chapter describes methods of guarantee valuation, reports estimates of guarantee values in different settings, and summarizes methods of guarantee accounting and their implications. While the old method recorded guarantees only when a default occurred, new methods (illustrated in the federal U.S. Credit Reform Act of 1990) seek to anticipate losses, create reserves, and channel funds through transparent accounts to ensure that costs of guarantees are evident to decisionmakers.

Loan guarantees that cover some or all of the risk of debt repayment have, in the past, been frequently used by governments to pursue a variety of policy objectives, including protecting bank depositors, promoting exports and foreign investment by domestic firms, supporting ailing industrial sectors, and even bailing out specific firms in financial distress. Today, an important goal is the financing of infrastructure. Rather than directly financing infrastructure projects, governments, especially in developing countries, are increasingly using guarantees to stimulate private lending to such projects. Partial guarantees—or guarantees targeted to specific policy or regulatory risks inherent in infrastructure sectors—mitigate those risks that the private sector cannot evaluate or will not bear. At the same time, such partial guarantees can substantially diminish the financial obligation of the government, where the only alternative is for the government to fully finance the project and bear all risks.

Researchers find that loan guarantees are of significant value, providing substantial comfort to lenders, especially as the underlying risk and the term of the loan increase. A guarantee's value to a lender, however, implies a cost to the government. Such a cost, and the consequent obligation, are not always explicit, but are nevertheless real. When providing a guarantee, a government incurs a *contingent* liability, or a liability that is conditional on some future event. Although contingent liabilities do not demand immediate payment, future obligations are expected, and these require careful accounting and administration. When the magnitudes of liabilities incurred are large and not adequately accounted for, payments resulting from default can lead to significant intergenerational inequity (Iden 1990).

This chapter does not examine the arguments for supporting specific policy objectives through guarantees. Rather it takes as its starting point the provision of a guarantee and focuses on the requirements for managing obligations that consequently accrue. To that end, the chapter: (1) highlights the financial characteristics of guarantees, (2) describes methods of guarantee valuation and reports estimates of guarantee values in different settings, and (3) summarizes existing and emerging methods of guarantee accounting.

Most governments do not account for the contingent liabilities that are incurred when an investment is guaranteed. Government budgets are typically on a cash basis, thus a *direct loan* of $100 made from government revenues is recorded as an outflow of $100. But a *government guarantee* of a $100 loan made by a private lender is recorded as a zero outlay, since nothing has been spent in that accounting period. The guarantee is accounted for only when a default occurs and the obligation has to be honored. Fiscal prudence is maintained by setting a largely arbitrary upper limit on the total value of guarantees. Guarantees are counted against this upper limit in various ways, including, in extreme cases, at the full face value of the underlying loans guaranteed plus interest payments due, even though the expected probability of default is significantly less than one.

History shows that guarantees do get called and, along with their significant implicit subsidy values, have a serious impact on budgeting. Defaults on guaranteed loans for infrastructure projects in the 19th century arose partly from poor design of guarantees—all risks were transferred to the government—but in recent decades, guarantees have been an important policy instrument in the United States (Eichengreen: chapter 4). Guarantee programs include loan guarantees to corporations, deposit insurance, mortgage guarantees, and trade and exchange rate guarantees. During the 1970s, contingent liabilities of the U.S. government grew at an extremely high rate. These liabilities did not show up explicitly in the budget; however, during the late 1980s, policymakers and the public felt the cost of such liabilities, particularly of the federal deposit insurance scheme that followed the crisis in the savings and loan industry (Bosworth, Carron, and Rhyne 1987; Iden 1990; CBO 1989; and Towe 1993). That crisis began the search for more prudent accounting concept methods. Similarly, defaults on loan guarantees in Canada during the 1980s led to new budgetary practices for accounting of contingent liabilities.

A systematic accounting system is needed to accurately reflect government liabilities and to improve the government's resource allocation. Guarantees should be recorded in the budget at the present value of their expected payments minus guarantee fees received. Such a methodology creates a more accurate picture of government liabilities (and implicit subsidies) and provides the government with a tool to decide between alternative projects.[1] Such procedures have been implemented, to varying degrees, in the United States in 1992 under the requirements of the Credit Reform Act and also in Canada. Other countries considering increased use of guarantees are actively examining the prospects of introducing a new accounting methodology for guarantees. Introducing the new methods in the United States revealed significant hidden subsidies and redirected funding among competing programs.

This chapter brings together two streams of research on valuing guarantees and on accounting for a government's contingent liabilities. Although a significant body of research exists on valuing contingent claims such as futures, options contracts, and other exotic derivative securities, the application of these pricing techniques to government liabilities is recent (Lewis and Pennachi 1994; Kau, Keenan, and Muller 1993; Ronn and Verma 1986).

---

1.   Similarly, loans provided by the government should, for budgetary purposes, be recorded at the value of the subsidy rather than at the full value of the principal amount.

Researchers have also independently looked at the issue of budgeting for such liabilities. However, there is no single treatment of valuation and accounting of contingent liabilities. Bringing the studies together in one overview increases understanding of contingent claims and should also provide policymakers with benchmarks and guidelines for decisionmaking. Examples are drawn primarily from developed countries—especially the United States—where substantial experience has accumulated. The analytical methods and findings should be of value to developing countries, too, since their use of guarantees is increasing.

After describing the financial characteristics of guarantees, this chapter then summarizes several studies evaluating gains from loan guarantees. Principles for management of contingent liabilities are outlined, and developments under the U.S. Credit Reform Act are then described and illustrated with the case of the U.S. Eximbank. The last section highlights the potential benefits of government guarantees, but cautions that effective deployment requires risk sharing with beneficiaries, valuation of liabilities incurred, and strict accounting.

Financial Characteristics of Loan Guarantees

For illustrating the nature of a guarantee, it is useful to begin by considering a risk-free loan (or a loan that carries no risk of default). Such a loan is equivalent to a risky loan with a loan guarantee

Risk-free loan = Risky loan + Loan guarantee.

The above identity holds when the guarantee is iron-clad, that is, when there is no risk that the guarantor will default on its commitments. In practice, no guarantee is completely free of default-risk and its value depends ultimately on the creditworthiness of the guarantor. To the extent that governments are more creditworthy than private guarantors, government guarantees are more likely to be honored. However, governments can also renege on their commitments. Mechanisms such as escrow accounts can be used to bolster the credibility of a guarantee; however, they also add to the cost of financing.

For our immediate purpose, however, it is useful to assume a "risk-free" guarantee—one that definitely will be honored. Consider, then, an example adapted from Merton and Bodie (1992). A borrower buys a loan guarantee for $1, then borrows $10 at the risk-free rate of 10 percent after surrendering the guarantee to the lender. Thus, the borrower effectively receives $9 in return for a promise to pay back $11. The implicit rate (in this case 22.22 percent) reflects both the risk-free rate as well as a charge for the guarantee. The transaction could also be viewed as the lender making a default-free loan of $10 and providing a guarantee on that loan as well for one dollar. Since the risk-free borrowing rate is 10 percent, the premium (22.22 -10 = 12.22 percent) reflects the default risk of the borrower as perceived by the lender.

Maintaining Incentives

When a guarantee is provided, the incentives of the debt holders in monitoring the performance of the firm are diluted or even eliminated. For example, government guaranteed loans for infrastructure projects in the late 19th century were not monitored, leading to diversification of funds and frustration of public interests (Eichengreen: chapter 4). Different approaches can be used to maintain the incentives, although in each approach one or another objective is foregone.

Consider a guarantee that covers only part of the risk. Using our example above, if the borrower obtains a partial guarantee, then its cost of borrowing should be between 10 percent (for completely risk-free) and 22.22 percent (when all risk is borne by the lender). A partial guarantee has positive incentive effects. Since only part of the transactions are covered by the guarantee, the borrower has an incentive to be efficient and the lender has an incentive to monitor the borrower's activities. For example, auto insurance deductibles give a driver the incentive to drive carefully. Similarly, the World Bank's guarantee covers only a portion of the risks, leaving intact incentives for the private parties to contain and manage commercial risks.

Risks due to adverse selection, or the inability of lenders to distinguish between good and bad risks, leads to rationing of credit. By guaranteeing only a portion of the risks, guarantors are able to create a filter that attracts those better positioned to assess and manage risk. Also, the guarantor can add value where it has credibility and expertise in project and financial analysis. If the guarantor has the expertise to evaluate projects at a cost lower than other financial institutions, then costs due to adverse selection can be reduced further.

Exploiting the structure of the debt to maintain incentives can be an alternative or complement to using partial guarantees. For example, if debt has senior and junior components, with senior debt holders having the first right on debt repayments, then a guarantee of senior repayments dilutes incentives for risk mitigation (Jones and Mason 1980). This occurs because, once guaranteed, senior debt holders lose their monitoring incentives. The incentives of junior debt holders are more complex. In general junior debtors have a continuous, and even increasing, incentive to monitor, especially if the guarantor is perceived as unable to impose a discipline on the senior creditors. However, being costly, the extent of monitoring will depend on expected benefits. When the value of the firm is low relative to its debt, junior debt holders also have reduced incentives to monitor because they foresee limited gain from improved performance of the firm. By the time senior debtors have been repaid, the value of the firm's assets may be close to exhaustion.

In contrast, guaranteeing junior debt strongly maintains the incentives of the senior debtors to remain diligent. (This conclusion apparently conflicts with the finding of a 1988 study by Selby, Franks, and Karki, but in that study, guarantee of junior debt is accompanied by a *de facto* guarantee of senior debt and so the incentive effects disappear.) Even when appropriately structured to maintain the incentive effects, however, Jones and Mason (1980) note that the cost of guaranteeing junior debt is higher than the cost of guaranteeing an equal amount of senior debt. This occurs because the existence of prior claims (senior debt) increases the likelihood of a payment default on junior debt. One suggestion they offer to minimize the cost of the guarantee is to include restrictions on dividend payments as part of the guarantee covenants.

Guarantee as a Put Option

A guarantee may also be viewed as a put option. A risk-free loan, which we noted above is equivalent to a risky loan and a guarantee, is also equivalent to a portfolio of a risky loan and a put option. A put option gives the owner the right, but not the obligation, to sell an asset for a pre-specified price (the exercise price) on or before a certain maturity date. A guarantee is a put option on the assets of the firm with an exercise price equal to the face value of the debt.

Consider the following: let V be the value of a firm and F be the face value of its debt. For simplicity, assume there are no coupon payments and all the debt matures on a specified date. Also consider a put option purchased by the lender on the assets of the firm, with an exercise price F. As a practical matter, the put option need not be on the assets of the firm itself, since these are unlikely to be liquid and tradable; rather, the goal should be to identify other assets that are heavily correlated with the value of the firm. These may include the prices of the firm's inputs and outputs (Babbel 1989).

Two scenarios are possible, one where the value of the firm is less than F and the other where it is greater than F. When V is greater than F, full repayment of debt can be expected and the put option is not exercised so its value is zero. However, when V is less than F, then the put option is exercised and has a net value of F-V, with the lender receiving the exercise price, F, for assets that are worth V. Also, when V is greater than F, the value of the risky bond is F. But when V is less than F, the value of the bond is V since debt holders are priority claimants on assets of the firm. The value of the risk-free bond is always F, by definition. The difference between the value of the risky bond and the risk-free bond is, as table 8.1 shows, also the value of the put option.

Therefore, from the above analysis it follows that

Value of risky loan = Value of risk-free loan - Value of put option.

But we also know that

Value of risky loan = Value of risk-free loan - Value of loan guarantee.

A comparison of the above two equations indicates that the value of the guarantee can be estimated by computing the value of the put option.

Identifying a guarantee as an option serves both a substantive and a practical purpose. Though the value of a guarantee could apparently be measured as the present value of future guarantee payments, in practice this is not possible except in the simplest cases because the guarantee value depends on parameters that are changing over time. The guarantee, or option, value is thus sensitive to factors such as the time to maturity, the volatility of the underlying asset, the value of the underlying asset, and the claims of other debt and equity holders. To capture the time-varying effects of these and other parameters, a fully specified dynamic model is

Table 8.1. Guarantee as a Put Option

	$V > F$	$V < F$
Value of risky debt	F	V
Value of put option	0	F-V
Value of risk-free debt	F	F

needed, as in contingent claims, or option pricing, analysis.[2] The use of present value methods is also complicated by the fact that the discount rate to use for contingent claims such as loan guarantees is not apparent. The appropriate discount rate should reflect only systematic risk (or risk that is inherent in the market and cannot be diversified away), but for contingent claims such as call-and-put options, no methodology exists for estimating a measure of their nondiversifiable risk.

Academics and practitioners have therefore relied on methods that price contingent claims as functions of more fundamental claims such as stocks and bonds. Contingent claims valuation methods have been extensively used to value loan guarantees. Deposit insurance provided by Federal Deposit Insurance Corporation in the United States is a major example (Ronn and Verma 1986, Pennachi 1987a, Pennachi 1987b). In box 8.1, we present a brief description of the well-known Black-Scholes option pricing methodology.

Value of Guarantees to Lenders and Other (Indirect) Beneficiaries

When a full or partial guarantee is provided to a lender, the risk of repayment is lowered, resulting in lower interest charges. Studies show that the pecuniary value of guarantees—the full extent of the possible saving in interest costs—is often very large. As may be expected, the value of a guarantee increases with the volatility (or risk) of the underlying asset or credit, the size of the investment, and the time to maturity. Guarantee values of 15 percent of the underlying debt are not uncommon and can often be much larger in risky and long-maturity situations.

The value of a guarantee is shared by the guaranteed debt holder, the borrower, and others who have claims on the assets of the firm. The actual recipients of the guarantee may benefit little from the guarantee, unless the provision of the guarantee was *unexpected*. Equity holders benefit indirectly because they are able to borrow at a lower rate. Non-guaranteed debt holders, however, may be worse off.

A clarification is in order. Guarantee values referred to here are the *gross* values, or the effect that guarantees have on reducing spreads charged by

---

2.   Option pricing techniques are a class of contingent claims valuation methods. Contingent claims analysis usually refers to the general framework for "pricing" or costing out various claims that are contingent on certain triggering events or conditions but are not necessarily linked directly to a tradable security. Options pricing, on the other hand, is viewed as the subset of contingent claims analysis associated with pricing financial option products based on an underlying tradable security.

Box 8.1. *The Basic Black-Scholes Option Pricing Analysis*

A guarantee is valuable to a lender because, if the borrower fails to meet debt repayment obligations, the guarantee ensures precontracted payments. Because the lender has, in effect, an option to sell the debt at a pre-agreed price, a guarantee is akin to a put option. Such an option—which can be on various underlying assets (bonds, stocks, currencies, or commodities)—gives its owner the right to sell that asset for a specified price (called the exercise price) on or before a certain date. If the option can be exercised only at maturity, it is referred to as a European option; in contrast, an American option can be exercised anytime prior to maturity.

The price paid by the owner of the option is referred to as the option premium. A fair premium is equal to the present value of the cash-flows from the option. The methodology used to compute this premium is referred to as option pricing or, more generally, as contingent claims valuation.

In 1973, Fisher Black and Myron Scholes achieved a significant breakthrough when they determined the premium for a European stock option in terms of parameters that are directly observable or may be estimated using historical data (the current price of the underlying asset, the volatility of the return on the asset, time to maturity, the exercise price of the option, the risk-free rate of interest). Assumptions underlying the Black-Scholes analysis for stock options include: (1) the stock price follows a particular stochastic—Ito—process and pays no dividends during the life of the option; (2) given the price today, the stock price in the future has a log-normal distribution; (3) the risk-free rate of interest and the asset volatility are constant; and (4) there are no transaction costs or taxes.

Consider, as an illustration, a put option on a stock whose current price is $100, the exercise price is $90, the risk-free interest rate is 10 percent per year, the volatility is 50 percent per year, and the option expires in six months. The Black-Scholes formula prices such an option at $6.92. A higher exercise price, longer time to maturity, and greater volatility would lead to a higher option price.

Underlying the Black-Scholes valuation model is the concept of *no arbitrage*—alternative assets with identical future cash-flows and risk characteristics should have the same price today. A central result in modern corporate finance, the Modigliani-Miller theorem on the equivalence of debt and equity, is also based on this concept. In the context of options, the basic method employed relies on being able to form, at a specific moment in time, a riskless portfolio of the option and the underlying asset. The no arbitrage condition implies that such a riskless portfolio will earn the instantaneous risk-free interest rate and thereby determines a partial differential equation that describes the evolution over time of the relevant variables. It is possible to form the riskless portfolio by appropriately choosing the number of stocks and options in the portfolio. Since both the underlying stock and the option are affected by the same sources of uncertainty, there is a correlation between the stock price and the option price; hence, the riskless asset is formed by buying either the asset or the option and selling the other.

Subsequent researchers have been able to relax the Black-Scholes assumptions and extend the conditions under which derivative securities can be priced. Cox and Ross (1976) discuss option pricing under alternative processes, including processes with jumps. Merton (1976) discusses option pricing when the underlying returns are discontinuous. Geske (1979) discusses valuation of compound options (a stock option is compound when, for example, it is valued not by the stock price, but by the underlying value of the firm). Roll (1977) derives an analytical formula for American call options with stocks whose dividends are known. Hull and White (1987) discuss option pricing on assets with stochastic volatilities.

Source: Hull (1993), Black and Scholes (1973), and Merton (1973).

bond holders and other lenders. Since the guarantee holder pays a premium or a fee for the guarantee, a *net* value calculation must be made to determine if the gain from lower financing cost is greater than the fee paid. Implicit in the discussion below is that a net positive gain accrues to the guarantee recipient, and this net gain results from the assessment made by the guarantor that the market valuation of the project risk is greater than the true risk (the guarantor in turn spreads its risks of default over a large number of projects). Bland and Yu (1987) who estimated the cost of borrowing minus the guarantee fee (for 445 insured and 694 uninsured bonds offered in 1985) found the net gain to be positive and inversely related to credit ratings.

The discussion in this section is organized by the method of guarantee valuation. The first method is the "rule of thumb" approach, which uses the market value of the debt (or relevant underlying variables) and compares it with a risk-free asset to determine the value of guaranteeing the risky debt. The method is approximate in most cases since it does not account for the changing value of the assets. However, it may be the only practical approach when sufficient data is not available. The second method is the market-valuation method, where similar assets with and without guarantees are compared, and it is assumed that the market accounts for the value of the guarantee. Finally, results of studies using option pricing methods are surveyed. Procedures for estimation of option values differ depending on: (1) specific features of the underlying credit (such as whether the debt is junior or senior), and (2) specific features of the guarantee (such as whether the guarantee is partial or full and whether it is available for the full time to maturity).

Rule of Thumb Methods

To illustrate the principles of guarantee valuation, Merton (1990b) estimated the implied value of loan guarantees for ten corporate bonds as the difference between the known *market price* and an estimated *default-free price* (table 8.2). These bonds were not actually guaranteed, but carried an implied cost of being guaranteed.

On May 19, 1990, none of these ten bonds were in default and the market prices used were the closing prices reported in *The Wall Street Journal* (May 11, 1990). The default-free prices of these bonds were estimated by discounting the expected principal and coupon payments at 9 percent, approximately the rate on treasury bonds and notes on that date.[3] To estimate

---

3.   The present value of a claim is its value in current dollars. The price of a bond is the present value of future cash flows (principal and coupon payments) discounted at an appropriate rate that reflects the risk of these cash flows. If there is no default risk associated with payments, then the appropriate discount rate is the yield on treasury securities of similar duration.

Table 8.2. Implied Values of Guarantees on Corporate Bonds

Bond	Years to maturity	Default-free price	Market price	Implied value	Percentage of market price
		Bond price ($)		**Guarantee value ($)**	
Continental Airlines	6	109.12	66.00	43.12	65.3
MGM/UA	6	118.24	63.38	54.86	86.6
Mesa Capital	9	127.36	95.50	31.86	33.4
Navistar	4	100.00	89.00	11.00	12.4
Pan Am	4	147.23	58.63	86.60	51.1
RJR	11	88.80	70.88	17.92	25.3
RJR Nabisco	11	141.35	76.88	64.47	83.9
Revlon	20	117.25	80.75	36.50	45.2
Union Carbide	9	102.89	92.25	10.64	11.5
Warner Communications	3	124.11	97.00	27.11	27.9

Note: Implied guarantee value = default free price - market price
Source: Merton (1990b).

the value of the guarantee as the difference between the market price and the default-free price, Merton also assumed that there are no call provisions, i.e., none of these bonds could be retired prior to maturity. If such call features or other options are present, the rule of thumb method is inappropriate and option pricing methods are needed.

The estimated implied value of the guarantees is rather high, varying from a low of 11.5 percent to a high of 87 percent of the market price. One explanation is that the bonds chosen were of lower grade. Moreover, the benchmark here is completely risk free, which is rarely the case, and often the guarantees in practice are partial in nature.

A simple back-of-the-envelope calculation of this type is appropriate when the guarantee covers the full term of the debt. In such a situation one can convert the risky debt into risk-free debt and compute the value of the guarantee as the difference between the two. However, in most situations, such as when guarantees are partial in terms of coverage (for example, covering only interest payments), secondary market debt prices do not indicate the default probability of each payment, and it is more appropriate to use contingent claim valuation methods.

Despite its limitations, the rule of thumb method is used because the detailed information needed for more sophisticated valuation is often not available. One application is in sovereign risk assessment by U.S. agencies providing guarantees to investors or exporters. Effective in 1993, federal agencies such as Commodity Credit Corporation (CCC), Export-Import Bank (Eximbank), and Agency for International Development (AID) are required to operate under a uniform sovereign risk assessment method, primarily to compute subsidy costs for budgetary purposes. The problem here, unlike in the Merton example, is that the market price of the underlying sovereign debt is not known. The procedure thus requires the use of credit rating methods to slot the debt into established rating categories and estimate the risk premium as equal to the premium of traded bonds in the same category.

A two-step process is followed: first, countries are placed in risk categories, and then subsidy costs for each category (and varying time periods) are established. A sovereign risk rating scale from 1 to 11 has been established.[4] A score of 1 indicates that payment problems are unlikely, and a score of 11 indicates severe expected losses on most debts. The rating is transformed into a risk premium representing credit risk for a particular country. The interagency group has correlated its ratings with ratings of Moody's and Standard and Poor's. Once a country is slotted into a particular risk category, a risk premium is calculated as the historical average of the risk premiums of commercial bonds (with same ratings) over investment grade bonds. The subsidy cost is calculated as the difference between the present value of loan payments at the treasury rate and a rate that is the sum of the treasury rate and the risk premium. Some of the estimates obtained are shown in table 8.3. As the maturity and the risk level rise, the expected gross cost of the guarantee increases. To protect against future payments from such large contingent subsidy costs, either fair premiums or appropriations are required to be set aside in reserves.

Market Values with and without Guarantees

Where comparable instruments with and without guarantees are traded, guarantee values are the difference in prices between the two securities on the assumption that the market has fully assessed the coverage provided by the guarantee. Such is the case where standardized guarantees are issued, for example, with municipal infrastructure investment programs in the United States. Market valuation is also possible where market values of a security exist before and after a guarantee.

---

4.   The eleven categories are A, B, C, C-, D, D-, E, E-, F, F-, F-- .

Table 8.3. *Subsidy Cost Rates for Different Risk Ratings and Loan Maturities*

Risk category	Subsidy rate [(subsidy cost divided by loan size)x100]			
	1 year	5 years	10 years	30 years
A	0.2	0.8	1.3	3.1
B	0.4	1.2	2.1	3.6
C	0.8	2.3	4.1	9.7
C-	1.8	4.5	6.5	13.6
D	3.7	8.7	11.2	20.4
D-	5.2	11.4	16.1	27.5
E	8.0	16.4	24.6	38.6
E-	11.6	23.0	33.4	48.9
F	17.9	33.9	46.5	61.8
F-	23.4	42.4	55.6	69.6
F--	32.4	54.6	67.3	78.4

Source: GAO (1994).

Hsueh and Kidwell (1988) studied the Texas School Board Guarantee Program, which received a full faith and credit guarantee of the State Government, raising the credit of the bond issued to a AAA rating. They found that interest cost savings are highest for low-rated bonds. Savings ranged between a high of 98 basis points for bond issues rated Baa prior to credit enhancement to 40 basis points for bond issues originally rated A; districts rated AA did not achieve any cost savings. The risk-free interest rate prevailing was just over 9 percent, implying a greater than 10 percent savings in interest costs for the lower grade bonds. The study also found that there are many more bidders for bonds that have a low intrinsic credit rating but are accompanied by a state guarantee. Of note to public policy was that as the supply of AAA rated bonds increased following the introduction of the guarantee program, municipalities not covered by the program had to pay about 50 basis points more than those benefiting from the guarantee.

Private insurance firms also provide guarantees of local government debt repayments. Typically, however, their coverage is limited to a portfolio of bonds that has relatively low levels of default risk. In contrast, public guarantors are compelled to take on greater risks for equity considerations (Hsueh and Kidwell 1988). Quigley and Rubinfeld (1991) examine the cost of borrowing following credit enhancement via private insurance (guarantees) in the after-market for municipal bonds during 1987-1989. They observed the same bond with and without a guarantee and found, on average, that insurance lowered the yield on municipal debt by 14 to 28 basis points for unrated bonds or bonds rated Baa-1 or lower, relative to an average yield-to-maturity of 7.8 percent for an uninsured bond. The lower gains from private insurance in the after-market, compared with those from Texas state guarantees discussed previously, suggest that the inherent risk of the bonds insured in the after-market is lower and the gains smaller.

A study of loan guarantees used to bail out Chrysler Corporation shows that the U.S. Government's commitment to alleviate the company's financial distress made a very significant difference to financing costs (Chen, Chen, and Sears 1986). The method adopted measured returns to the company's equity and debt following specific government announcements and actions toward implementing the guarantee program. Both the announcements and specific actions resulted in gains to equity and bond holders. An interesting finding is that the gains to equity owners were greater than gains realized by debt holders who were directly guaranteed. The authors suggest that, as residual claim owners, equity holders benefit significantly even when the guarantee is targeted only to debt repayments. Their finding justifies an innovative pricing approach used for the guarantee. In the past, when the government had bailed out corporations in financial distress (such as Lockheed in 1971), the taxpayers had, in effect, taken the downside risk but had not gained from the upside when the companies recovered. Pricing for the Chrysler loan guarantee corrected this asymmetry and included not only a 1 percent fee on outstanding debt but also warrants on the company's equity.

A study on loan pricing in the context of project finance also finds that guarantees create significant value to the project (Kleimeier and Megginson 1994). The mean spread over LIBOR in the sample loans was 100 basis points. A loan that had a guarantee benefited from a reduction in spread of 45 basis points. A limitation of this study, however, is that it does not distinguish between the extent of guarantee provided and the source (host government, export-import bank, or private sponsor).

Applying the Theory of Contingent Claims to Guarantee Pricing

Unlike the market-based analysis described above, which compares several slightly different instruments to arrive at "implied" guarantee values, contingent claims models focus on valuing the guarantee based on the underlying dynamics of the assets and liabilities behind the guarantee. If these underlying dynamics conform to a broad class of models, contingent claims analysis allows us to estimate—through numeric simulation or direct computation—the value of the guarantee based on the pay-out structure implied by the guarantee. In evaluating firm-specific guarantees, input into a contingent claims model typically includes the market value of the firm's assets, the book value of the firm's debt, the volatility of the underlying assets and liabilities, and the time horizon of the guarantee. (For an explanation of contingent claims analysis see box 8.1 and Merton 1990a.)

An early application of option pricing methods for pricing guarantees is by Sosin (1980) and this is a useful starting point because the main findings are echoed in other studies. The guarantees he examined had provisions similar to the steel program that was initiated in June 1978 by the Department of Commerce of the U.S. government to guarantee loans to firms in the steel industry.[5] The guarantee program was meant for instances where financial assistance was not otherwise available. The maximum amount guaranteed was 90 percent of the value of the loan. At least 15 percent of the cost of the project was to be supplied as equity capital or as a loan repayable in no less time than the guaranteed loan. There was no charge for the guarantee.

The value of a guarantee and who benefits from it depend on the structure of the financing. Under the steel program, the new debt, which received the guarantee, was subordinate to the existing debt. As a result, the guarantee had no value for senior debt holders. Holders of the new subordinated debt received the guarantee but also had to accept lower returns. The main gain thus went to the equity holders who benefited from the lower interest rates on the new debt and also as residual claimants to the value of the firm.

The value of the guarantee is shown to be most sensitive to the underlying risk of the firm (s) and the maturity of the loan. Table 8.4 shows the guarantee value as a ratio of the new investment; it is illuminating also to view the guarantee benefits in terms of interest savings.

Guarantee values are low when risk and maturity are low, but they can rise very rapidly to substantial levels. For a 10-year loan, the value of the guarantee is 3.7 percent of the value of the new investment when the standard deviation of asset values is 0.15, but it rises to 35.4 percent when the standard deviation rises to 0.35. Similarly, as loan maturities increase, guarantee values become extremely large. This is intuitive, since the value of any option goes up with maturity because there is a higher probability of the option being exercised.[6] Note that the highest interest savings are in the hundreds of basis points. The guarantee value also rises when the firm is highly leveraged (not shown in table 8.4, but reported by Sosin). This follows because, as the share of debt in financing rises, the conditional probability of default on junior debt rises.

---

5.   The authors mention that the first recipient of the guarantee program was Korf Industries, which received a guarantee for 90 percent of the $21,250,000 loan extended to it by 16 banks.

6.   The model used by Sosin to price the guarantees is based on Merton (1977).

Table 8.4. Sensitivity in Guarantee Values and Interest Rate Benefits

	Guarantee value (G/I)			Interest rate benefit (basis points)		
σ	5 years	10 years	15 years	5 years	10 years	15 years
0.15	0.1	3.7	13.8	3	48	141
0.25	3.7	18.6	35.6	93	216	467
0.35	12.5	35.4	54.2	157	663	893

Note: G/I is the ratio of guarantee value to size of investment; I (size of investment) =20, σ is a measure of the project's riskiness.
Source: Sosin (1980).

Another application of option pricing method for pricing guarantees is by Baldwin, Lessard and Mason (1983). The authors illustrate the use of contingent claims analysis for determining the value of guarantees for two firms with very different characteristics: a guarantee on a $200 million loan to International Harvester (IH) and to Dominion Textiles (DT). The relevant firm characteristics are in table 8.5.

The value of the guarantee was obtained via numerical simulations as outlined in the paper by Jones and Mason (1980). Even though the guarantee is for the same amount, one can clearly see that the value of the guarantee is higher for International Harvester, because of its high business risk, which is also reflected in the low market value of the equity in relation to the value of the firm. In addition, the current liabilities in relation to firm value are also much higher for International Harvester. These factors add up to a higher probability of default for International Harvester—hence a higher guarantee value.

Table 8.5. Risk Profile and Guarantee Value
($ million)

	IH	DT
Business risk (standard deviation of annual returns in percent)	40	20
Current liabilities	$2,330	$178
Long-term obligations	$1,866	$220
Annual payouts	$304	$41
Market value of equity	$247	$153
Value of firm	$2,618	$584
Value of guarantee	$166	$10

Source: Baldwin, Lessard, and Mason (1983).

In an assessment of a U.K. government guarantee of corporate debt, Selby, Franks and Karki (1988) estimate the value of a loan guarantee to International Computers Limited (ICL). In March 1981, the British Government guaranteed a £200 million new borrowings by ICL. The motives were two-fold. ICL was a major employer with 24,000 employees; it was also the sole manufacturer of computers in Britain and the government did not want ICL to be taken over by a foreign company. The existing debt was of various maturities.

Since ICL debt was not actively traded, Selby, Franks and Karki measured the value of the firm indirectly. Using the market value of equity and standard deviation of return on equity—which they estimate to be 1.0—the authors numerically estimate the market value of the firm's assets and the standard deviation of return on these assets.[7] For a loan maturity of two years, the value of guarantee was estimated as £83.38 million, assuming that new debt was junior to existing debt. Of this, over half (£42.56 million) is a subsidy to the project, which, in turn, is over a fifth of the value of the loan. The rest of the guarantee value (£40.83 million) accrued to senior bondholders. This wealth transfer to senior bondholders followed from the structure. Default on the junior debt triggers early redemption of the senior bond at its face value. The longer the maturity of the senior bond, the lower the prevailing market value of the bond is likely to be relative to its face value and the higher the wealth transfer to senior bondholders. Such a structure negates the usefulness of guaranteeing junior debt since, by *de facto* guaranteeing of senior debt, the incentive of senior bondholders to monitor the firm's performance are diluted, if not eliminated.

When guaranteed debt has the same seniority as unguaranteed debt, the transfer to nonguaranteed bondholders is much less and can even be negative since they have to share the proceeds of the assets with the guaranteed debt holders. Also, since prior claims are eliminated, the subsidy value of the guarantee falls to just over 10 percent.

Another application of contingent claim valuation for pricing guarantees is to value interest payment guarantees on developing country debt (Borensztein and Pennachi 1990). Using results from option pricing theory, the market price of the interest payment guarantee is estimated as if the guarantee were to be traded in financial markets.

The value of the guarantee is estimated as a portfolio of two put options. When underlying conditions are good, all debt payments can be made and the guarantee is not called (this they represent as buying a put with exercise price D [1+ij], where D is the principal of the debt and ij is the interest rate

---

7. The transformation is based on a relationship derived by Merton (1974).

applicable for the jth payment). When conditions are especially poor, then the full guarantee on all interest payments would be called (modeled as a short position in a put with exercise price D). The authors of this approach proxy country debt conditions using the price of the developing country debt in secondary markets. A feature of their estimation, which is not present in the earlier studies cited, is that they allow for the interest rate to vary, creating an additional source of uncertainty that raises the value of the guarantee.

The guarantees referred to are four-year guarantees on a floating rate perpetuity with semiannual coupons tied to the six-month U.S. Treasury bill yields. The results of their estimation indicate that the value of a hypothetical current interest payment guarantee for four years ranges between the full value of interest payments when the market price of that debt is about 30 cents on the dollar to half of all interest payments when the market price of debt is 60 cents on the dollar. The high values of the guarantees essentially reflect the very low market valuation of the debt and the low variance found in the history of debt values (making it unlikely that values would increase enough to prevent triggering the guarantee).

The option price approach reveals a higher value of the four-year interest payment guarantee than would the "rule-of-thumb" approach. Thus the market values the debt at a higher level (and hence has a lower implicit value of the short-term interest payment guarantee) because it is more concerned—and more optimistic—about long-run repayment.

Management of Contingent Liabilities: General Principles

In the past, guarantees were often implicitly treated as free and were recorded in government budgets only when a guarantee was called to make good on a payment default. At the time the guarantee was made, no liability was recorded in government accounts and hence no reserves were created for the contingency that the guarantee may be called. Seguiti (1988) draws attention to budgetary practices in Italy, where even though interest subsidies by the government are accounted for in the budget, guarantees are reported if and only if default occurs. Prior to the Credit Reform Act of 1990, contingent liabilities were not recorded in the U.S. budget.

Experience with loan guarantees in Canada makes the case for proper accounting. In the first half of the 1980s, about C\$3 billion were spent in paying off the guarantees or in providing supplementary budget finance to beneficiaries of guarantees. To guard against such contingencies in the future, the Canadian government instituted management and budgetary procedures in 1986 to minimize the risk of large disruptive payments.

The studies reviewed in the previous section demonstrate that, far from being "free," guarantees are of great value. A guarantee's value to investors and lenders implies a cost to the provider. When markets have full information, the value is identical to the cost (expected payment to cover default). Where market perceptions are more pessimistic than warranted, the cost may be less than the value. Thus, except when the market assessment is truly out of line with underlying conditions, governments providing guarantees must prudently manage their exposures.

General principles for managing contingent liabilities include: sharing risks with private lenders to ensure they have incentive to monitor the projects, charging fees to create the right incentives for use of guarantees and to build reserves in the event of default, and finally, instituting a rational system of accounting.

Risk Sharing with Lenders

The principle of risk sharing with the lender is becoming more widely accepted and practiced. For guarantees benefiting private firms or projects, it is common to limit the guarantees to debt payments and not cover equity, since equity holders are presumed to be willing to take on greater risks in return for a higher expected return. Though equity may not be explicitly covered, as discussed, it benefits from the guarantee to debtholders.

Further risk sharing occurs when less than 100 percent of the debt or only a limited timespan during the life of the debt are covered. In Canada, risk sharing is an explicit part of the government's guarantee policy, and an attempt is made to minimize the government's exposure. Developing country governments seeking private power projects have also sought to keep their exposure limited to sovereign or political risks, requiring the private investors to bear commercial risks. However, because the power purchaser is often a government agency with a poor credit rating, the government ends up taking the commercial risk as well. Appropriate policy reform that privatizes the power company and allows commercially viable tariffs will be needed to ultimately shift commercial risk to private parties. Thus effective risk sharing is a function of policy reform.

Charging for Guarantees

Government guarantees are often not priced and, when they are, there is no clear rationale to them. For example, in the program for supporting the steel industry described by Sosin (1980), no fees were charged. Guarantees provided by governments to cover political risks in infrastructure projects are also typically free. In some instances, this is beginning to change. Export credit agencies traditionally provided risk coverage at low cost and incurred large losses. Now export credit agencies are beginning to charge guarantee fees based on the riskiness of the underlying credit. While the fees tend to vary substantially, they can be as high as 10-15 percent of the value of the loan (Zhu: chapter 6).

Pricing of guarantees is highly desirable because it creates a market test for guarantees, reduces the inevitable temptation of private lenders to seek all available guarantees, shifts the cost of guarantees to the consumers of services provided rather than to the general taxpayer, and provides ongoing information on the value of available guarantees.

In addition to charging a fee for guarantees to cover downside risk, governments may seek to share in the upside potential through the acquisition of warrants. This was the case in the Chrysler loan guarantee. The possibility of using such warrants is also an element of the Canadian government's policy on loan guarantees, though this option has so far not been used.

Accounting Principles

Consider a prior situation when guarantees are (implicitly) assumed to have no costs in the year the commitment is made. In fact, if fees are collected, the guarantee program actually reduces the budget deficit. This creates an incentive to issue guarantees. In particular, guarantees are preferred to loans, which are counted at their full face value. A more appropriate accounting system based on the expected net present value cost commitment of a government places loans and guarantees on an equal footing.

A simple numerical example illustrates the basic issues. Consider a direct loan of $1,000 and a loan guarantee for an underlying loan of the same amount. Assume that the subsidy costs for both are $200 each.[8] The guarantee carries a fee of $10. Table 8.6 displays the budget authority and outlay figures that would be recorded under a cash budget system as it existed in

---

8.   In this example, as in the rest of this chapter, we make no attempt to assess the relative merits of direct loans versus loan guarantees as instruments of government support. The example assumes that the subsidy value under either instrument is the same. Liability under either instrument can be reduced by appropriate structuring. A guarantee can be partial, providing coverage only against specific triggering events or requiring copayments, as discussed above. But risk-sharing is also possible where direct loans are provided by the government if a condition of the loan is significant equity participation by private interests.

Table 8.6. *Accounting for Loans and Guaranteed Loans, before and after Accounting Reform*

	Budget authority	Outlay
Before accounting reform		
Direct loan	1,000	1,000
Loan guarantee	0	-10
After accounting reform		
Direct loan	200	200
Loan guarantee	200	200

Source: Adapted from CBO (1991).

the United States prior to credit reform, as well as the figures recorded under an expected net present value cost budget system currently employed for the U.S. budget.[9] Thus, prior to accounting reform, the full amount of the direct loan is recorded in the budget authority and outlay. No budget authority is recorded for the loan guarantee, however, since no cash outflow is presumed. In fact, the guarantee fee of $10 is recorded as a negative outlay or an inflow.

However, since the underlying opportunity cost to the government is the same under either action, the loan and the guarantee should be recorded at their subsidy cost of $200. Thus the new accounting system decreases the outlays for loans and increases outlays for guarantees in the year of disbursement. The subsidy appropriation of $200 for the guarantee and the guarantee fee of $10 must be set aside as reserves, which earn interest. This amount covers future claims due to defaults by borrowers. A contingent liability program is *funded* when the premiums for the guarantees and reserves created through budgetary appropriations are equal to the expected payments. Liabilities are *fair* when the premiums are paid for by those who benefit from the guarantees (Towe 1993).

Valuing Contingent Claims

A key task is to value contingent claims that arise from issuing the guarantee. A useful first step is to distinguish between two types of guarantees (as in Canada): guarantees for programs and guarantees for *ad hoc* projects. Programs provide guarantees to a large pool of risk bearers (as in student

---

9. The budget authority permits a government agency to enter into financial obligations depending on which expenditures or outlays are undertaken.

loan or mortgage programs). In contrast, *ad hoc* guarantees are made to specific companies in financial distress, where the government views the rescue of the company to be in the national interest, or for high risk new development. This rationale is not unlike that advanced in developing countries for attracting private finance to infrastructure projects.

For programs, assessment of contingent liabilities is usually straightforward and is often based on the history of defaults. However, when past data is not available, or when it is not a reliable guide to future liabilities, a forward-looking risk-based assessment needs to be made. Where appropriate, option-pricing models can be an aid in specifying underlying asset dynamics to estimate risk-based premia. Today, the U.S. government is beginning to use these sophisticated methods to measure costs of government contingent claims. Option-pricing methods can also be used for *ad hoc* projects where the project or the firm has either directly measurable market values and riskiness measures or appropriate proxies (Babbel 1989).

However, option-pricing methods have limited applicability for newer projects because such projects do not have sufficiently long histories to provide needed data. Market-based methods are also typically not possible because there do not exist enough traded securities with and without guarantees to estimate guarantee values. Instead, more direct measures of default need to be estimated.

One procedure could be to use methods employed by credit rating agencies. These agencies categorize project risks in great detail to place projects in a rating category that summarizes the risk of default. Traded securities in that risk category could then be used to estimate the value of the guarantee as the difference between the value of risk-free debt and the present value of risky debt of a similar maturity. Where even those estimates are not possible, it is still worth imputing an approximate cost to guarantees. In Canada, a requirement on the part of all government departments seeking *ad hoc* guarantees from the Finance Ministry is that they set aside 25 percent of the value of the underlying loan from their regular appropriations. Future payments, resulting from defaults, are charged against the amounts set aside. This creates a clear opportunity cost for the beneficiary department when seeking a guarantee. The value of 25 percent was arrived at somewhat arbitrarily and therefore does not differentiate risks by projects. With experience, greater refinement of valuation will occur. It is also well to remember that even when estimates are more "sophisticated," they suffer from a series of measurement errors stemming from inappropriate assumptions on the loss distribution and the parameters of the distribution. Hence, all estimates need to be subjected to stringent sensitivity tests.

Moreover, the value of the contingent claim depends not only on the underlying risk but also on the time period over which the risk is covered. The longer the period of coverage, the greater the exposure, and, therefore, the value of contingent claims recorded in the budget for otherwise identical projects would be higher for the one with longer duration debt. A corollary of the time dimension of guarantee valuation is that the value of the contingent claim will change (typically decline) over time. Not surprisingly, the U.S. Credit Reform Act requires a continual valuation of contingent liabilities. Although potential claims decrease because of the passage of time, they may increase because certain risks have been accentuated.

U.S. Credit Reform Act

To illustrate and elaborate on the principles outlined in the previous section, we present here the salient features of the U.S. Credit Reform Act of 1990. The presentation begins with the objectives of this Act and its coverage. The system of new accounts created to implement the Act is also described. Finally, we illustrate the budgetary implications of this Act for the U.S. Export Import Bank.

Features of the Credit Reform Act

In 1990, the U.S. Government passed the Federal Credit Reform Act (CRA). The key objective of this Act is to measure more accurately the cost of federal credit programs. The Act requires that the cost of interest subsidies and defaults in credit programs be estimated on a discounted present-value basis when new credit is extended and that these costs be recorded in the federal budget. By estimating the subsidy cost of federal credit—and reflecting it in the budget—credit programs are made equivalent to other federal spending in the budget. When appropriately implemented, the CRA lays the basis for a more rational and efficient allocation of budgetary resources.

The CRA applies to almost all federal loan and loan guarantee programs. However, federal insurance activities (such as deposit insurance, pension insurance, crop insurance, flood insurance) are excluded from credit reform.

Under the CRA (beginning fiscal year 1992), the budget reflects the budget authority and outlays needed to cover the subsidy cost associated with new loans and loan guarantees. In their annual request for appropriations, federal agencies include estimates of subsidy costs for new loans and guarantees. According to the CRA, the subsidy cost of a loan guarantee is "the present value of cash-flows from estimated payments by the government (for defaults and delinquencies, interest rate subsidies, and other payments) minus estimated payments to the government (for loan origination and other fees, penalties, and recoveries)" (GAO 1994). Subsidy costs for a particular loan or loan guarantee are charged against the appropriation of the federal agency. New loans seeking a guarantee cannot be disbursed unless the amount of the subsidy has been appropriated by Congress. The full subsidy cost is recorded as an outlay when the loan or the guaranteed loan is disbursed. Recall that, prior to credit reform, the budget recorded no outlays when private loans were guaranteed. In addition, the CRA mandates that costs of credit assistance be re-estimated and reflected in the budget at the beginning of each fiscal year following the year in which the disbursement was made.

Not everyone agrees that the CRA was a wise move. For instance, Weil (1992) argues that budgetary accounting is a veil that does not necessarily have substantial implications in a world where the government and all agents discount actions undertaken. Thus, whether the guarantee is accounted for at the start or when the default occurs should not influence taxes or welfare, though under the CRA budget, deficit estimates will be higher earlier on (compared with the previous system) and lower at later points in time. Weil concedes that when agents are "myopic," reserving against contingent liabilities induces the right behavior. He adds that the CRA introduces accounting inconsistencies by including only some guarantee programs and excluding others.

Dropping large-ticket programs (such as deposit insurance) from the purview of the CRA indicates a political imperative to restrict the levels of budgetary deficit. For this reason, he is skeptical of the subsidy calculations that will be made for programs under the CRA. In particular, he cautions against the use of option-pricing techniques, which are highly sensitive to the assumptions used. Finally, Weil notes that when the government does guarantee a loan, it does not always have to self-insure by taking the guarantee on its own books. Where possible, it should sell the guarantee, thereby eliminating the need to continuously monitor the loan performance and make revenue adjustments in response.

In a comment, Taylor (1992) argues that the CRA was but one element in meeting the objectives of the 1990 Budget Act, which created caps on discretionary spending and linked entitlement spending with taxes. The consequent system required that any new entitlement program be paid with a cut in other programs or an increase in taxes. Excluding loan guarantees from the discipline imposed by the CRA would have led to an explosion of loan guarantees, given the caps being placed on budgetary spending. Although the inconsistency created by not including all guarantee and insurance programs under the CRA is undesirable, the exclusion of loan guarantees from budgetary discipline would be worse.

System of Accounts

The Credit Reform Act created five accounts for each federal agency that administers credit programs. These are: (1) the credit program account, (2) the financing account, (3) a liquidating account, (4) the noncredit account, and (5) a receipts account. Subsidy costs are to be expressed in terms of budget authority and outlays in the program and the financing accounts. There are separate financing accounts for loans and guarantees.

Figure 8.1. System of Accounts Under Credit Reform

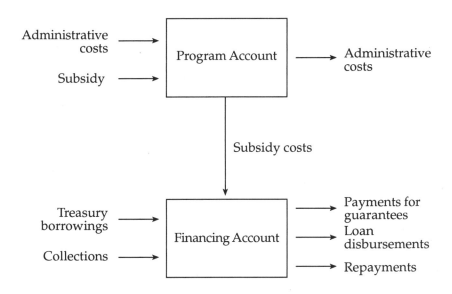

Source: GAO (1994).

The program account of the beneficiary agency receives appropriations from the U.S. Congress for administrative and subsidy costs of a credit activity (figure 8.1).[10] For the agency, the budget authority is equal to the appropriations, and its outlays are the subsidy costs that occur when the loans are disbursed. Thus, in their annual request for appropriations, the agencies need to include estimates of subsidy costs for new loans and guarantees. If an agency exhausts its subsidy appropriations in a fiscal year, it cannot provide further credit assistance in that year. When a loan or a guaranteed loan is disbursed, the financing account receives the subsidy costs from the program account. In addition, the financing account records borrowings from the Treasury, guarantee fees, recoveries from past loans, and payments due to defaults. If the subsidy estimates are accurate, the financing account inflows and outflows should balance over time.

The liquidating account is a temporary account that handles liabilities incurred through loans and guarantees made before October 1, 1991, continuing the cash treatment used before the CRA. The account has permanent, indefinite budget authority (that is, it does not need annual appropriation) to cover any losses. The noncredit account is for noncredit activities such as grants, which were earlier included with credit accounts. The receipts account collects any negative subsidies for cases where the federal activity shows a profit.[11]

Budgeting for Eximbank

Here we illustrate how credit reform affects budgeting for U.S. Export Import Bank (Eximbank). The Eximbank guarantees loans made by lenders to exporters of U.S. goods. Prior to credit reform, the Eximbank's net cash-flows were recorded in the unified budget. Measures of new credit assistance were reported in the credit budget, which placed limits on new loan obligations and guaranteed loan commitments. The appendix to the president's budget reported Eximbank's income statements and balance sheets. The operating income in any year lumped together payments from decisions reached in many different years. Thus, the account system did not provide even a rough estimate of the cost of credit assistance in any given period.

---

10. Details of budgeting for administrative costs under credit reform can be found in CBO (1992).

11. When subsidy costs are negative, no appropriations are required. For such a program, the negative budget authority and outlays are transferred from the financing account and recorded in the federal budget as proprietary receipts. These receipts are not available for use by the agencies unless the authority to do so is provided by law.

Table 8.7. Budgetary Treatment of Eximbank
(millions of dollars)

	Pre-credit reform outlay	Post-credit reform outlay
Existing revolving fund	-823.1	
Program account		264.8
Financing account (loans)		425.6
Financing account (guarantees)		-458.5
Liquidating account		-1,014.0

Source: OMB (1995).

Table 8.7 presents how credit reform would affect accounting for Eximbank in the unified budget. Before credit reform, the Eximbank revolving fund would have simply shown net outlays of - $823.1 (administrative expenses would have been paid from a separate salaries and expense account). The negative outlay represents receipts in excess of disbursements. Under the provisions of credit reform, the estimated subsidy costs (sum of the subsidy cost for loans and guarantees) would be reflected in the budget in Eximbank's program account and would be separated from Eximbank's nonsubsidized cash flows. When the loan or guaranteed loan is disbursed, the financing account would receive the subsidy cost for that particular loan. The liquidating account will handle all loans and guarantees made before October 1, 1991.

The outlays would consist of disbursements of tied aid, disbursements of subsidy costs associated with credit assistance, and payment of administrative expenses. All other cash flows would be treated as a means of financing and be recorded on the financing account, which is not part of the budget.

Conclusion

As instruments for supporting private enterprise and attracting private finance to priority endeavors, guarantees provide significant value. Their value increases with the underlying riskiness of the project and the maturity of the loan being guaranteed. This survey shows that the value in the high-risk, high-maturity loans can be worth hundreds of basis points of interest costs or, equivalently, expected default payments can be a very substantial portion of the loan.

Any policy using guarantees thus needs to address several trade-offs. By guaranteeing the lending the government takes on the risk of default and thereby reduces the incentives of the lenders and project sponsors to actively monitor project performance. To create the incentive for continued project monitoring as well as for filtering out those who have a low ability to manage risk, governments seek to share risks with private lenders by guaranteeing less than the full loan. The amount of risk sharing in the cases surveyed has not been large, but governments are increasingly conscious that they need to lower their exposure and, as the Canadian example shows, there is likely to be greater movement in this direction. The value of the guarantee also depends upon the structure of financing. Guaranteeing junior debt creates incentives for senior debt holders to be vigilant, but raises expected costs to the guarantor.

The high value of loan guarantees, losses experienced, and trends toward greater budgetary discipline have led to countries adopting a more rational approach to accounting for subsidies. While the old method recorded guarantees only when a default occurred, new methods seek to anticipate losses, create reserves, and channel funds through transparent accounts to ensure that costs of guarantees are evident to decisionmakers. The phenomenon of credit reform is relatively new. Although problems exist in estimating subsidy costs, we believe that over time it will be easier to estimate these costs more precisely. Better data would enable predictions of future performance and would also allow sophisticated contingent claim valuation methods for pricing the guarantees.

The growth of contingent liabilities, especially those associated with guarantees to lenders and other investors in private infrastructure projects, has become a source of concern in many developing countries. Some governments have chosen to restrict guarantees severly or even deny them. Guarantees against certain risk are often required, however, to finance the project. When guarantees must be provided, the methods described in this chapter become relevant. The use of these methods is under serious consideration in the Philippines and Columbia. In the first instance, the methods adopted are likely to be less sophisticated than some of those described here; however, any effort at good housekeeping will be a step in the right direction.

Acknowledgments. We are grateful for the help and comments received from David Babbel, John Denis, Robert Hill, Michael Klein, Subodh Mathur, Murray Petrie, Marvin Phaup, Steve Pilloff, Stephen Shapar, Christopher Towe, Alfred Watkins, and especially Christopher Lewis. Anonymous reviewers and

Moshe Syrquin also provided useful guidance. An earlier version of this chapter appeared in the February 1996 *World Bank Research Observer* 11(1): 119–42.

Bibliography

Babbel, David F. 1989. "Insuring Banks against Systematic Credit Risk." *The Journal of Futures Markets* 9(6): 487–505.

Baldwin, Carliss., Donald Lessard, and Scott Mason. 1983. "Budgetary Time Bombs: Controlling Government Loan Guarantees." *Canadian Public Policy* 9(3): 338–46.

Black, Fisher, and Myron Scholes. 1973. "The Pricing of Options and Corporate Liabilities." *Journal of Political Economy* 81(3): 637–59.

Bland, Robert L., and Chilik Yu. 1987. "Municipal Bond Insurance: An Assessment of its Effectiveness at Lowering Interest Costs." *Government Finance Review* June: 23–26.

Borensztein, Eduardo, and George Pennacchi. 1990. "Valuation of Interest Payment Guarantees on Developing Country Debt." *International Monetary Fund (IMF) Staff Papers* 37(4): 806–24.

Bosworth, Barry P., Andrew S. Carron, and Elisabeth H. Rhyne. 1987. *The Economics of Federal Credit Programs.* Washington, D.C.: Brookings Institution.

Chen, Andrew., K.C. Chen, and R. Stephen Sears. 1986. "The Value of Loan Guarantees: The Case of Chrysler Corporation." *Research in Finance* 6: 101–17.

Congressional Budget Office (CBO). December 1989. "Credit Reform: Comparable Budget Costs for Cash, and Credit." Washington, D.C.: U.S. Government Printing Office.

_____. January 1992. "Budgeting for Administrative Costs under Credit Reform." Washington, D.C.: U.S. Government Printing Office.

Cox, John C., and Stephen A. Ross. 1976. "The Valuation of Options For Alternative Stochastic Processes." *Journal of Financial Economics* 3(112): 145–66.

General Accounting Office (GAO). 1994. "U.S. Needs Better Method for Estimating Cost of Foreign Loans and Guarantees." GAO/NSIAD/GGD-95-31, Washington, D.C.: U.S. Government Printing Office.

Geske, R. 1979. "The Valuation of Compound Options." *Journal of Financial Economics* 7: 63–81.

Hsueh, Paul L., and David S. Kidwell. 1988. "The Impact of a State Bond Guarantee on State Credit Markets and Individual Municipalities." *National Tax Journal* 41: 235–45.

Hull, John. 1993. *Options, Futures and Other Derivative Securities*, Second Edition, New York: Prentice Hall.

Hull, John, and A. White. 1987. "The Pricing of Options on Assets with Stochastic Volatilities." *Journal of Finance* 42(2): 281–300.

Iden, George. 1990. "Contingent Liabilities of the Federal Government—Their Economic Effects and Budgetary Treatment." A paper for the annual meeting of the Allied Social Science Associations, Dec. 30, Washington, D.C.

Jones, Philip E., and Scott P. Mason. 1980. "Valuation of Loan Guarantees." *Journal of Banking and Finance* 4: 89–107.

Kau, J., Donald Keenan, and Walter Muller. 1993. "An Option-Based Model of Private Mortgage Insurance." *Journal of Risk and Insurance* 60(2): 288–99.

Kleimeier, Stefanie, and William Megginson. 1994. "Loan Pricing in Project Finance." University of Georgia, Athens, Georgia.

Lewis, Christopher M., and George G. Pennachi. 1994. "The Value of Pension Benefit Guaranty Corporation Insurance." *The Journal of Money, Credit, and Banking* 26(3):735–53.

Merton, Robert C. 1973. "The Theory of Rational Option Pricing." *Bell Journal of Economics and Management Science* 4(1): 141–83.

_____. 1974. "On the Pricing of Corporate Debt: The Risk Structure of Interest Rates." *Journal of Finance* 29(2): 449–70.

_____. 1976. "Option Pricing when Underlying Stock Returns are Discontinuous." *Journal of Financial Economics* 3(112): 125–44.

_____. 1977. "An Analytical Derivation of The Cost of Deposit Insurance." *Journal of Banking and Finance* 1: 3–11.

_____. 1990a. *Continuous-Time Finance.* Oxford: Basill Blackwell.

_____. 1990b. "The Financial System and Economic Performance." *Journal of Financial Services Research* 4(4): 263–300.

Merton, Robert C., and Zvi Bodie. 1992. "On the Management of Financial Guarantees." *Financial Management* 21(Winter): 87–109.

Office of Management, and Budget (OMB). 1995. "Appendix to the Budget of the United States Government, Fiscal Year 1996." Washington, D.C.

Pennachi, George. 1987a. "Alternative Forms of Deposit Insurance: Pricing and Bank Incentive Issues." *Journal of Banking and Finance* 11(2): 291–312.

_____. 1987b. "A Reexamination of the Over- (or Under-) Pricing of Deposit Insurance." *Journal of Money, Credit and Banking* 19(3): 340–60.

Quigley, John M., and Daniel L. Rubinfeld. 1991. "Private Guarantees for Municipal Bonds: Evidence from the after Market." *National Tax Journal* 44(4): 29–31.

Roll, Richard. 1977. "An Analytical Formula for Unprotected American Call Options with Known Dividends." *Journal of Financial Economics* 5(2): 251–58.

Ronn, Ehud, and A. Verma. 1986. "Pricing Risk-Adjusted Deposit Insurance: An Option-Based Model." *Journal of Finance* 41(4): 871–95.

Seguiti, Maria Laura. 1988. "An Italian Perspective on U.S. Federal Credit Reform." *Public Budgeting and Finance* 8(4): 54–67.

Selby, M. J. P., J. R. Franks, and J. P. Karki. 1988. "Loan Guarantees, Wealth Transfers and Incentives to Invest." *The Journal of Industrial Economics* 37(1): 47–65.

Sosin, Howard B. 1980. "On the Valuation of Federal Loan Guarantees to Corporations." *Journal of Finance* 35(5): 1209–21.

Taylor, John. 1992. "The Budgetary Arithmetic of Loan Guarantees and Deposit Insurance: A Comment." *Carnegie-Rochester Conference Series on Public Policy* 37(December): 123–26.

Towe, Christopher. 1993. "Government Contingent Liabilities and Measurement of Fiscal Impact." *How to Measure the Fiscal Deficit: Analytical and Methodological Issues*, Mario I. Blejer and Adrienne Cheasty, eds., Washington, D.C.: International Monetary Fund.

Weil, Philippe. 1992. "The Budgetary Arithmetic of Loan Guarantees and Deposit Insurance." *Carnegie-Rochester Conference Series on Public Policy* 37(December): 97–122.

Index

(Page numbers in italics indicate material in tables or figures.)

pricing, 204-8; guarantees as put options, 196-98; maintaining incentives of debt holders, 195-96; market values with and without guarantees, 202-204; rule of thumb methods of guarantee valuation, 200-202; value of guarantees to lenders and other beneficiaries, 198, 200

Financial performance of utilities, misleading, 145

Financing of power generation projects, 173; Hopewell Energy Corporation (Philippines), 175-78; Shajiao C (China), 180-81, *182*; sources for financing in Asia, 174-75; YTL Corporation (Malaysia), 178-80

Financing of transportation projects, 181; Bangkok Second State Expressway, 184-85; Don Muang Tollway (Bankok), 185-86; Guangzhou-Shenzhen Superhighway (China), 187-89; mitigating risks in, 189-90; Tate's Cairn Tunnel project (Hong Kong), 183; Toluca Tollway (Mexico), 186-87

Fire protection: in France, 27; in United States, 15

Foreign exchange, risk and, 164-65

Foreign export credits, 175

Foreign investment: most effective inducement for, 150; telecommunications and attracting, 42

Foreign ownership of privatized utilities, 50-51

France, infrastructure in, 24, 27-28

Free public services, 29

Fuel taxes, 8

Ghana, telephone service in, 44

Government, role of, 4, 30

Government guarantees, 110-11, 117, 118-22; failure to honor, 163; *see also* Guarantees

Government subsidies, 108, 110, 117-18

Great Britain, infrastructures in, 24-26; *see also* United Kingdom

Guarantees, 175; accounting methods for, 193, 208; completion, 163; credibility of, 194; vs. export credits, 158-59; in government budgets, 193, 208, 210-11; local gov-

ernment, 163; option pricing methods for pricing of, 205; premium rates of ECA, 159-60; as put options, 196-198; sovereign, 162-63; *see also* Financial characteristics of loan guarantees; Government guarantees; Loan guarantees

Guarantee valuation, rule of thumb methods for, 200-202

Guatemala, foreign direct investment in, 169

Highways. *See* Roads

Highway Trust Fund (U.S.), 14

Home-owner associations (U.S.), 9

Hong Kong, financing for Tate's Cairn Tunnel project in, 183

Hopewell Holdings Ltd., 175-76, *177*, 178, 180

Hungary, telecommunications in, 55

Incentives to minimize costs, 132n

India: early railway bonds in, 118-19; financing power plants in, 164; irrigation charges in, 139; long-distance telecommunications in, 56; Madras Canal finance problems in, 122; National Water Policy of, 141; projected power needs of, 174; telephone waiting lists in, *44*

Indonesia: decentralization in, 48; financing for Paiton power projects in, 163; irrigation in 139, 142; need for capital market mechanism in, 189; projected power needs in, 174; revenue from road users in, 138; telecommunications in, 48, 144; vehicle taxes in, 139; water and sewerage services in, 131

Industrial plants, treatment of waste from (U.S.), 11

Information: asymmetric, 109, 111-17; influence of (on financing), 109-10

Infrastructure finance, distributional aspect of, 134

Infrastructure investments: lessons from the history of, 123-25; in 19th century, 108-9

Infrastructure services: pricing for efficient provision of, 136-37; public provision of, 130-31